Mission Ukraine

Mission Ukraine

The 2012–2013 Diplomatic Effort to Secure Ties with Europe

MACIEJ OLCHAWA

McFarland & Company, Inc., Publishers
Jefferson, North Carolina

This work was first published in Polish as *Misja Ukraina* (Wydawnictwo RM, 2016).

LIBRARY OF CONGRESS CATALOGUING-IN-PUBLICATION DATA

Names: Olchawa, Maciej, 1983– author.
Title: Mission Ukraine : the 2012–2013 diplomatic effort to secure ties with Europe / Maciej Olchawa.
Other titles: Misja Ukraina. English
Description: Jefferson, North Carolina : McFarland & Company, Inc., Publishers, 2017 | Includes bibliographical references and index.
Identifiers: LCCN 2017034395 | ISBN 9781476669380 (softcover : acid free paper) ∞
Subjects: LCSH: European Union—Ukraine. | Kwaśniewski, Aleksander. | Ukraine—Relations—European Union countries. | European Union countries—Relations—Ukraine. | Ukraine—Relations—Poland. | Poland—Relations—Ukraine. | Ukraine—History—Euromaidan Protests, 2013–2014. | Ukraine Conflict, 2014– | Ukraine—Politics and government—21st century.
Classification: LCC HC240.25.U38 O4313 2016 | DDC 341.242/209477090512—dc23
LC record available at https://lccn.loc.gov/2017034395

BRITISH LIBRARY CATALOGUING DATA ARE AVAILABLE

ISBN (print) 978-1-4766-6938-0
ISBN (ebook) 978-1-4766-2897-4

© 2017 Maciej Olchawa. All rights reserved

No part of this book may be reproduced or transmitted in any form or by any means, electronic or mechanical, including photocopying or recording, or by any information storage and retrieval system, without permission in writing from the publisher.

Front cover image of Soviet Army monument with graffiti, in Bulgaria, Ukraine © 2017 Anton Chalakov/iStock

Printed in the United States of America

McFarland & Company, Inc., Publishers
 Box 611, Jefferson, North Carolina 28640
 www.mcfarlandpub.com

To Marta,
for being there no matter what

Table of Contents

Preface	1
Introduction: The Most Influential Lobbyist of Ukraine in the World	5
I. Ukraine in Aleksander Kwaśniewski's Geopolitical Strategy	15
II. The European Union's Special Envoy to Ukraine	35
III. "Russia Won't Stop": The Russian Factor in the Disintegration of Ukraine	113
IV. The West's Strategy	125
Epilogue: In the Center of the Whirlwind	137
Chapter Notes	145
Bibliography	167
Index	169

Preface

"How did you become interested in Ukraine?" is a question I have been asked on numerous occasions while living in the U.S., Poland, and Belgium. In all honesty, I didn't plan on studying Ukraine. After graduating from Loyola University Chicago in 2006, I went abroad to pursue an MA in European studies and I moved to Kraków to learn more about Poland. But ever since the 2004 Orange Revolution, I increasingly began following the political and social developments in Kyiv. Once in Kraków, I couldn't resist enrolling in Ukrainian studies, although I knew very little about this former Soviet Union country. In order to be admitted into the program and pass the entrance exam at the Jagiellonian University, I spent the summer giving myself a crash course on Ukraine's history and politics. The geopolitical eye-opener was Zbigniew Brzezinski's 1996 essay "Ukraine's Critical Role in the Post-Soviet Space," published by Harvard Ukrainian Studies.

Although I wasn't anywhere near grasping several hundred years of this country's saga, my admission interview responses must have impressed the director of the Ukrainian studies program, professor Włodzimierz Mokry, because he concluded: "You'll get the results next week. But between the two of us, you can already celebrate with a pint of beer." That was exactly what I did, and my Ukrainian journey commenced in the fall.

The idea to write *Mission Ukraine* originated a few years later in a conversation with Professor Mokry after my second book, *Stars and Trident*, was published shortly before the Eastern Partnership Summit in November 2013. Since 2008, I had been living in Brussels and working as a policy adviser in the European Parliament, focusing on Ukraine and the Eastern Partnership. Until the very end, we hoped Ukraine would sign the Association Agreement (AA) with the EU. At that time,

Preface

we couldn't have predicted the birth of the Euromaidan, the annexation of Crimea and the war in Eastern Ukraine.

Mission Ukraine is a case study of the EU's special envoy mission led by Aleksander Kwaśniewski and the former president of the European Parliament, Pat Cox, and their efforts to secure a European path for Ukraine. I wanted to display the intricate diplomatic and political "game of chicken" played between the European Union and Viktor Yanukovych in which the president of Ukraine swerved at the last second. In late November 2013, it was not Brussels that backed out of the Association Agreement; instead, it was Yanukovych who refused to sign the historic pact with the European Union. The Cox-Kwaśniewski mission played a key role in these events because it was part of the EU's last, all-out effort to save the AA, which gave millions of Ukrainians hope of a European future for their country. Yanukovych's decision terminated the European perspective for Ukraine and led to the protests that became known as the Euromaidan. This book addresses several key questions, including: Did Yanukovych really intend to sign the Association Agreement with the EU or was he just using it to receive concessions from the Kremlin? Was it a mistake on the part of the EU to make Yulia Tymoshenko's release a condition for the signing of the AA at the Eastern Partnership summit in Vilnius?

My research relied heavily on speeches, reports, statements, official documents, and newspaper, television, and radio interviews. However, the most valuable information came from interviews that I conducted both on and off the record. My ability to roam the EU's corridors in Brussels and Strasbourg, as well as my trips to Ukraine prior to 2014 (I was an election observer in the 2010 presidential race and organized several fact finding missions for EU officials), gave me a good backdrop to the politics at play. Several fascinating firsthand accounts have been published about the Euromaidan; however, this book focuses on the politics and diplomacy leading up to the Revolution of Dignity.

Mission Ukraine also examines the role of Aleksander Kwaśniewski in the European integration of Ukraine as well as his geopolitical strategy focused on a deeply integrated EU, which can be a global player only if it is truly united. The book provides a history of Kwaśniewski's involvement in Ukraine, beginning with his role in the Orange Revolution in 2004–2005. Along with Javier Solana, the EU's High Representative for Com-

Preface

mon Security and Defense Policy, and Valdas Adamkus, the president of Lithuania, Aleksander Kwaśniewski played an important part in negotiating a peaceful settlement following the disputed presidential elections. Moreover, I discuss Kwaśniewski's outlook on the annexation of Crimea and the war in Eastern Ukraine, and offer an analysis of his recommendations for Ukraine's relations with the Euro-Atlantic community.

This work, first published as *Misja Ukraina* in Polish, is an amalgamation of my academic and professional experience that would not have been possible without the guidance of several individuals. I would like to take this opportunity to express my utmost gratitude to Włodzimierz Mokry, who has constantly supported me. I also wish to thank Michael Khodarkovsky from Loyola University Chicago, who taught me about the complex history of Russia and the Soviet Union, which allowed me to better understand contemporary Ukraine. My understanding of the collapse of empires and my perception of Ukraine's strategic geopolitical role was, and continues to be, profoundly shaped by Alexander J. Motyl. I am very grateful for his help and encouragement. I am glad to have been able to count on the support of Rafał Godlewski, Paweł Kowal, Paweł Purski, Christopher Kamyszew, and the entire Prescient team in Chicago. I am particularly indebted to Bart Galica for his friendship.

The talented Jakub Piasecki was the book's first reviewer and translator. I wish to thank him for his merit and for significantly improving this text. I am also thankful for Asha Underiner's hard work in editing *Mission Ukraine*, her meticulous attention to detail, and her valuable feedback. Ireneusz Bil of the Amicus Europae Foundation helped me along every step of the way and I am very thankful for his assistance and patience.

Most of all, I would like to express my gratitude to President Aleksander Kwaśniewski, who revealed to me what was happening behind the scenes of his mission and answered my numerous questions.

A proper "thank you" to my sister, brother, and parents would require writing another book dedicated solely to that purpose, but I hope they know how grateful I am for everything.

My wife not only helped me revise the book and offered advice, but also made this project possible. Her strength and determination are a great source of energy. For that, as well as for countless other things, I am grateful and I would like to dedicate this book to her.

Introduction: The Most Influential Lobbyist of Ukraine in the World

> *My predecessor, Aleksander Kwaśniewski—and this is something I must admit, despite our many differences—was very effective in Ukraine at that time, and he played a key role in resolving the conflict between the old regime and the opposition.*[1]
>
> —Lech Kaczyński

> *Trust cannot be won overnight. It is not like I could get there and say, "My name is Kwaśniewski. I am the president of Poland and now I am going to help you." It does not work that way.*[2]
>
> —Aleksander Kwaśniewski

> *If Poland had more than one Aleksander Kwaśniewski, Ukraine would have joined Europe a long time ago.*[3]
>
> —Arseniy Yatsenyuk

Standing in front of the grandiose columns of the Ukrainian Foreign Ministry's headquarters in Kyiv, Aleksander Kwaśniewski noticed that his colleague, Pat Cox, was visibly exhausted after a long day of meetings and negotiations. It was almost 11:00 p.m. on a frigid February night in 2013. The former president of Poland turned to his friend from Ireland and said, "Don't worry, Pat. Look: they've got a lot of empty space on this square—an ideal place to put up statues of you and me."[4]

Pat Cox had every right to feel tired. This exchange took place during the twelfth visit of the Cox-Kwaśniewski mission to Ukraine, initiated by the European Union in June 2012. Every couple of weeks, Cox would fly from Dublin to Amsterdam, Amsterdam to Vienna,

Introduction

As the president of Poland, Aleksander Kwaśniewski (left) met with Pat Cox when Cox was the president of the European Parliament. Strasbourg, May 13, 2003. © European Union 2003. Source: EP.

Vienna to Kyiv, and finally to Kharkiv aboard a small private plane provided by the Ukrainian authorities. The time spent in the air must have been sufficient to prepare himself for negotiations with Ukraine's president, Viktor Yanukovych. He would meticulously review his notes from previous meetings, although he would never be able to feel entirely confident, because he never knew what to expect from the Party of Regions. Before the European Parliament's mission, Cox had never been to Ukraine. He did not speak Russian or Ukrainian. As a full-blooded democrat, the liberal Irish statesman experienced a culture shock when he came face to face with Ukrainian politics. Corruption, blackmail, deceit and the overwhelming power of oligarchs were only part of Ukraine's political landscape, which is why Cox needed to rely on somebody who was familiar with Ukraine.

Aleksander Kwaśniewski did not top the list of potential candidates for the job. "I know I was not the first person they called. It was Prodi. Prodi told me about it himself," recalls Kwaśniewski.[5] But Romano Prodi, the former Italian prime minister and former president of the European Commission, did not undertake the challenge. He was never particularly interested in Ukraine, and was well aware of the lan-

The Most Influential Lobbyist of Ukraine in the World

Kwaśniewski (left) describes Pat Cox (right) as a fully-fledged democrat who is true to his principles, who enjoys life, meeting people, networking, and exploring the world. This photograph shows Poland's president during his official visit to the European Parliament. Strasbourg, May 14, 2003. © European Union 2003. Source: EP.

guage barrier. At the same time, the European Union needed someone who was recognized internationally and who could act efficiently to defrost the Kyiv-Brussels relationship.

In October 2011, Yulia Tymoshenko was sentenced to seven years in prison following charges of abuse of power during her tenure as prime minister. In March 2012, she was also charged in connection to the so-called "tax case." Tymoshenko was charged with misappropriation of public funds, tax evasion, and forgery.[6] It was obvious that both cases were politically motivated, which is why the European Union could not accept that the former prime minister, former presidential candidate, and the leader of the largest opposition party was thrown behind bars.

In June 2012, the European Union attempted to seize the initiative and remove the hurdles that stood in the way of a new political and economic agreement between the EU and Ukraine. The imprisonment of the former prime minister constituted the single greatest challenge, which is what led to the concept of sending envoys to Ukraine.

Introduction

The president of the European Parliament, Martin Schulz, and the Party of Region's Mykola Azarov, then-prime minister of Ukraine, came up with the initiative of creating a special mission. Soon afterward, the notion was proposed that the former president of Poland should be one of the emissaries. Initially, Schulz argued that the operation should focus primarily on the Tymoshenko case. However, Kwaśniewski managed to convince him to widen its scope: "I told him it was not enough. We need a broader context. That is why we argued to include monitoring of judicial and legal reforms."[7] Schulz agreed, and when it was announced that Kwaśniewski and Cox would become the European Parliament's representatives, he said he hoped that "their mission will be a breakthrough that will help Ukraine to address problems concerning the rule of law and the independence of judiciary," and "will contribute to restoring mutual confidence in EU-Ukraine relations."[8]

Formally speaking, the main objective of Kwaśniewski's mission was to assist Ukraine in its judicial and legal reforms, its electoral reform, and the eradication of selective justice. Over time, the mission turned into the European Union's main weapon in its showdown with the regime of Viktor Yanukovych. It was an unprecedented game of politics and diplomacy, with Ukraine's future—either European or Eurasian—as its stake.

Aleksander Kwaśniewski believed from the start that "there was no other way for Ukraine, but to carry on and sail through the stormy waves in order to reach the European harbor."[9] The mission was about reaching tangible objectives through negotiations with both the government and the opposition, so that Ukraine as a state—not as a president, a government, or a political party—could sign the Association Agreement with the EU at the upcoming Eastern Partnership summit scheduled to take place in Vilnius, Lithuania, in November 2013.

Even though Tymoshenko's case was the starting point, the actual objective of the mission was about Ukraine's historic chance—its European integration. Moving closer to the EU through the Association Agreement was of momentous importance to Kwaśniewski. That is why, when he spoke in the European Parliament in October 2013, the former president of Poland argued:

> It is beyond a doubt that we are approaching a historic moment. Comparisons with the 1991 referendum on independence make perfect sense. Many observers were surprised, as were the Ukrainian voters themselves, with the

results. With a turnout close to 80 percent, over 90 percent of those who took part in the referendum supported Ukrainian independence.[10]

In 1991, Ukraine chose to break away from the Soviet Union and Russia. Over 20 years later, Kwaśniewski's mission was supposed to enable another historic event. Over the course of a year and a half, Kwaśniewski aspired to secure a place for Ukraine among the EU's closest allies. During that time, he participated in 28 visits, spending almost 80 days in Ukraine, and over 20 days in Brussels and other capital cities, such as Washington and Berlin. According to Martin Schulz, the mission lasted 150 working days, with Cox and Kwaśniewski spending "more time with each other than with their wives."[11]

Kwaśniewski met with Yanukovych 18 times and spoke with him for at least 50 hours.[12] He attempted to convince Ukraine's president to allow Tymoshenko to receive medical treatment abroad, most likely in Germany. But the talks grew increasingly difficult, as Russia used its trade embargo to apply more and more political and economic pressure on Ukraine. Still, anything was possible in the early days of November, and there was a chance the deal would still be signed. On November 14, Kwaśniewski stated in Brussels: "I do not want to make any assumptions, but if the draft law on hospitalization abroad is ready, chances are fifty-fifty. But nothing can be done without hard work. We will keep on working."[13] However, time was running out, and the day of the summit in Vilnius was approaching.

On November 21, one week ahead of the Eastern Partnership summit, the government of Mykola Azarov announced that work on the Association Agreement was put on hold. On the following day, around two thousand people gathered on Independence Square (*Maidan Nezalezhnosti*) in Kyiv. That was the eve of Euromaidan, which became Ukraine's second revolution since it regained its independence. This pro–European revolution, which started when Viktor Yanukovych rejected the process of European integration, instantly transformed into a movement against the status quo. It became an uprising against all the illnesses that were ailing Ukraine: against the schizophrenic political elites, living lives of luxury in their parallel world of prodigious power; against the cancer of corruption, which preyed upon what was left of the state's integrity; against the tuberculosis of social injustice and backwardness, which choked all hope of a better future in a developed and

Introduction

democratic European country, which Ukraine's youth longed for. Many believed that the Association Agreement and deeper relations with the European Union were the best medicine that Ukraine could take. When Yanukovych ripped away their remaining hope, Euromaidan was born.

The result of this brave uprising included sniper fire on the streets of Kyiv, the martyrdom of the Heavenly Hundred, Yanukovych's escape, the Anschluss of Crimea by Russia and the war in Eastern Ukraine. The number of casualties has reached thousands.

Nobody knows how this story will end for Ukrainians and their nation. This book is about how it all began, and about Aleksander Kwaśniewski's role in Ukraine's struggle.

* * *

In November 2013, the Institute of World Politics conducted an opinion poll. The Kyiv-based institution surveyed around 50 Ukrainian and foreign experts about their assessment of the most influential lobbyists working for Ukraine. Their evaluation included the following categories: longstanding commitment to Ukraine's interests, promoting Ukraine on international platforms (such as international conferences, foreign mass-media appearances, etc.) and longstanding support for Ukraine's European integration. Forty-seven participants voted for Aleksander Kwaśniewski. The former president of Poland gathered more votes than the EU's Commissioner, Štefan Füle (ranked 2nd); the Klitschko brothers (ranked 3rd); Sweden's foreign minister, Carl Bildt (ranked 5th); the president of Poland, Bronisław Komorowski (ranked 7th); Poland's foreign minister, Radek Sikorski (ranked 8th); and the European Parliament's chairman of the delegation to Ukraine, Paweł Kowal (ranked 10th). According to the Institute of World Politics:

> Experts underlined the titanic effort undertaken by the former co-president of the European Parliament's observation mission (Kwaśniewski and Cox), aimed at sustaining the dialogue between Kyiv and Brussels.... Despite his obvious connections to the famous Ukrainian philanthropist (who also features [on] our list), it is right to call Kwaśniewski Ukraine's most loyal friend in Europe.[14]

There are not many politicians in Europe, and even in the world, who understand the changes that took place in Ukraine as well as Aleksander Kwaśniewski. And only a few comprehend the tragic historical burden dragging down Ukraine. For that reason, Kwaśniewski is one of the few international politicians who are experts on Ukraine. His experience as president of Poland has been an invaluable asset in this regard. Kwaśniewski held the top job between 1995 and 2005 during the time when Poland determined its strategic interests and worked toward them. Over the course of a decade, not only did Poland undergo political and economic transformation, but, thanks to those changes, it became a member of NATO in 1999 and, five years later, was admitted into the EU. It was over the same ten-year period that Ukraine improved its relations with the West. The most pivotal event was the signing of the Charter on a Distinctive Relationship with the North Atlantic Alliance at the 1997 summit in Madrid.

Despite some objections and concerns, Poles reached an internal political consensus concerning their nation's NATO and EU membership. Regardless of political affiliation, almost all elected officials and the people who voted them into office agreed that Poland's place was in the Euro-Atlantic community. The same cannot be said about Ukraine. During the time Aleksander Kwaśniewski managed Poland's relations with its Eastern neighbor, Ukraine was pulled between Moscow, Brussels, and Washington, D.C. Given Ukraine's historical, economic, and political connections with Russia, the adoption of this multi-vector policy might have seemed rational. It was, however, a de facto alibi, which justified apathy and backwardness. Ukraine's presidents and governments, one after another, failed to undertake reforms; instead, they created a peculiar mixture of post–Soviet dysfunction, corruption, and the oligarchs' absolute power. This was the Ukraine Kwaśniewski had to deal with as Poland's president. So why did he bother to support Kyiv's European ambitions?

Aleksander Kwaśniewski argues that he is interested in Ukraine's affairs because that is what good neighbors do. "If Ukraine wants to be independent, if Ukrainians need reliable partners and good advice, if they need an open door to Europe, that is exactly what we should give them."[15] That understanding is the reason why he remained deeply engaged in Ukraine's affairs throughout his term, as a mediator during the Orange Revolution and later as the European Union's special envoy.

In the global theater of politics, Aleksander Kwaśniewski plays a double-hatted role. He acts as Ukraine's ambassador in Europe and the United States, and as ambassador of the transatlantic community in Ukraine. The ability to compare Ukraine's affairs to experiences of those countries with which his interlocutors may be more familiar makes it easier for him to reach Western audiences. To that avail, he draws historical and cultural parallels between Ukraine and Russia. But, even more importantly, he underlines glaring contrasts separating the two neighbors.

> I've explained this to many Western politicians and I've told them that the problem with Ukraine is a combination of the *homo sovieticus* syndrome, which is common among all societies of the former Communist bloc, because for 70 years they all existed within the Soviet Union. What is even more significant in Ukraine's case is the *homo peripheriacus* syndrome. Anyone who wanted decent education and a career had to go to Moscow. This situation undermined the Ukrainian people's self-esteem and blurred any distinctions between them and the Russians. But this situation has been changing. All it took to realize we are dealing with a nation characterized by a profound national, linguistic, and cultural identity was just a few years of Ukraine's independence. The Orange Revolution further augmented Ukraine's national identity.[16]

Kwaśniewski also compares Ukraine to Poland. Due to his background, his political career, and direct engagement in pivotal moments of Poland's recent history, Kwaśniewski is apt at depicting both the similarities and the differences between the two countries' experiences. Western politicians are not overly familiar with Central and Eastern Europe. Still, terms such as "Solidarity," "Martial Law," and "Round-Table Talks" are more familiar to them than "Sixtiers" and "Rukh." That being said, Kwaśniewski makes frequent references to Poland's history.

When Kwaśniewski attended a conference in Berlin in early 2014, people asked him about the difficulties faced by Ukrainian protesters. In order to explain the phenomenon of the Maidan, Kwaśniewski underlined the differences between Solidarity's protests of the 1980s and Martial Law, and the conflict taking place on Kyiv's Independence Square. In its struggle for change, Solidarity could resort to mass protests and coordinated strikes. That is because factories and other places of employment belonged to the state. This is not an option in Ukraine, believed Kwaśniewski, because most people there are employed by private companies. Therefore, it is much more difficult to organize a strike and much easier to lose one's job. Moreover, the Catholic Church played an important part in Poland, whereas none of the three separate Orthodox Churches that operate in Ukraine enjoy the prominence and influence of Poland's Catholic Church during the days of the Solidarity movement.[17] Poland's struggle was not an easy one. But the challenges facing Ukraine are equally difficult. For that reason, Kwaśniewski depicts both differences and similarities between Poland and Ukraine. This way he can argue that Ukraine has to be given a chance and requires the West's support, just as Poland did in the past before it succeeded.

When he is confronted with doubts as to whether Ukraine can ever join the European Union, Kwaśniewski points out, "Poland signed the Association Agreement in 1991 and it only joined the EU in 2004, following 13 years of our allies' vehement support."[18] Poland's road to NATO and the EU was a bumpy one, and it was not covered overnight. Having gone through close to 50 years of communism, the state required comprehensive reforms in order to fulfill the democratic and free-market criteria of the transatlantic community. Despite numerous shortfalls and internal disputes over its pathological communist legacy, Poland has been pictured as an economic poster child. Poland's success story enables Kwaśniewski to defend Ukraine's pro–Western aspirations, and Poland's experience proves that the EU's expansion was a good, albeit pricey, investment.

At a press conference held in Spain at the time Poland was pursuing its EU membership, Kwaśniewski was asked by a journalist how he would explain to Spanish taxpayers that EU funding was going to be redirected from Madrid to Warsaw. "It's our turn," he replied. He would use the same argument when facing Polish taxpayers in 2015 or 2020: "It's Ukraine's turn."[19] "That's what the idea of European solidarity is all about. To some extent, that's what the EU itself is all about."[20]

Ukraine plays a pivotal role in Aleksander Kwaśniewski's geopolitical strategy, but it is the European Union that is at the epicenter. The EU's weaknesses are commonly known, but at the same time, it is a community that transformed the blood lands of Western Europe into the common field of democracy, welfare, and cooperation it is today. After the collapse of the Iron Curtain, which divided Europe for half a century, the European democracies invited a group of previously Soviet-dominated countries into their club. In the end, the united and democratic Europe survived and the communist superpower met its

Introduction

end. Aleksander Kwaśniewski has an explanation for this. He believes that the EU constitutes one of the most ambitious and successful geopolitical projects in history, not merely "an episode, like the U.S.S.R."[21] If the European Union wishes to become a meaningful global player, such as the United States and China, it is bound to deepen its integration and extend its scope of freedom. Ukraine has to be part of that expansion and it needs to decide for itself. According to Aleksander Kwaśniewski:

> If Ukraine wishes to modernize, it needs to team up with the European Union, not the Eurasian Union. The latter may be convenient within the current framework of cooperation and contemporary economic interests. The trade relationship between Ukraine, Belarus and Kazakhstan has a long history. But if you want to talk about modernization, Europe is the only option.[22]

In that case, what kind of Europe does Kwaśniewski have in mind?

I

Ukraine in Aleksander Kwaśniewski's Geopolitical Strategy

In order to uphold the greatest achievements of the Orange Revolution, we need to constantly remind the Ukrainian people that their ticket can take them in both directions: to Moscow and Brussels. If one day it turns out that the ticket to Brussels is invalid, we're going to have a problem.[1]
—Aleksander Kwaśniewski, November 2005

I've been dealing with Ukraine for over twenty years and I've learned that the most important thing is patience.[2]
—Aleksander Kwaśniewski, November 2013

United States of Europe

By appointing Aleksander Kwaśniewski as its special envoy, the European Union chose a man who feels comfortable in two different worlds: the East and the West. He is well known in Brussels and in Kyiv, and can communicate with elites in both Washington, D.C., and Astana. This familiarity has enabled him to formulate a complex and realistic geopolitical strategy. Whether or not the EU will be able to fight for Ukraine depends on what the EU becomes in the years to come. Aleksander Kwaśniewski's vision of the EU's future is clear.

The nature of the European Union's relationship with Ukraine depends highly on the desired nature of its development. Should it be a casual club where its member states meet for non-binding consultations, or should the relationship be tighter, along the idea of an ever-closer union? The academic and political debate on the EU's future has been going on ever since the EU's foundations were laid out. It concerns both the Union's shortcomings as well as its achievements. For the opponents of European integration, EU institutions are nothing but a bureaucratic behemoth, prone to overregulation detrimental to member states' competitiveness. For Aleksander Kwaśniewski, the EU entails something completely different:

> The European project is one of the greatest and one of the most successful—perhaps even the most successful—projects created by mankind in the past couple of hundreds or even thousands of years. This project enabled former enemies (that is nation states, which had fought the bloodiest wars in history) to communicate, to unite, to create a common market, and to build a social unity. It is due to these achievements that Western Europe has enjoyed peace, security, and open borders for 70 years. The Union can proudly say it has achieved remarkable reconciliation and understanding among its nations.[3]

According to Aleksander Kwaśniewski, the European Union's integration project is among the greatest achievements of our civilization, comparable to the creation of the United States of America by the Founding Fathers.[4] In a speech delivered at an Atlantic Council conference in Washington, Kwaśniewski argued that the EU's future is linked to its deeper integration: "That means stronger EU institutions and more common policy. To put it bluntly—and it is a catchy phrase—we need more Europe, not less Europe. We need more integration, not less integration."[5] Only through deeper integration will the European Union be able to face new challenges. Kwaśniewski claims that the EU needs to find its position on the international stage, characterized by multiple centers including China, Russia, the U.S., and Latin America. "If the EU is to have a stake in this world, it needs to be united, more integrated, and more populous than it is today."[6] "If we are to mean something in the geopolitical architecture of the 21st century, we need to stick together, because even the most powerful European states do not mean much on their own."[7] "When it comes to the EU's future, I am optimistic. I am confident the EU will not just overcome its crisis, but it will continue to develop when it's over. Joining the ranks of the United States and China, as main global players, should become our purpose."[8]

In 2012, at the Yalta European Strategy summit, Aleksander Kwaśniewski demonstrated the EU's strength by referring to the number of gold medals obtained by its member states at the Olympic Games in London. Overall, the United States won the highest number of medals, followed by China. If, however, the European Union were to

I. Ukraine in Aleksander Kwaśniewski's Geopolitical Strategy

Aleksander Kwaśniewski gives a speech during the Yalta European Strategy—YES conference in September 2012. Seated from left: Vitali Klitschko, Natalia Korolevska, Leonid Kuchma, Serhiy Tihipko, and Arseniy Yatsenyuk. © Yalta European Strategy, 2012, photographer Sergei Illin.

be classified as a single entity, it would have come in first. This situation exemplifies the EU's potential.[9]

Currently, the European Union is collectively led by the leaders of its member states' governments. If, however, "the process of the European integration deepens and the EU undergoes federalization, transforming into the de facto United States of Europe," the EU will be able to have its true leader, its own president.[10] Kwaśniewski is not certain whether such a perspective is realistic ("not for the next 20 years"[11]), but a federal European Union would become a significantly stronger global player. This process of federalization experienced a huge setback in June 2016.

On 23 June 2016, a referendum took place in the United Kingdom, which decided the country's future relationship with the EU. Commonly known as Brexit, voters were asked if they want the United Kingdom to remain in the European Union or leave. More than 30 million people went to the polls (a 71.8 percent turnout) and 52 percent voted to leave the EU.[12] This sent political and financial shockwaves throughout Europe and the world. The pound sterling immediately devalued and hit the lowest level against the dollar since 1985.[13]

The process of UK's departure from the EU will be a complicated one because it is a road that has never been traveled. Formally, after invoking Article 50 of the Treaty of Lisbon, the UK and the EU will have two years to negotiate this political and economic divorce. Unknotting a relationship that was held together since 1973 can be expected to be a prolonged and arduous process. In addition, the United Kingdom's own unity may come under jeopardy given that 62 percent of voters in Scotland and 55.8 percent in Northern Ireland voted to remain in the European Union. What will happen to the UK if Scotland, for example, holds another independence referendum to stay in the European Union? According to Aleksander Kwaśniewski, in a sense, Brexit "is the end of Great Britain" and marks "a great change for the European Union."[14]

Kwaśniewski believes that "Brexit is an event that could lead to the deconstruction of all that has hitherto given Europe peace, a sense of security, and growth." Brexit could be the beginning of a negative process.[15]

> We have gone through the great economic crisis that was comparable to the one in the 1930's. This is something that is overlooked in Europe. The crisis in the 1930's ended in war. For now, we haven't had a war, not even a revolution. We haven't had the inflation that generally comes as a result of these types of crises. What we do have is Great Britain leaving the EU. This isn't a tragedy yet, but is a big problem.[16]

One consequence of the crisis is the impoverishment of many Europeans and "people without prospects for the future don't vote for the status quo."[17] The status quo includes the continent's mainstream political parties that have been pro–European and were the driving force in integrating the EU's member states. The alternative includes the far-right, anti-immigrant, Eurosceptic parties that have gained influence not only in France and the Netherlands, but also across Scandinavia and Central Europe. That is why Kwaśniewski is of the opinion that "in this time of shock there will be an increase in nationalism and populism.... This shock will affect stock exchanges and currencies. Foreigners living in Great Britain will also experience problems."[18] Brexit's consequences will have a radicalizing effect on Europe and undermine its position on the world stage.

I. Ukraine in Aleksander Kwaśniewski's Geopolitical Strategy

Kwaśniewski believes that Brexit is everyone's loss: "Europe without the United Kingdom is a smaller Europe, a weaker Europe, a Europe that is worse off. The fact that a great country is leaving [the EU] could be the beginning of the destruction of the whole structure, the whole European project."[19] In his analysis, Kwaśniewski divides the post–Brexit reality into three stages.

Stage one: The next three years will be a period of shock and chaos in the European Union. Europe will be divided between countries in the mainstream with robust economies, like Germany, France, Italy or Sweden, and those that will remain in the peripheries. Stage two: This could potentially be the formation of a three-tier Europe. The first group would be composed of the EU six founding states that believe that the European project cannot fail. These leaders will not let the European project go to waste and feel a moral obligation to save it. Kwaśniewski argues that the leaders of these EU Member States will say to the rest, "We're integrating and you can get onboard or watch the train leave the station."[20] Kwaśniewski believes that they will not say this to the Eurozone countries, which make up the second group, because these countries know that unless they want to "commit economic suicide," they need to integrate. The third group will encompass the remaining countries that find themselves on the peripheries. Stage three: return to integration. Kwaśniewski is convinced that in a decade or two, there will be a return to the notion that European countries must work together in order to face competition from China, India, and the United States.[21]

Hopefully, it will not be too late for Europe to reunite itself around the EU's values. As always, Kwaśniewski remains cautious in providing overly optimistic analysis of the Brexit crisis: "I'm afraid that one day we'll reach a point of no return and afraid that we'll wake up in a world that is headed toward a major conflict."[22]

Building a Strong EU through Ukraine's European Integration

According to Aleksander Kwaśniewski, "solidarity is the foundation of Europe. If we question that, we don't stand a chance. We in Europe know all too well where national egotism can lead. We should stick to the plan to bring the Eastern countries into the orbit of our values."[23] A truly united Europe, based on the ideals of solidarity, is the right place for Ukraine, something that Kwaśniewski also argued in his October 2013 speech in the European Parliament.

> Ukraine is more than an excellent partner for an integrated Europe, which is open to other countries, to other people. It is a partner with deep European roots, a strategically important location, close to 50 million well-educated and dynamic people, with a significant number of young individuals, which we need more than ever. Ukraine is also a huge market that creates great opportunities for European investment and cooperation beneficial for both Ukraine and the entire European Union.[24]

Kwaśniewski said: "I am confident that Europe needs Ukraine's market. Moreover, Ukraine's roots are European. It is a Christian state, which played an important part in Europe's history."[25] The former Polish president also believes that if we keep saying "no" to Turkey and Ukraine, we will be the ones begging them to join in 10 years' time. There is just too much at stake when it comes to Ukraine and Turkey's potential.[26] A free Ukraine is not just what her neighbors need. A free, prosperous and modern Ukraine as part of the European community is what Europe needs.[27] "Europe needs Ukraine because of demographics, its market, and millions of Ukrainians, already working in the EU, including in Poland. As opposed to Russia and Belarus, Ukraine is prepared to accept our standards."[28] The EU's enlargement is not just in its best interest; it is also its mission.

Aleksander Kwaśniewski is of the opinion that the mission of the EU's enlargement should be embraced with hope and optimism: "Europe has the potential to develop if it is integrated and united; it has a chance to develop if we stop thinking only in terms of national interest and start thinking how to align those interests with Europe's."[29] The continent's strength and full potential can be unleashed, only if we do not barricade ourselves from the outside world by indulging our selfish desires: "Europe stands a chance if it is deeply integrated; Europe stands a chance if it is wider, greater, and more open to new countries that want to become members of the European Union."[30] It is crucial that aspiring EU member states wish to join the club voluntarily.

After all, Europe's integration and the EU's expansion have not been imposed on anyone. Regarding Ukraine's aspirations:

I. Ukraine in Aleksander Kwaśniewski's Geopolitical Strategy

> We are merely reacting to Ukraine's expectations. This may be in our best interest, but that's a different story. We're not trying to force anyone. If Ukraine decides to team up with Russia, there is nothing we can do about it. But today, Ukrainians want to team up with Europe. All relevant public opinion polls confirm their willingness to associate with the EU, and to join it in the future.[31]

According to Aleksander Kwaśniewski, "a lot of work is required within the EU, so that it is convinced that Ukraine's membership is in its interest. That is the job I've been trying to do."[32] This is not an easy task. Europe needs to understand that a strong, independent, and energy-sufficient Ukraine will be a reliable political and economic partner. This transformation, however, cannot miraculously happen overnight, which is why Kwaśniewski made it his personal mission to prove to the EU that Ukraine will require time and assistance. After all, the EU is powerful and wealthy enough to wait for returns on its investment.

The European Union constitutes the world's largest economy and the strongest trading bloc. By these standards, the EU is the main trading partner of 80 countries. In comparison, the United States is the main trading partner of 20 countries.[33] The free flow of people, commerce, and capital boost the EU's competitiveness and make it an attractive place for others. Moreover, the European welfare state system—despite its costs—provides a comfortable standard of living for its citizens. For more than two centuries, the idea of the American dream lured millions to the United States. But today, climbing the social ladder in Europe is easier and the gap between the rich and the poor is remarkably smaller on the Old Continent.[34] But everything has its price.

According to Zbigniew Brzezinski: "The European Union—with its aging population, lower rates of growth, even larger public debt than America's, and, at this stage of its history the lack of a shared 'European' ambition to act as a major power—it is unlikely to be able to replace America's once-compelling attraction or fill its global role." Moreover, the EU needs to face the prospect of ceasing to be the model for other regions: "Too rich to be relevant to the world's poor, it attracts immigration but cannot encourage imitation.... Too self-satisfied, it acts as if its central political goal is to become the world's most comfortable retirement home. Too set in its ways, it fears multicultural diversity."[35]

Aleksander Kwaśniewski agrees with Brzezinski's viewpoint, and argues that the European Union has to remain open to migration, both internal and external. If Europeans wish to stay true to their values, they cannot reject the people attempting to reach Lampedusa, the Italian island that has become a transit point for immigrants. Education frameworks, aimed at assimilating these people into the "European bloodstream," are necessary to avoid ghettoization. Kwaśniewski holds that the issue of migration and refugees will be one of Europe's main areas of conflict and internal debate.[36]

Europeans from those states that have yet to join the EU benefit from its existence in two ways. They can either emigrate to the EU or become citizens when their country of origin becomes a member. The latter option depends on the EU's openness and the potential members' ability to fulfill European standards.

Aleksander Kwaśniewski is of the opinion that the EU should remain open to Ukraine. At the same time, deeper cooperation requires sacrifices from both sides. Even before Euromaidan, Kwaśniewski argued that the Association Agreement is the right first step on the way to necessary changes in Ukraine, one that is going to take years to fully implement. It is Ukraine's chance for modernization, given that it suffers from numerous post–Soviet syndromes. Those ailments are much deeper than they were in Poland, since "fortunately, Poland was never a Soviet republic,"[37] Kwaśniewski claims. Thus, considering Ukraine's history and contemporary limitations, he is "far from being overly critical of Kyiv."[38] Kwaśniewski's leniency toward Ukraine does not mean that he offers excuses for the country's weaknesses. "I do blame Ukrainian political elites—all governments—for their tendencies toward animosity, instead of seeking compromise. Ukrainians are not familiar with the idea of building a nationwide consensus for the benefit of the whole society. Such weaknesses hamper Ukraine's development."[39]

Speaking in the European Parliament, Kwaśniewski said, "I am convinced that ... the Association will give Ukrainian citizens a sense of greater security and the rule of law."[40] Adopting European standards in a country, which for years was dominated and corrupted by the oligarchic system, is not easy. At the same time, Ukraine is not without blame.

> Ukraine is not an ideal country, nor will it be one for a long time to come. But we have the opportunity to introduce it to our standards. If we don't do that, Kyiv will follow the Russian and the Belarusian model. Ukraine was strongly under Russia's influence for centuries, and its people experienced a very brutal form of

communism. There are plenty of historical and geopolitical features and conflicts. Only a European strategy will help Ukraine emerge from the crisis. Fortunately, the country has a very lively civil society, which wants to be in the EU.[41]

Kwaśniewski believes that changes in Ukraine should be related to a generational change: "All this will require the young Ukrainian generation, which is not tainted by the Soviet legacy, to seize the initiative. A European perspective is the best thing that we can offer to Ukraine. This is how you can rebuild the country and its society."[42]

The proliferation of European standards, prosperity, and economic development are not the only things that are currently at stake. Today, it is about maintaining peace in Europe. Kwaśniewski notes that after the end of Cold War,

> It seemed like we made it to safety. Especially that more and more countries from our neighborhood want to share our values, our standards. They wish to respect human rights, respect the rights of minorities, and the rule of law. It seemed like we had reached the destination. Today, it's clear this process is not only incomplete, but that it has actually regressed.[43]

Unfortunately, Europe has not arrived at the "end of history." Following the ethnic cleansings in the Balkans in the 1990s, Russia's annexation of Crimea, and its military and logistical support of separatist forces in Eastern Ukraine are yet more examples of power politics making a comeback. Could this have been avoided? Not likely.

The crisis, which took place in Ukraine at the turn of 2013, was caused by the missed opportunities of 2004 and 2005. Opportunities were mostly wasted by Viktor Yushchenko and the Orange camp, but the European Union had its share of mistakes too. Ten years down the road, Ukraine was still corrupt to the bone. The values for which its society strived on the Maidan had been forsaken. For that reason, Ukrainians tend to refer to this event as the "so-called" "Orange Revolution," since it changed little. That is why they were forced to take matters into their own hands again, in what came to be known as the Euromaidan.

"Bon Chance, Alexandre": The Role of Poland's President in the Orange Revolution

Interviewed by the Polish Press Agency on the eve of the anniversary of the Maidan protests, Kwaśniewski said:

> The Orange Revolution was Ukraine's success and the birth of the country's civic society. With all due respect for the revolution's leaders and international mediators, credit has to be given to the Ukrainian people. They demonstrated extraordinary determination and bravery. They stood on the Maidan for days and fought for dignity despite freezing temperatures. The Orange Revolution was about dignity. Not about money, not about jobs, not about certain politicians.... The Orange Revolution was an event of great importance, and it cannot be wasted by political squabbles and electoral quarrels.[44]

Viktor Yushchenko made too many promises during the Maidan rallies. Especially too many promises of an economic nature, argues Kwaśniewski. After Yushchenko was elected, having won the rerun election for the second time, the former Polish president tried to warn him that "the festivities are over; it's time to get to work. The post-election expectations are sky-high. You need to use this enthusiasm and do something tangible."[45] Unfortunately, contrary to what Kwaśniewski had said, Ukrainian leaders shattered the dreams that had been inspired by what took place on the Maidan. Kwaśniewski must have felt this disappointment on two different levels: as president of Poland and as a politician directly involved in mediations between Kuchma, Yushchenko and Yanukovych. But despite the shortcomings of the Orange Revolution, at least the streets of Kyiv were not filled with blood, though it was a close call. Following the rigged elections in the fall of 2004, for the first time since Ukraine regained independence, the country found itself on the edge of an abyss.

The first round of the presidential election in Ukraine took place on October 31, 2004. Out of the 24 contenders, Viktor Yanukovych and Viktor Yushchenko led the race from the start. The first, coming from Donetsk, was prime minister at that time and had the blessing of President Leonid Kuchma. The latter was a former director of Ukraine's central bank. Despite this, neither of them was able to get the required majority.

The second round took place on November 21. Numerous reports of irregularities were noted and electoral fraud aimed to help Yanukovych was widely suspected. The United States and the European Union shared these suspicions. U.S. Secretary of State Colin Powell said that the results could not be recognized because the electoral process did not meet international standards and numerous reports on electoral fraud had not been investigated. Additionally, he made it clear to Kuchma

I. Ukraine in Aleksander Kwaśniewski's Geopolitical Strategy

that if the Ukrainian government would not take an immediate and responsible action, the country's relations with the U.S. would suffer.[46] Kyiv's relations with Washington had already hit rock bottom; therefore, Kuchma phoned Warsaw—the capital that he knew would not hang up on him.

Before the second round of the presidential election started, Kuchma called Aleksander Kwaśniewski on the day of his birthday and assured him that he would push for a fair electoral process. Kwaśniewski responded that the nature of the elections would define Kuchma's legacy among Ukrainians.[47] Kuchma made another phone call on Tuesday, November 23. This time he was not that calm. Yushchenko's supporters had been gathering on Maidan since Sunday. The "orange" camp mobilized crowds and concerts were being played on a makeshift stage. Kwaśniewski advised Kuchma that he should act as a moderator in order to boost Ukraine's image internationally.[48] On the same day, right before midnight, Viktor Yushchenko called the Polish president and requested his assistance in order to solve the political deadlock.

Kwaśniewski argued that both contenders—Yushchenko and Yanukovych—as well as Kuchma were equally responsible for Ukraine's unity: "They can pass the test, or fail it. If a civil war breaks out—and that is what I fear most—we're done."[49]

Ukrainian politicians found themselves in a risky situation, which could spin out of control and lead to bloodshed at any time. However, Kuchma still thought he would come out of it unscathed. He kept his distance and didn't even want to hear about any round-table talks.

Meanwhile, preparatory work was being carried out in Poland. Kwaśniewski delegated Jacek Kluczkowski, a minister in the chancellery of Poland's prime minister, and former ambassador to Moscow and presidential advisor, Stanisław Ciosek. They were joined by the head of the America Directorate at the Ministry of Foreign Affairs, Henryk Szlajfer; head of the Eastern Europe Department, Wojciech Zajączkowski; and presidential advisor on Ukraine, Olga Iwaniak. Former Ukrainian foreign minister Borys Tarasyuk arrived to Poland and, as Kwaśniewski recalled, "argued that my participation offered the only chance for a successful mediation."[50] Upon arrival in Kyiv, Polish envoys also held talks with Tarasyuk, who said: "You need to hurry. Kuchma may be willing to reach a compromise, but his influence among the security structures has been diminishing."[51]

At the same time, Kuchma and Yushchenko held telephone conversations with Javier Solana, the European Union's High Representative for Foreign and Security Policy, who had been probing EU member states whether getting involved in Ukraine's affairs was worth the effort. The EU's involvement was exactly what Aleksander Kwaśniewski was advocating. He had been trying to involve other European heads of states and EU representatives in order to avoid the perception that that crisis in Ukraine was a conflict between Poland and Russia. Kwaśniewski's interlocutors included: Dutch Prime Minister Jan Peter Balkenende (the Netherlands held the EU presidency at that time), Czech President Václav Klaus, and Austrian Chancellor Wolfgang Schüssel. Various European leaders were interested in Ukraine to a different degree. Kwaśniewski's conversation with the German Chancellor Gerhard Schröder was "cold." The Polish president tried to convince him to use his connections in Moscow to persuade the Kremlin that the policy of an iron fist would not do any good. Paris' reaction was equally indifferent. French President Jacques Chirac paid close attention to Kwaśniewski's analysis of the Ukrainian crisis, only to say: *"Bon Chance, Alexandre"* ("Good luck, Aleksander").[52]

Lithuania demonstrated the highest level of interest, as President Valdas Adamkus joined the ranks with Poland. On the Friday morning of November 26, Kwaśniewski landed in Kyiv. He subsequently met with Javier Solana and Leonid Kuchma before noon. Despite the fact that Kuchma had agreed to round-table talks the day before, he opened the meeting with a rant against the West and the opposition, blaming them for his country's poor situation. After ten minutes filled with insults, Kwaśniewski finally interrupted him and asked: "Leonid, should I just leave and head back for Warsaw?"[53] Kuchma was still agitated, but talking to him became gradually easier and easier. Every now and then, the discussion was interrupted by phone calls … from Moscow. Vladimir Putin was insisting that Russia should be represented in the talks. Finally, Kuchma assured Kwaśniewski he would participate in the negotiations.

Interviewed by *Polityka* magazine, Kwaśniewski recalls that he suggested that the sides convene at Mariyinsky Palace, near the

I. Ukraine in Aleksander Kwaśniewski's Geopolitical Strategy

Verkhovna Rada, the Ukrainian parliament. If the meeting did not take place at this location, Kwaśniewski thought that it would send a signal to the world that Ukraine is an odd country with three presidents—an acting one, an official one, and a president-elect—and no authority, as none of them can enter the president's residence. Kuchma said: "But it's being blocked." "So Yushchenko needs to unblock it. We have to get there," Kwaśniewski retorted.[54]

It seemed like everything had been prepared and the talks could start, but the round-table was nearly abandoned at the last minute. Kwaśniewski recollects:

> While we were leaving Kuchma's residence, we received intel about a rally of 40 thousand miners. It was scheduled before 3 pm. I was beginning to picture the fights in my head.... Our mission would have ended even before the negotiations started. I was saved by a twist of luck and my connections. The nine years of networking with all the Ukrainian politicians paid off. I got into the car with Jacek Kluczkowski, who had private phone numbers of a number of Ukrainian politicians. I managed to get a hold of Tihipko, Yanukovych's chief of staff, whom I had known. "Is it true what they say about the rally?" "Yes, nobody can control it anymore. Luhansk, Donetsk, and Kherson want to secede. It's over. Miners are revolting," he said. "Sir, I beseech you not to do it. We are about to meet at 4pm with Mr. Yanukovych. If you do that, you'll break off the talks. Please, do not do it under any circumstances." He got the message. I need to admit that Yanukovych did the right thing. He went to see the miners and told them to abort the mission.... That half hour was critical. Had the worst happened at that time, who knows where Ukraine would be today.[55]

Luckily, Kwaśniewski had known Serhiy Tihipko for many years. He helped him develop official connections in Paris, Berlin and other capitals. Kwaśniewski reminisces: "Sometime, it would all be about whether or not you had someone's phone number. Being able to reach an important politician's mobile phone ... would decide whether you could negotiate and even stop bloodshed. It would determine future developments for the next few hours or even the next few weeks."[56]

Soon after Kwaśniewski managed to put out a fire, another one would be started. He was supposed to meet Yushchenko's team at 3 p.m., but they suddenly said that they would not sit at the same table with Yanukovych. "In that case, who would you like to talk to?" inquired Kwaśniewski, Adamkus and Solana. "We can speak with Kuchma." The mediators attempted to convince them that Kuchma was an outgoing president and—despite everything—Yanukovych was an important partner who had gained millions of votes.[57] They finally said "yes" and turned out to be much better prepared than Yanukovych's team.

The Ukrainian round-table talks started after 5 p.m. Among the European mediators present were Kwaśniewski, Adamkus, Solana, and secretary general of OECD, Ján Kubiš. The Ukrainian side was represented by Kuchma; Yushchenko; Yanukovych; speaker of the Verkhovna Rada, Volodymyr Lytvyn; and the former speaker of the Parliament and first president of independent Ukraine, Leonid Kravchuk. Putin made sure that speaker of the Russian Duma, Boris Gryzlov, was present. Kuchma moderated the meeting.

Sitting to Solana's right and in front of Kuchma and Kwaśniewski, Yanukovych argued fervently that the elections were fair. Yushchenko, who was at the opposite side of the table, presented examples of electoral fraud. Yanukovych kept on insisting that the election was fair. It was at that time when Kwaśniewski suggested a hypothetical situation: Let's assume a second round is underway. It's business as usual until 4 pm and the turnout is 40 percent. An earthquake takes place at 4 pm and nobody's able to vote anymore. What do we do? Logically speaking, the election is not over and voters still need to be given a chance to make the final decision. After all, it can't be ruled out that Mr. Yanukovych will win, said Kwaśniewski.

> **Kwaśniewski**: Was the election fair?
> **Yanukovych**: Yes, fair.
> **Kwaśniewski**: And you're a million votes ahead?
> **Yanukovych**: Yes, one million.
> **Kwaśniewski**: In that case, why are you afraid of a repeat of the second round?
> **Yanukovych**: Because it's complicated from a legal standpoint.
> **Kwaśniewski**: It is complicated. However, there are times when new developments need to be taken into consideration.[58]

Yanukovych fell into his own trap. His team did not want to be outdone by Yushchenko's team. When Yushchenko reported 700 electoral protests against fraud in Eastern Ukraine, Yanukovych's men reported 7,000 in the West. Kwaśniewski asked if the 7,000 examples of fraud were not a good enough reason to repeat the second round.

Following three hours of talks, three points—for which Kwaśniewski had pushed from the start—were agreed upon: dialogue would be main-

I. Ukraine in Aleksander Kwaśniewski's Geopolitical Strategy

tained, force would not be used, consensus must be reached in accordance with Ukrainian law. In the evening, they all met at an informal dinner at Kuchma's residence.

Even though everyone agreed that force should not be used, Yanukovych clearly did not believe his own words. On Saturday, he insisted that Kuchma should use force to deal with the unrest in Kyiv's city center. "You have become very brave, Viktor Fedorovych, to speak to me in this manner," retorted Kuchma. "It would be best for you to show this bravery on Independence Square," he added.[59] Kuchma was not convinced that the use of force was the best option, but that did not mean that such a solution was out of the question. Anything could have happened Friday night. On that day, hard-cast bullets and tear gas were distributed to around 10,000 troops of the Ministry of the Interior. Their job was to deal with the crowd on Maidan.[60] Yushchenko was promptly informed about this development by certain individuals within the Ukrainian security services. Kuchma's phone would not stop ringing. On the U.S. ambassador's request, Secretary of State Colin Powell tried to reach Kuchma, but he would not answer. Kwaśniewski tried to call the president too.

Luckily, the Ministry of Interior did not resort to force. The military and security services were increasingly more divided, which frightened Kuchma. On Monday, the threat was beginning to gradually fade away. On Wednesday morning of December 1, the second round of the round-table talks commenced. It was still unclear whether a repeat of the elections would take place. Yushchenko insisted on invalidating the second round, but Yanukovych would not have it. Finally, Lytvyn laid out a proposal: a reform of the electoral legislation pertaining to presidential elections and a rerun of the second round, should that be the Supreme Court's decision. The constitution would also be changed and a new government would be formed based on the points above.[61] The constitutional amendments were supposed to diminish the presidency to the benefit of the premiership, which did in fact happen two years later.

Yushchenko was accompanying Kwaśniewski when he left the meeting room. A crowd of people wearing orange scarves, orange jackets and orange hats was chanting Yushchenko's name. He said: "The president of Poland is here with me." "Polshcha! Polshcha!" the crowd replied. "They would have done anything for him. That's how much they trusted him," recalls Kwaśniewski. "That's when I told him: 'Remember Viktor, the enthusiasm will run out of steam eventually. It's up to you to manage it wisely.'"[62]

Pressure was rising as the Supreme Court's ruling was awaited. On December 3, the decision was made to repeat the second round on December 26. Even though Kuchma "had been running around like a headless chicken for weeks,"[63] three days after the ruling was proclaimed, he decided to respect the Supreme Courts' decision. Kuchma announced that the following round of the round-table talks would take place on December 6.

The final meeting started on Monday evening and lasted six hours, until early morning of the following day. The government's resignation, demanded by Yushchenko, was the bone of contention. In the end, Kuchma did not dismiss the government, but it was agreed that Yanukovych would take a three-week leave during the campaign period. Deputy Prime Minister Mykola Azarov was to be in charge of the government during that time.

It was agreed that, in accordance with the Supreme Court's decision, there would be a rerun of the second round of the election, the legislation governing presidential elections would be amended and new members of the Central Electoral Committee would be appointed. The Verkhovna Rada voted in favor of the changes on December 8. Two months later, Viktor Yushchenko was sworn in as Ukraine's new president. The Orange Revolution was over.

When he was president, Yushchenko said: "I consider Aleksander Kwaśniewski's active involvement during the Orange Revolution to be a significantly important episode of his political career. I am confident that his input and his strategic vision were a remarkable contribution to the victory of Ukrainian democracy and the end of a fierce political crisis."[64]

Former U.S. ambassador to Ukraine, Steven Pifer, in his insightful work entitled, "European Mediators and Ukraine's Orange Revolution," analyzes the Kwaśniewski-Solana tandem as a swift and efficient model, which the European Union could apply to deal with other potential crises. Their success was possible because it was a fusion of the EU High Representative's authority with the personality of a head of state

I. Ukraine in Aleksander Kwaśniewski's Geopolitical Strategy

who benefited from personal connections and the ability to interact with other presidents on an equal basis.[65] Pifer also believes that

> by virtually all accounts, Kwaśniewski made the most creative contributions. As one person present at the roundtable described it, Kwaśniewski understood what was going on and was the mediator most inclined to get into discussions on substance. He spoke Russian, was most attuned to the politics of the situation, and could draw upon his own experience as a participant in the 1989 Polish roundtable negotiations. Moreover, among the mediators, Kwaśniewski had the closest personal relationship with Kuchma, whom he had known since 1996, and with whom he could deal on an equal basis (president-to-president). As a Ukrainian involved in the process commented, Kwaśniewski was a political equal who could pull Kuchma aside and say: "C'mon Leonid, you can't mean that," and Kuchma would listen.[66]

Close personal relations with Kuchma helped Kwaśniewski dissolve a number of tensions. They shared a decade of experience of mutual cooperation as heads of state. They knew each other well and, given the way things are in Ukraine, they must have had quite a few shots of vodka together. But difficult subjects related to sensitive historical issues were not overlooked. In 2003, the year of the 60th anniversary of the Volhynia massacres, Kwaśniewski delivered a speech at a renovated Catholic cemetery in the town of Poryck. "Family members, of those who were murdered, are here today. They wish to mourn their relatives and bury them with dignity," said Kwaśniewski. Addressing Kuchma, the Polish president added:

> Mr. President, we are grateful to all the empathic Ukrainian people who understand this. We would like to thank you for your words filled with sympathy, remorse, and friendship. We appreciate the attitude demonstrated by independent Ukraine, acting as our host here, willing to reflect together with us on the tragic history that we share.[67]

Kuchma replied, "We have gathered here to condemn violence and put an end to the veil of silence surrounding these events."[68] He did not unequivocally condemn the Ukrainian Insurgent Army (UPA), as demanded by the families of the victims, but given all the disparity in perceptions between Poles and Ukrainians, the process of reconciliation was moving in the right direction.

At that time, Kuchma felt like he owed a lot to Kwaśniewski. The Polish politician was among the very few leaders who did not sever ties with Kuchma after the so-called "Cassette Scandal." Mykola Melnychenko, an officer of the Security Service of Ukraine (SBU), recorded Kuchma's conversations for one year, between October 1999 and October 2000. These recordings led to a terrible deterioration of Kyiv's relations with Brussels and Washington, especially after Melnychenko was granted refugee status by the U.S. in April 2001. The audio materials contained Kuchma's conversations with his associates, including the president's suggestions that someone should "take care of" the investigative reporter Georgiy Gongadze.[69] The decapitated body of the Georgian journalist was found on November 2000. He was reported missing in Kyiv on September 16. The link between Gongadze's case with the ruling regime was made public on November 28 by the chairman of the Socialist Party Oleksandr Moroz. Another thing that disturbed the United States was the suspicion that Ukraine sold the Kolchuga passive early warning radar to Saddam Hussein.

The Kolchuga system detects and analyzes electromagnetic signals emitted by planes and vessels and enables detecting planes without the use of traditional radars.[70] In consequence, a fighter pilot is not aware of being located. According to Carlos Pascual, the U.S. ambassador to Ukraine at that time, Washington suspected Kyiv of selling Kolchuga as early as in March 2002. Melnychenko's recordings from July 2000 were the source of the intelligence. One day after the accusations were made public, the U.S. announced it would suspend its $54 million aid program for Ukraine.[71] The level of ostracism with which Kuchma had to deal was so high that President George W. Bush refused to sit next to him at a meeting of the Euro-Atlantic Partnership Council, during the NATO summit in Prague in 2002. Given that both the United States and Ukraine start with the letter "u" and seating arrangements were determined alphabetically, Bush and Kuchma would sit together. But at the Americans' request, the organizers found a not-so-subtle, but nonetheless diplomatic, solution. English names of countries were replaced with their French versions. Therefore, the representative of *Les États Unis* was not seated next to the president of *L'Ukraine*. Kwaśniewski was the only NATO leader who did not agree with this kind of attitude towards Kuchma.[72] Kuchma had more luck during dinner at the Prague Castle when he sat at the same table with George W. Bush, separated from the American president by Kazakhstan's head of state, Nursultan Nazarbayev.[73]

In 2004, Kuchma did not wish to leave a messy legacy and to be

I. Ukraine in Aleksander Kwaśniewski's Geopolitical Strategy

remembered as the one who set Ukraine on fire. On the other hand, he was not prepared to lose his influence and his possessions. His actions at the time suggest he was disoriented. He sought both Kwaśniewski and Putin's council. The solution suggested by the Russian president was simple: under such circumstances, one should proclaim martial law or hand over power to the president-elect. "Well, how on earth do I hand over power to him, Vladimir Vladimirovich? He's just a Donetsk bandit,"[74] Kuchma reportedly replied. His relations with Yanukovych were gradually deteriorating. At the same time, Kwaśniewski appealed for compromise and moderation. He also managed to maintain the trust of both sides of the dispute.

Kwaśniewski's road in politics proved to many in Ukraine that someone who had launched his career and climbed the career ladder in the communist system could still be able to find his place in a new, democratic state. Moreover, a person like that was able to win elections! Each time Ukrainians would go to polls, left-wing politicians would bring up Kwaśniewski as a shining example. Oleksandr Moroz, who portrayed himself as "Ukraine's Kwaśniewski," constantly talked about the "Polish route" for the left wing.[75]

After the Orange Revolution, when inquired whether he would be able to build a European-style social democracy, Moroz said: "Aleksander Kwaśniewski's communist background did not stop him from becoming a democratically-elected president of Poland. His position, in the old system, was even higher than mine. But Poland respects its president."[76] Kwaśniewski's story could be brought up by Ukrainian politicians with various backgrounds. Some of them—such as Moroz— would emphasize that an ex-communist, social democratic politician was capable of winning elections. Others—such as Yushchenko, who was leaning towards the West—underlined that President Kwaśniewski supervised Poland's accession to NATO and the EU. He was whoever Ukrainians wanted him to be.

When Yushchenko attempted to convince Kwaśniewski to address the Maidan crowd, he declined. The Polish politician explained he had to maintain the illusion of neutrality for as long as he remained engaged in the process of resolving the conflict:

> I need to be able to talk to everyone. I wouldn't want to allow anyone to argue that I was at the square, the crowd cheered, and now they've got me. That's

what we agreed on—together with Adamkus and Solana—that we'll stick to our roles as moderators for as long as necessary. Our job was to facilitate dialogue and answer the phone, no matter which side of the conflict called us.[77]

This farsightedness enabled Kwaśniewski to undertake another mediating mission in 2012. Given the seeming success of the Orange Revolution, no one would have thought that Yanukovych would be elected president in 2010. Had Kwaśniewski failed to maintain the illusion of neutrality (despite his clear inclinations) and openly supported the orange camp, his participation in the European Parliament's mission, organized seven years later, would not have been possible. Not everyone, however, appreciated Kwaśniewski's involvement. Moscow didn't even try to hide that there would be consequences.

> After the first round of negotiations, when we started to find a common ground, I knew there would be a price to pay. That's why I asked myself: Is it worth it and does it even make sense to engage? And I decided that the mission had to be concluded. I have no regrets, despite the price that will likely have to be paid because politicians in several capitals will be angry.[78]

Due to his involvement in the Ukrainian round-table talks, Kwaśniewski lost his chances for a prestigious, international post to which Poland could have aspired after his term as president. He admits: "If anything was within reach at that time, it was the position of the United Nation's Secretary General. But my chances were gone after my involvement in the Orange Revolution in Ukraine. You can't get that job without Russia."[79] In 2005, Kwaśniewski took part in the World War II Victory Day parade on the Red Square. In 2014, he said:

> I wouldn't go there today because of what happened in Ukraine. But Poland's support for the Orange Revolution in 2004 had a cast a shadow on the Victory Day celebrations at that time. Putin held a grudge against me because of my support for the Orange Revolution. A debate whether I should go at all was taking place in Poland at that time. I still believe I made the right call. We demonstrated our willingness to respect a ceremony that was so important for Russia. We demonstrated our openness to dialogue.[80]

Being open to discussion with anyone who would like to join the negotiating table defined Kwaśniewski's attitude during the Orange Revolution. If Ukraine had not wasted its opportunity, he would not have had to undertake another mission in 2012. Given the way things developed, he had no other choice but to try to resolve another crisis.

II

The European Union's Special Envoy to Ukraine: The Cox-Kwaśniewski Mission

Finding an explanation for what is going on in the heads of Ukraine's leaders, and what sort of decisions will be taken, is a task for psychics, not analysts.[1]
—Aleksander Kwaśniewski

If there is a green light from Pat Cox and Alexander Kwaśniewski there will be a green light for Ukraine in Europe. Without a green light from them, there will not be a green light.[2]
—Carl Bildt

For over two decades, EU-Ukraine relations resembled a plot of a Brazilian soap opera, infested with ridiculous twists. Ukraine was having an affair with both the West and the East, but in fact, it was moving in neither direction. Kyiv flirted with Brussels with its willingness of a closer political and economic cooperation. At the same time, it was drifting towards Eurasian, not European, standards; using its multi-vector policy as an excuse for lackluster progress on reforms, corruption and poor democratic standards were pushing Ukraine close to the Russian model. Meanwhile, the EU had its own problems. In 2012, Aleksander Kwaśniewski reminded: "Let us not forget that the European Union has a lot to deal with. Kyiv's future is not its only concern. We are going through a financial crisis, facing Greece and Spain's problems. But we have not given up on Ukraine, because it still has loyal friends among European states, Poland in particular."[3]

Despite its own problems and its dissolution and weariness with Ukraine, the EU did not stop supporting it. At that time, a new political and economic agreement embodied an important attempt toward deeper bilateral relations. Since 1994, the Partnership and Cooperation Agreement (PCA) constituted a basis for EU-Ukraine relations.[4] After years of engagement within its framework, both sides decided to deepen their cooperation. In March 2007, negotiations of the New Enhanced Agreement (NEA) were launched. It was later called the Association Agreement.

According to Ukrainian diplomats and European negotiators, the political part of the Association Agreement was practically completed in the first half of 2011.[5] The negotiations of the economic part of the agreement—the Deep and Comprehensive Free Trade Area (DCFTA)—were a more complex issue. According to the European Commission, facilitating trade and promoting social standards in order to boost investment in Moldova, Georgia, Azerbaijan, Armenia and Ukraine (The Eastern Partnership countries) constituted DCFTA's main objective.

In September 2011, *The Wall Street Journal* published an editorial entitled "The Future of Ukraine is With the European Union," written by Viktor Yanukovych.[6] On the day of the celebration of the 20th anniversary of Ukraine's independence, Yanukovych declared that EU membership was his country's priority. But the case of Yulia Tymoshenko practically brought deeper integration with the EU to a halt. The Ukrainian prosecution carried out two trials against the former prime minister. It was clearly following the orders of Yanukovych's political party. On September 11, 2011, Yulia Tymoshenko was convicted on accounts of abuse of office while she was prime minister. In accordance with paragraph 365 of the penal code, the court in Kyiv sentenced her to seven years in prison and a fine of 195 million dollars. The so-called "gas case" verdict was upheld by the Court of Appeals' decision of December 23, 2011, and by the Court of Cassation on August 29. Besides Tymoshenko's negotiations of gas prices with Russia related to the abuse of office, the court began presiding over the so-called "tax case" on March 28, 2012. Tymoshenko was accused of misappropriation, tax evasion, and forgery.[7]

Aleksander Kwaśniewski is of the opinion that the arrest and conviction of Yulia Tymoshenko was politically motivated, despite the fact that there may have been a legal basis if, indeed, she had abused power

II. The European Union's Special Envoy to Ukraine

by stamping the deal without prior consultation with the council of ministers. The former Polish president points out two aspects. The first one was revenge, as Yanukovych and his posse hated Tymoshenko. The second one—fear: "They knew that Tymoshenko was the only person capable of organizing a meaningful opposition against Yanukovych. After all, she collected an impressive number of presidential votes when she was a party leader." At that time, Batkivshchyna was the only truly European political party because the remaining ones were either regional or oligarchic in nature. Only Batkivshchyna managed to build its structures in all of Ukraine (its support rate varied geographically, but it was present everywhere). Because of this, it was a threat to Yanukovych.[8] From the EU's point of view, it meant that Ukraine's political system was drifting towards Belarusian, not European standards. There was also a humanitarian dimension of the Tymoshenko case.

Rape, violence, overcrowding, and corruption are common in Ukrainian jails, where the personnel abuse inmates physically and mentally. It was clear from the start that Tymoshenko's case would attract international attention, which is why it was important to make it look like her conditions were not that bad. Tymoshenko's cell did not look like the 8 square meter room filled with up to 20 inmates, "without windows, with laundry drying underneath the ceiling, and with walls infested with carcinogenic mold."[9] As reported by Małgorzata Nocuń:

> The penitentiary assured me that Tymoshenko could not complain about the comfortable conditions. Her cell was spacious, with neat furniture, and kitchen cabinets. But those imagines were contrasted with pictures of a bruised Tymoshenko and her lawyer's statements on the allegedly inhumane treatment of his client. He claimed that the lights in Lady Yu's little cell never went out and her every move was being monitored round the clock. Tymoshenko suffered from pains in the back and did not receive proper medical attention. Painkillers did not do the trick and it turned out that a guard had inflicted her bruises.[10]

The European Union found it unacceptable that the former prime minister, former presidential hopeful, and the leader of the largest opposition party was locked up. Even if the gas deal were indeed questionable, signing an unfavorable agreement would lead to political, rather than criminal, consequences in any normal European country. As argued by the statement regarding Yulia Tymoshenko issued on May 2011 by the High Representative's spokesperson, there were "suggestions of political motivation behind these cases." The statement notes:

> The EU will continue to underline to the Ukrainian authorities the need for respect for the rule of law, incorporating fair, impartial and independent legal processes. We note the danger of provoking any perception that judicial measures are used selectively, and we stress the importance of ensuring the maximum transparency of investigations, prosecutions and trials. We consider these principles especially important in a country with which we intend to enter into a deeper contractual relationship built upon political association.[11]

In June 2011, the European Parliament adopted a resolution on the case of Yulia Tymoshenko and former government officials. MEPs concluded that the EU had consistently underlined the necessity of respect of the rule of law and strongly advised against any use of the penal code for political gains. The EU reacted in a much harsher manner after the arrest of Tymoshenko itself. On August 5, 2011, Catherine Ashton, the High Representative, and Štefan Füle, the EU's Commissioner for Enlargement and European Neighborhood Policy, issued a joint statement. The document expressed their extreme concern with the developments, which took place at the Pechersk District Court that led to the arrest of Yulia Tymoshenko.[12] But apart from issuing additional written statements, Brussels did not really know what else to do.

A new idea was finally conceived in the spring of 2012. On May 16, Ukraine's Prime Minister Mykola Azarov visited Brussels. He might have felt a bit out of place. Less than two weeks before his arrival, Herman Van Rompuy told Euronews, "the Prime Minister of Ukraine announced he would come to Brussels, we said: 'Stay home!'"[13] Despite this, Azarov went to Brussels and met with the president of the European Parliament, Martin Schulz. He complained that relations with the EU were in a deadlock and—after all—Tymoshenko was a criminal, who was acting against the law, which resulted in huge losses for Ukraine. Moreover, her Christian Democratic political allies blocked Kyiv's European integration in Brussels. Having listened to the same old story of the Party of Regions, Schulz ran out of patience and said, "Enough is enough!" and added that despite the fact that Ukrainian authorities only had themselves to blame for this problem, he was ready to send an observation mission to Ukraine. It was supposed to assist Ukrainians in areas where they could not deliver themselves: remove the remaining

II. The European Union's Special Envoy to Ukraine

obstacles on the way to the Association Agreement, which in reality meant resolving the Tymoshenko crisis. There was one condition, though. Schulz demanded a promise that Ukraine would fully cooperate and provide the mission with complete access, no matter which door would have to be opened. Azarov needed a minute to think about it … and to call Kyiv. When he returned to the meeting room, he said, "Deal!"

The same evening, Schulz and Azarov held a press conference and announced the commencement of the parliamentary mission. The name of the special envoy (only one person initially) was to be announced shortly.

Why wasn't the Party of Regions concerned with the notion of the EU's envoys rummaging through their courts' documents? Why weren't they disturbed by the idea of having foreign visitors in their government departments and prisons? The truth is that Yanukovych and his government had nothing to lose. By saying "yes" to the EU's mission, they demonstrated their openness to cooperate and gained more room to maneuver in their dealings with Russia. The mission also benefited Schulz. Even though Tymoshenko's situation seemed hopeless, the president of the European Parliament could not just let it go. His ambitions went well beyond the chamber of the EP.

Schulz is a heavyweight politician and an EP veteran. He was first elected MEP in 1994 and has been building his position and influence ever since. Between 2000 and 2004, he was chairman of the German Socialist (SPD) delegation in the European Parliament. Following the 2009 European elections, he took the helm of the Socialists and Democrats Group, the second largest political faction in the EP. In the everlasting competition among the EU's institutions (and their leaders), Schulz advocated for more powers for the Parliament. This would often require engaging in a fierce confrontation with the Commission and the Council. He usually has a stern expression and does not refrain from acerbic language when he grills heads of Member States and European Commissioners. One of his speeches sparked Silvio Berlusconi to outrageously retort that Schulz would be perfect for the role of a capo in a movie about a death camp.

Even though the European People's Party (EPP) was the largest political group during the EP's 2009–2014 term, a sort of gentlemen's agreement has been upheld for years. It resembles the German "grand coalition" between Christian Democrats and Socialists (S&D). That is why following Jerzy Buzek's two-and-a-half-year term, Martin Schulz took over the European Parliament's presidency in 2012. He had to make the most of the little time he would have in order to prove himself as a politician capable of assuming the post of president of the European Commission.

A few months before the 2014 European elections, the Party of European Socialists nominated Schulz as its candidate for the top job. The new president would replace José Manuel Barroso, whose term was about to end. The deal was as follows: should the Christian Democrats prevail, Jean-Claude Juncker would preside over the Commission; if the Socialists should win, Schulz would be given the job. In the end, Juncker came out on top, but that does not change the fact that in 2012 Schulz's odds were good. Therefore, the German politician could not simply ignore Ukraine, and the mission was a perfect tool to demonstrate that he was a statesman who took matters into his own hands and found solutions to the EU's greatest challenges.

Aleksander Kwaśniewski has a high opinion of Martin Schulz. "I believe he has been—for many years—the first president of the EP who comprehends the political nature of the institution and his own role."[14] Given that there was not much the head of the EU's diplomacy, Catherine Ashton, and the commissioner in charge of relations with Ukraine could do, Schulz wanted the European Parliament to undertake the mission impossible. Following the announcement of the mission's launch on May 16, 2012, the German politician started to look for the right person for the job.

As mentioned before, Romano Prodi declined, even though he might have seemed like the perfect candidate. The former Italian prime minister and former president of the European Commission was an experienced politician on both the national and European level. Moreover, he was affiliated with the Socialist faction, which had always had better relations with the Ukrainian "blues." The Party of Regions would not tolerate anyone from the EPP, Tymoshenko's political ally. Someone other than Prodi had to be chosen.

Kwaśniewski's name came up next. However, his candidacy had to be supplemented, so that everyone in both Kyiv and Brussels would be happy. Pat Cox turned out to be the balancing factor. Cox might

II. The European Union's Special Envoy to Ukraine

have been a Liberal Democrat, but his party had joined the EPP. The former president of the European Parliament had experience in European politics, which complemented Kwaśniewski's experience on the national level. Moreover, the balance between the West and the East was also maintained.

> I am delighted that Pat Cox and Aleksander Kwaśniewski have accepted my proposal to go to Ukraine to monitor court proceedings involving Ms. Tymoshenko on behalf of the European Parliament. Mr. Cox and Mr. Kwaśniewski are personalities of high international repute. They command respect for their excellent record in foreign and domestic politics. They enjoy wide support across all political forces in the European Parliament. I hope their mission will be a breakthrough that will help Ukraine to address problems concerning the rule of law and the independence of judiciary. I hope it will contribute to restoring mutual confidence in EU-Ukraine relations.[15]

In December 2011, at the EU-Ukraine summit, European leaders and Yanukovych declared that a consensus had been reached regarding the contents of the Association Agreement. In March 2012, the document was initialed (the trade-focused DCFTA was initialed in July 2012). Nevertheless, mutual trust between Brussels and Kyiv was practically non-existent and Yanukovych—along with his Party of Regions—had broken a number of promises. Kwaśniewski argued:

> We remember all the promises. None of us—at least not me—suffers from amnesia. We have been asked by Martin Schulz to be here today with the European Parliament's observation mission. We wish to hold talks with all the parties involved in this conflict. At the same time, we are searching for solutions that will help us make sure the Ukrainian achievements—such as the initialing of the Association Agreement—won't be squandered. This is a pivotal moment. If we do not find a political way out of this dead-end street, all the positive achievements may be wasted.[16]

Ukraine found itself in a tricky situation. The Association Agreement with the EU had been initialed, but its conclusion was frozen by political factors. "What can be done to enable Kyiv to free itself from its own trap? We're looking for a solution."[17]

During the next 18 months, Kwaśniewski participated in 27 missions, including 80 days in Ukraine and at least 20 more days in Brussels and other capitals. The former Polish president claimed, "the nature of the mission was discreet; we did not hold any official positions."[18] The Cox-Kwaśniewski mission was rather different than the one undertaken in the wake of the Orange Revolution. In 2004, both the opposition and President Kuchma invited Kwaśniewski, which fostered his mission's legitimacy, given that "in order for the mission to be successful, it needs to be accepted by both sides."[19] Less than a decade later, he was again a special envoy to Ukraine.

During the Orange Revolution, the mission was focused on electoral fraud. The stakes of the mission commenced in June 2012 were significantly different: it was about Ukraine's future: "I don't think I need to convince anyone of my support for Ukraine's European aspirations. After all, that was the goal of Pat Cox and my visits on behalf of the EU."[20] Kwaśniewski assumed the role of an impartial mediator of a political dispute, but he openly admitted he was supportive of Ukraine's decision to join the West. On the other hand, he did not act as anyone's political consultant and was not politically affiliated with either of the camps. Not even the pro–European one.

Martin Schulz (middle), with Pat Cox (left) and Aleksander Kwaśniewski, announces the launch of the European Parliament's special mission and notes, "I am delighted that Pat Cox and Aleksander Kwaśniewski have accepted my proposal to go to Ukraine." Brussels, June 7, 2012. © European Union 2012. Source: PE-EP.

II. The European Union's Special Envoy to Ukraine

The objective of the mission was to reach tangible results by consulting both the government and the opposition, so that Ukraine could sign the Association Agreement. In order for that to happen, the Yulia Tymoshenko case had to be resolved. At the time, Kwaśniewski and Cox faced some criticism in Ukraine. The argument was that their assessment of the situation would be political, rather than legal, as they were not experts on the Ukrainian justice system and, in effect, did not possess the qualities and expertise necessary for leading the mission.[21]

Tymoshenko's case was obviously politically motivated, but Kwaśniewski did not intend to ignore Ukraine's legal system: "If you asked me if I see any instant solutions to this problem, I'd say that I don't. It's going to take patience and numerous talks. Even if we don't consider Ukraine's legal system to be completely impartial, we can't just ignore it. We need to adhere to certain rules and procedures."[22] Given that the former Ukrainian prime minister's sentence was legally binding, Kwaśniewski was of the opinion that "the issue requires a legal solution. That requires political will. It's a highly complicated matter, which depends upon the Ukrainian government's common sense."[23]

A month prior to the start of the mission, Kwaśniewski openly stated that Yanukovych should allow Tymoshenko to seek medical attention abroad. When he said these words, Western European politicians were contemplating whether they should boycott the 2012 Euro Cup. Kwaśniewski was vehemently against the idea. He claimed a boycott would only affect the Ukrainian people, who would consider it an affront to Ukrainian society and its ambitions. "Instead of resorting to a boycott, we should rather intensify the dialogue. We should make it clear that what has been going on around Yulia Tymoshenko and her former cabinet members is unacceptable."[24] Kwaśniewski had the opportunity to follow his own advice during the course of the 2012 Euro Cup.

The first Ukrainian visit of the EP's special envoys was preceded by collecting and analyzing information pertaining to the legal dimension of the case of Ms. Tymoshenko and Yuriy Lutsenko. "We will now analyze the documents together with our legal team. The upcoming week will be all about paperwork," said Kwaśniewski.[25] On June 11, Kwaśniewski and Cox met in Kyiv with Tymoshenko's daughter, her lawyer, and former deputy prime minister, Hryhoriy Nemyria. Then they spent three hours with Viktor Yanukovych. They discussed the details of the gas deal, signed by Tymoshenko in January 2009, and its consequences. The envoys also met with Prime Minister Azarov and a number of other officials: the Minister of Justice, the Minister of National Health, representatives from the prosecutor's office, the Security Council, and even doctors. "It was clear Kyiv took the mission seriously," said Kwaśniewski.[26] Indeed, the Ukrainian authorities did not take the mission lightly and an ad-hoc intergovernmental unit was created specifically to assist the envoys' work and provide access to documents, people and facilities. The individuals who were assigned to this unit were Deputy Head of the Secretariat of Cabinet of Ministers of Ukraine, Serhiy Kamyshev (Ukraine's ambassador to China between 2004 and 2009), and Advisor to the Cabinet of Ministers of Ukraine, Vadym Pozharskyi.

The government was divided between two factions, a pro–Russian and pro–European camp. Both sides saw Ukraine's interests (and often their own) as either with Moscow or Brussels. Kwaśniewski recognized this from the outset and knew that the pro–European camp could potentially help in getting Ukraine past the ongoing political impasse. Some of these individuals remained behind the scenes, but provided the mission with official and unofficial support.

On June 11, Kwaśniewski was invited to watch the Ukraine-Sweden soccer match. That is where he met Mykola Zlochevsky, former Minster of Ecology and Natural Resources of Ukraine. According to some accounts, Pat Cox was not sure if going to an informal setting like a Euro Cup game was the best idea. But Kwaśniewski did not mind and allegedly said, "I'm in Ukraine. I'm among friends."[27] At halftime, Ukraine and Sweden were tied 0:0.

Mykola Zlochevsky was among Ukraine's largest gas producers. He resigned in April 2012 and was transferred to a secondary position at the National Security Council while the ministry was handed down to Eduard Stavitsky, a person loyal to the Yanukovych "family." (Stavitsky later ended up on Interpol's international wanted list.) Meanwhile, Zlochevsky focused his efforts on creating an independent pro–Western private gas producing company. Kwaśniewski knew that the political dependence of Ukraine (and of its entire political establishment) on Russian gas was so overwhelming that the Kremlin could easily use

II. The European Union's Special Envoy to Ukraine

economic leverage over Kyiv through its state monopoly and businessmen close to Vladimir Putin. The price for natural gas in Ukraine was the highest in Europe and yet the country's dependence on Gazprom's energy was rising. The Ukrainian national team began losing 1:0 after a goal in the 52nd minute.

The Ukrainian government did not want an all-out confrontation with Russia and Vladimir Putin over gas; however, it did not mind if individual businessmen would take the risk trying to extract Ukraine's own energy resource. At that time, there were very few independent gas producers in the country and Viktor Yanukovych and the oligarchs close to him were in control of most of these companies. Zlochevsky was not in that camp because apparently he saw potential somewhere else: in Europe. Three minutes after the first goal, Ukraine came back. It was 1:1.

Aleksander Kwaśniewski was of the opinion that creating a strategy aimed at securing Ukraine's energy independence that would not only diversify its energy supplies, but also change the principles of the internal policies regarding domestic exploration and production of natural gas. It seems that he and Mykola Zlochevsky had similar views. In the 62nd minute, Ukraine scored a winning goal. The game ended 2:1.

Kwaśniewski and Cox met with Yulia Tymoshenko for the first time during their second visit to Ukraine (June 24–26, 2012). They talked for about three hours in the hospital in Kharkiv, with doctors and representatives of the prosecution and the penitentiary. In the following months, Kwaśniewski would attend a number of trials and he would meet with Tymoshenko or her daughter almost every time he visited Ukraine. His conversations with the former prime minister drew a great amount of media attention. Journalists would inquire about what she said and how she was doing. But Cox and Kwaśniewski would not comment and only revealed basic information.

> First of all, Pat and I agreed to play the role of impartial referees. Secondly, we did not want to let anyone—neither Yanukovych, nor Tymoshenko —manipulate us. Both wanted to have us on their side. Finally, there was the risk that the media would manipulate our statements and we did not have the luxury of time to hold extended press conferences and make potential corrections to any misquoted statements. It was all happening so fast and anything could have hit the news.[28]

In June, Cox and Kwaśniewski monitored the proceedings of the Kharkiv court during the third trial of the "tax case" and in Kyiv at the second trial regarding the cassation of the "gas case" charges. The turbulent trials were filled with tension, as demonstrated by statements of Serhiy Vlasenko—Tymoshenko's lawyer. One year earlier, when his client was tweeting on her iPad, and occasionally verbally offending the judges, he proclaimed, "They're a bunch of criminals. Some of them wear prosecutor's uniforms, others black robes. I beseech you, slaves in robes, do not forget that you represent the court."[29]

"The prison and courthouse were among the first places Cox visited in Ukraine," recalls Kwaśniewski. Although Tymoshenko was not present in the Kharkiv court, her lawyers, who were criticizing the judges and the prosecution, were there. Cox could not speak Russian, so he relied on interpretation. He finally turned to Kwaśniewski: "Aleksander, is it true what they are telling me?" "Yes, it's true," replied Kwaśniewski. "In my country, Ireland, they would be charged with contempt of court." The former Polish president was not as shocked as Cox, who "watched the whole spectacle wide-eyed."[30]

Apart from attending trials and meeting with Prime Minister Azarov, Kwaśniewski and Cox spent five hours on talks with Prosecutor General Viktor Pshonka and his deputy, Renat Kuzmin. They also met with the U.S. ambassador and Canadian diplomats.

Another five-day mission to Ukraine took place from July 9 to July 13. Kwaśniewski and Cox monitored Tymoshenko's trials and attended the trial of Yuriy Lutsenko. They spent two hours in a hospital in Kharkiv, where they spoke with the former prime minister, met with her lawyer, doctors, and the hospital's administration. As reported by Kwaśniewski, the enclave was fully controlled by Ukraine's penitentiary services and Tymoshenko did not have access to phone calls, the Internet, or newspapers. She could only watch two television channels, a public and private one. She read books extensively. Kwaśniewski said Tymoshenko amazed him because despite "limited access to information, she maintained acute judgment."[31] The hospital (which was more of a prison) did not deprive her of her political gut and her understanding of unfolding events on the other side of the bars. Therefore, apart from monitoring her medical condition, Cox and Kwaśniewski listened closely to her assessments of the political situation in Ukraine.

II. The European Union's Special Envoy to Ukraine

The visit to Kharkiv was followed by a trip to the capital city. They spent five hours in the Kyiv prison, speaking with Yuriy Lutsenko and Valeriy Ivashchenko, their wives and their lawyers. Having visited Mykola Azarov, Kwaśniewski and Cox spoke with heads of the EU's diplomatic missions to Ukraine, NGOs[32] and representatives of the opposition, including the former minister of foreign affairs, Borys Tarasyuk.

Cox and Kwaśniewski returned to Ukraine on July 22. They attended the trial again and visited Tymoshenko in the Kharkiv hospital. This time, they also met with Valeriya Lutkovska, the Ukrainian Ombudsman. Speaking with the Ukrainian prime minister, Kwaśniewski repeated that the mission would closely monitor Tymoshenko's trial.[33] Just as he had promised to Martin Schulz, Mykola Azarov was not trying to impede the envoys' work. On the contrary, Cox and Kwaśniewski informed Schulz that Azarov's "personal engagement has been indispensable in opening hospital, prison and institutional doors and in providing access to a large volume of relevant documents."[34]

Kwaśniewski (second from right) meets with Štefan Füle (left), the EU's Commissioner for Enlargement and European Neighborhood policy. Brussels, October 2, 2012. © European Union 2012. Source: PE-EP.

And there were plenty of documents to go through. Pat Cox, a perfectionist, read through hundreds, maybe even thousands, of pages related to the proceedings against Tymoshenko. Cox has a habit of taking meticulous notes during meetings. Some say he had a dozen or so notebooks filled with notes at the time the mission was coming to an end. Ukrainian prosecutors were well aware of the fact that Cox and Kwaśniewski were supported by the EU's lawyers. They also realized quite quickly that they could not just deceive the envoys, because Cox would consult his notes and say: "Hold your horses, gentlemen. Only a few months ago you said something completely different." With another mission behind his belt, Cox enhanced his understanding of Ukraine.

The fifth visit to Ukraine, including Kharkiv, Kyiv and Yalta, was held between August 13 and August 17, 2012. It was during that time that the verdicts on the case of Yuriy Lutsenko and the appeal of Valeriy Ivashchenko were reached. On August 14, the Court of Appeal in Kyiv reduced the sentence from five years in prison to a one-year probation period. The EP's envoys spoke with President Yanukovych for four hours. They also took part in meetings with the speaker of the Verkhovna Rada Volodymyr Lytvyn, Viktor Yushchenko, and Oleksandr Moroz. Kwaśniewski knew them very well from the days of the Orange Revolution.

In October 2012, the European Parliament extended the Cox-Kwaśniewski mission for the first time: initially, only until the end of the year. On October 2, during the meeting of the European Parliament's main decision-making body—the Conference of Presidents—the special envoys presented their views on the "humanitarian, legal and political aspects in relation to the legal proceedings against Ms. Yulia Tymoshenko, Mr. Yuriy Lutsenko and Mr. Valery Ivashchenko."[35]

The meeting was followed by a press conference. Martin Schulz informed the media that the mission would be extended at least until the end of 2012, even though it would be suspended for the duration of the electoral campaign and the upcoming parliamentary elections in Ukraine, so that "Mr. Kwaśniewski and Mr. Cox won't be used instrumentally by either of the sides."[36] Despite the fact that the former acting minister of national defense, Valeriy Ivashchenko, was released from prison, Kwaśniewski argued that the humanitarian objective of the mis-

II. The European Union's Special Envoy to Ukraine

sion had not been accomplished. Only the release of Yulia Tymoshenko would be a complete success: "Yulia Tymoshenko is still in the hospital, which is still better than prison."[37]

Kwaśniewski concluded that the European Court of Human Rights in Strasbourg might be helpful in resolving the case of the former prime minister and acknowledged that critical opinions on the Ukrainian judiciary were spot-on. On the other hand, he brought up the potential of Ukraine's European integration and how it could benefit the Union: "Even though this is not going to be easy and is going to take time, I believe there is a chance for the implementation of European values. I am much more optimistic when it comes to Ukraine than other countries,"[38] he maintained.

The former president of Poland underlined that the parliamentary elections, scheduled for October 28, would be a final litmus test for Ukraine's future: "Without free and fair elections we have no chance to continue this dialogue, we have no chance to go forward."[39] Aware of the fact that Kwaśniewski and Cox had not published a concluding report, the German newspaper, *Frankfurter Allgemeine Zeitung*, wrote:

> Kwaśniewski has been instrumental in making Tymoshenko's trial look trivial. He has delayed the presentation of the official report on the trial, which he has been working on with the former president of the European Parliament, Pat Cox, so as not to present it before the elections. By doing so, negative opinions—which, according to this paper's preliminary findings, will be included in the report—will not be able to reach members of election observation missions and influence their findings.[40]

Aleksander Kwaśniewski rebutted these accusations, claiming that the article was inaccurate: "We were not stalling; we simply presented a preliminary report, because the mission is not over yet. Also, we did not wish to publish it and make a fuss about it, because it would have been abused by both sides of the dispute."[41] Moreover, Kwaśniewski underlined that the preliminary report that he presented in the European Parliament argued that the imprisonment of Yulia Tymoshenko was casting a shadow over the elections. No matter how apposite and procedurally smooth the elections would have been, it would still be impossible to deem them completely free when "the leadership of the opposition party is behind bars."[42] Kwaśniewski also emphasized, "we met with the president on four different occasions and spoke with him—together with Pat Cox, as no other talks were held—a dozen hours or so. We also spent roughly the same amount of time talking to Yulia Tymoshenko."[43] According to the former president, isolating Ukraine would have been the worst call that could have been made. "*FAZ* and certain German politicians suggest that we should isolate Ukraine and treat it like Belarus. If we had followed their advice, today we would have another Belarus, only in Ukraine."[44] Kwaśniewski presented a few examples of other countries where isolation did not attain the desired effect: "Isolating Cuba has only led to it being ruled by the Castro brothers for over 50 years; in the isolated Belarus, Lukashenko has ruled as an autocrat for over a dozen years and the opposition is not even represented in the parliament."[45] The former Polish president argued that the situation in Ukraine was different, because it had been treated differently:

> Isolation would lead to the same situation that we're dealing with in Belarus: the undemocratic and detrimental to Belarusian society rule of Lukashenko. In today's Ukraine, however, the opposition collects half of the parliamentary vote. The Belarusian opposition is not represented by a single parliamentarian, and they held elections a few weeks ago. That is a big difference. I do not wish for the Belarusian scenario to be repeated in Ukraine. Pursuing such a policy by anyone in Europe would be a mistake.[46]

Following the October parliamentary elections, it did not come to Ukraine's isolation. However, the Council of the European Union expressed its "concern that the conduct of the 28 October parliamentary elections presented a mixed picture with several shortcomings and constituted a deterioration in several areas compared to standards previously achieved."[47] The vote count was taking days and the opposition parties (Batkivshchyna, UDAR, and Svoboda) threatened they would boycott the results, if the authorities continue to "steal" ballots. In the end, the Party of Regions prevailed.

Cox and Kwaśniewski arrived to Ukraine on November 6. The official results had not been announced yet, and the battle over parliamentary seats was still fierce. It was at that time that they met for the first time with Jan Tombiński, the new EU ambassador to Ukraine. His predecessor from Portugal, José Manuel Pinto Teixeira, concluded his four-year term in August 2012.

Pinto Teixeira was not overly popular in Ukraine. He had a fall out

II. The European Union's Special Envoy to Ukraine

with the Party of Regions and the Ukrainian government due to his undiplomatic statements about President Yanukovych. In February 2012, he was even summoned by the Ukrainian Ministry of Foreign Affairs. Kyiv had complained to the EU that the ambassador's statements "do not correspond to the traditions of international relations in diplomacy.... The issue is not just the tone of ambassador Teixeira's remarks, but the fact that a person sent to Ukraine as a diplomat ... is trying to get involved in the political process."[48] The European External Action Service backed its envoy and argued that the note of the Ukrainian MFA constituted an attack of a personal nature against the EU's ambassador and his professionalism. Whether Pinto Teixeira was right in his critical assessment of Yanukovych is another matter. The problem was that his statements shut down any communication between the EU and the Ukrainian government and president, who, after all, had been elected by the Ukrainian people in elections deemed legitimate by the European Union. Teixeira admitted he had never had a personal meeting with Yanukovych during his tenure in Ukraine.[49] His network in Kyiv was very limited and he never really tried to expand it. As Kwaśniewski and Cox were urging for the signing of the Association Agreement during dozens of meetings, the pessimistic Pinto Teixeira was convincing the Ukrainian media that chances were very slim. Clearly, he was not doing anything that could potentially tip the scales in Ukraine's favor.

By the time Pinto Teixeira's tenure was over, he had only met with Cox and Kwaśniewski once—in July, during their fourth visit to Ukraine. The lack of support on the part of the EEAS can be justified by its initial attitude toward the EP's mission. Kwaśniewski explained: "Who was our mission's main opponent? Ms. Ashton's team because they considered it an attempt to rid them of their prerogative. But given Ms. Ashton and her subordinates' passivity, these accusations weren't way off."[50]

According to Kwaśniewski, the first significant change in the EEAS' attitude could be noticed right after the appointment of the new ambassador. For as long as it was Pinto Teixeira, "it was a disaster. He was then delegated to Cape Verde, or someplace, and that is where he belonged," says Kwaśniewski. "The arrival of Jan Tombiński, an experienced diplomat, was a change for the better."[51]

Tombiński had served as ambassador of Poland to Bosnia and Herzegovina, Slovenia, and France. In 2007, he was appointed Poland's ambassador to the European Union. Those were the busiest days of the Polish diplomatic representation in Brussels, since Poland held the presidency of the Council of the European Union in the second half of 2011. There are 130 EU diplomatic missions worldwide and they all report to the High Representative for Foreign and Security Policy. All the member states wish to delegate their own representatives to head missions in countries and regions that they find strategically important. It should be noted, though, that these diplomats represent the entire EU, not just their countries of origin. Following the nomination of Catherine Ashton in 2009, the European External Action Service, created by the Treaty of Lisbon, was beginning to take shape. Another round of ambassadorial nominations also took off. Poland sent its diplomats to Jordan, South Korea, and later to Saudi Arabia, important countries from the EU's point of view, but none of them had been eyed by Warsaw specifically. Tombiński's nomination was a game changer in this regard. "Tombiński is an extraordinary diplomat," according to Kwaśniewski, and his nomination was beneficial to the president's mission.

For the president's 58th birthday, Yanukovych sent Kwaśniewski wishes and called him "Ukraine's loyal friend." He added: "For many years, you have actively supported our country's integration with the European Union. I am confident that thanks to your support, Ukraine will successfully reach its goal of European integration and join the European family, where it belongs."[52] Yanukovych sounded optimistic, contrary to most EU leaders.

On December 10, 2012, the Council of the European Union issued another statement expressing its concern over politically motivated verdicts aimed against members of the former government. It concluded that the trials were not carried out in accordance with international standards and that all the rulings issued by the European Court of Human Rights and the Council of Europe, concerning the standards the detainees were being held under, as well as their access to medical attention, should be implemented. Moreover, it was argued that there was need for dialogue with the opposition and reform of the electoral system, as well as a necessity to guarantee fair access to media to elec-

II. The European Union's Special Envoy to Ukraine

toral candidates. The Council also declared that the association agenda was necessary for a future implementation of the Association Agreement and the free trade agreement, especially in regard to electoral reforms, judicial reforms, and constitutional reforms. What was remarkably important is that the EU reaffirmed its "willingness to sign the already initialed Association Agreement," as soon as Ukrainian authorities "demonstrate determined action and tangible progress" in the aforementioned reforms. It could be signed "possibly by the time of the Eastern Partnership Summit in Vilnius in November 2013."[53] Kyiv was running out of time.

In the meantime, Prime Minister Mykola Azarov was celebrating his 65th birthday in Kyiv. His reappointment as the head of government must have felt like a birthday present. Kwaśniewski and Cox met him again during their 11th visit to Ukraine (December 17–19, 2012). At this time, Pat Cox conveyed Martin Schulz's letter in which the president of the European Parliament wrote: "Mr. Prime Minister, I would like to congratulate you on your appointment as prime minister of

Press conference following the extraordinary meeting of the Conference of Presidents. Strasbourg, February 6, 2013. © European Union 2013. Source: EP.

Ukraine. Accept my sincere congratulations and wishes for successful work in this post. I look forward to our future successful cooperation."[54] Azarov was just as cordial. At the end of December, he gave compliments to the EU's envoys, noting that these "extraordinary and experienced European politicians have impressed me with the actions they undertook in order to help our country. At the same time, they have made an effort to maintain a balanced and impartial position."[55] Speaking with Martin Schulz over the phone, Azarov said that Pat Cox and Aleksander Kwaśniewski had been actively supporting the process of Ukraine's European integration and the Ukrainian government highly valued their advice.[56] Close associates of Yulia Tymoshenko also appreciated the mission's achievements.

In December 2012, Eugenia Tymoshenko said:

> Today, like never before, we need Poland's support and the support of its political elite. Therefore, I would like to express my gratitude to Aleksander Kwaśniewski, who has been leading the European Parliament's mission to Ukraine, fighting for Yulia Tymoshenko and Yuriy Lutsenko's freedom. Together with President Pat Cox, President Kwaśniewski has been doing his best to free the prisoners and rehabilitate them politically.[57]

Six months had passed since the mission was launched. Kwaśniewski did not visit Ukraine in January; instead, he went to Brussels. Following his meeting with Martin Schulz on January 9, Kwaśniewski confirmed that the overall opinion on the necessity to carry on the mission was justified. He believed it should be continued "until its main objective is accomplished. November of this year, when the Association Agreement is to be signed in Vilnius, currently seems like the appropriate stopping point."[58] Kwaśniewski argued that among the mission's achievements was the creation of "an effective channel for communication and dialogue." In addition, the envoys managed to earn the trust of both the government and the opposition. "We have maintained open lines of communication with the entire opposition. Giving it up at this stage, when there's still so much to be done, would be a mistake."[59]

On February 4, the emissaries visited Yuriy Lutsenko at the penal colony in the Chernihiv Oblast and visited Yulia Tymoshenko in the Kharkiv hospital the following day. That same day, they met with Viktor Yanukovych.[60] Three weeks later, Yanukovych was expected to make an appearance at the EU-Ukraine summit. However, he was not antic-

II. The European Union's Special Envoy to Ukraine

ipating a warm welcome. It was speculated throughout the entire previous year whether the talks would even take place. The annual summit was originally scheduled for December, but it was postponed for the first time in its 15-year history. At the end of December, European Commission President José Manuel Barroso had a conversation with Yanukovych and decided that the meeting would take place in Brussels, at the end of February.

On February 25, sitting right in front of the Ukrainian president, Herman Van Rompuy brought up the precise criteria that Kyiv had to fulfill in order to sign the Association Agreement. The main issues included selective justice, elections, and a reform of the association agenda. Van Rompuy underlined that the EU was calling on Ukraine to undertake "determined action and tangible progress in these areas at the latest by May this year."[61] Thus, Yanukovych had three months to sort out Lady Yu's case.

Meanwhile, in the United States, only three days after the summit, Kwaśniewski was lobbying for Ukraine. In late February, the former president of Poland argued: "My message here in Washington and in Europe is that the West needs Ukraine, and Ukraine needs the West—in economic, political, and military terms."[62] Kwaśniewski arrived to the U.S. directly from Kyiv. Given that he only had a few hours between landing and the conference at the Atlantic Council, the moderator jokingly offered him a Red Bull.[63]

Speaking at the Atlantic Council, Kwaśniewski stated: "I'm afraid sometimes [when] discussing the problem of Ukraine. Of course, my knowledge is much deeper [than that of] my partners in Europe or in the United States, but sometimes I have the impression that in our part of the world, ... we are thinking about Ukraine with a lot of stereotypes, too many stereotypes." Consequently, Kwaśniewski argued that it was important to be able to understand what is good and what is bad in Ukraine and to talk about it. The Judiciary's low credibility is a problem, and despite numerous reforms, "if we speak about Ukrainian courts, Ukrainian prosecutors, Ukrainian quality of law, ... this system is much closer to Soviet style, not to European style. And I know that this opinion sounds quite tough, but it's true."[64] The selective justice implemented against Yulia Tymoshenko and the former interior minister, Yuriy Lutsenko, posed the greatest challenge. Kwaśniewski admitted at the time, "It's absolutely impossible to say that we watched only a pure judiciary.... The political intention is quite obvious in these two cases. And today to find a solution for this case is not easy, because we have three levels of the problem." Kwaśniewski believed that these levels were legal, political, and psychological. The third element concerned the nature of relations between Tymoshenko and Yanukovych, which he labeled as, "quite difficult."

Kwaśniewski also discussed U.S.-Ukraine relations:

> I think it would be good if here in Washington we ... understand that it is really time for a strategic decision. That it is not the time that we can wait and wait to see whether something will happen or not. And that is a real struggle, and that is a struggle which is about the future of Ukraine, where Ukraine will be, part of the Western zone, Euro-Atlantic zone, or part of a Euro-Asian union or some kind of structure.... This time we have no more possibilities to postpone or to wait for some development of the situation. Now is the time of decisions.[65]

Kwaśniewski also argued that Ukraine's economy was in terrible shape and it required the International Monetary Fund's intervention. If the IMF does not have anything specific to offer, Kwaśniewski explained, Ukraine would be tempted to join the Customs Union in order to get cheaper gas. "We don't speak about a small amount of money; we speak about really the future and some kind of 'to be or not to be' for Ukraine in the next month."[66] The former president of Poland appealed to the EU and the U.S. to send a signal of solidarity to Ukraine, if it made progress:

> The European Union should say, well, we are prepared to sign the Association Agreement in November this year and now it's time for this homework. And the IMF, with the support of the United States, should say, "OK, we are ready to go back to Kyiv to discuss all details of a new agreement with the IMF giving some financial support for you if you will fulfill the necessary conditions and [undertake the] necessary reforms."[67]

Kwaśniewski underlined the fact that he could not discuss any details related to the potential release of Yulia Tymoshenko: "We continue our mission, and I cannot show you the kitchen of our difficult work." Still, he argued that a solution should be found in May. "We have to find a solution. What kind of solution? Theoretically, hypothetically, we can discuss a lot of possibilities, but we'll see what will happen next, in the next weeks," he relayed at the Atlantic Council. Judiciary reforms had to be adopted by the parliament: "We should

II. The European Union's Special Envoy to Ukraine

not be naïve.... It's absolutely necessary to change the role of the general prosecutor because ... the position of general prosecutor in the Ukrainian system is from the past. It's absolutely from the Soviet Union time. That is maybe the most influential person in Ukraine, sometimes more influential than the president."

Kwaśniewski argued that reforms would take time and require patience because they could not be carried out overnight. "We have to change the system of the education of lawyers. We have to change the mentality of the people. We have to change a lot of things, which will take time." Both sides of the Atlantic Ocean should provide Ukraine with relevant support.

> You Americans, we Europeans, we have to decide now, because what is the real alternative for Ukraine? ... Well, we cannot accept you in our community because you are not prepared enough with all these legal elements, rule of law, et cetera, et cetera. And what is the alternative? Ukraine in the Customs Union. Ukraine in the Eurasian Union. Of course it means that not one of our values, not one of our standards ... will exist in this Eurasian Union. So the alternative is that we have to accept Ukraine today with changed and reformed laws, but with time to fill this with real substance.[68]

Kwaśniewski was very familiar with the position of American diplomats in Ukraine. During the tenure of his mission, he met with the U.S. Ambassador to Ukraine, John F. Tefft, nine times and twice with his deputy, Geoffrey R. Pyatt. Washington appreciated Kwaśniewski's role, as demonstrated by Pyatt's statements. The diplomat applauded Ukraine's attempts aimed at implementing changes, which would enable the signing of the Association Agreement with the EU. At the same time, he underlined that the problem of selective justice had to be dealt with:

> We very strongly support the Cox-Kwaśniewski mission. We are very hopeful that the Government and its European interlocutors will find a formula to meet the conditions that the European Community has established, including putting an end to the practice of selective prosecutions. And that means dealing with the question of Mrs. Tymoshenko. The specifics of that is a complicated legal issue. The Ukrainian Government, working with Cox and Kwaśniewski and the European Governments, will have to find a way forward—and it's not my place to assign what that route forward is.[69]

Another analysis was to be presented to the European Parliament's political factions in April. This time, Cox and Kwaśniewski were to meet with MEPs in Strasbourg. Since Tymoshenko was still imprisoned and it did not seem like this was going to change, not everyone was satisfied with the mission's progress. The EP's envoys faced criticism from the very start, but this time some officials in Brussels wanted to call off the mission altogether.

Rebecca Harms, the leader of the Green political group in the European Parliament, had been voicing her discontent for months. "I think that we need to set conditions [to extend] the mandate, and a report [on the mission's work] should be published. This is being discussed only behind closed doors, and there is no change in Ukraine,"[70] she said. Despite the envoys' best efforts, Harms argued: "I get the impression that the mission has not achieved its goal, at least as we had hoped."[71] Harms' actions may have been driven by a hidden agenda, due to her political infighting with Martin Schulz. But the question remains: was she right in claiming that the mission achieved no significant objectives?

"There was a justified concern, that Yanukovych would use the mission as a tool because he would be able to hide behind it and say: 'What's the problem? They are still working. Let them work.'"[72] However, the mission did lead to the release of two political prisoners. Yuriy Lutsenko was pardoned on April 7, 2013, and released immediately. Before that, the former acting minister of defense, Valeriy Ivashchenko, was set free and his travel ban was lifted on August 14, 2012. The mission's opponents found it difficult to argue with such tangible results. Had the mission not been able to show these achievements, labeling it ineffective would have been much more convincing. "This argument would have been justified, had we not set them free." Additionally, over time, it became clear that a lot was done to help Tymoshenko. "At that stage of our mission, we might not have set Tymoshenko free, but we made her life much easier. Our presence guaranteed that nothing bad would happen to her."[73]

In Strasbourg, Cox and Kwaśniewski presented their report, where they informed that Yulia Tymoshenko was being hospitalized with the supervision of female guards and without video monitoring. What was also comforting was that, due to her condition, she would not be moved to a penal colony and she did not have to be present for her trials. Cox and Kwaśniewski underlined that since December 2012, they had also closely monitored the case related to the charges against Batkivshchyna's

II. The European Union's Special Envoy to Ukraine

legislator, Hryhoriy Nemyria, as well as the charges against Tymoshenko's legal representative, Serhiy Vlasenko (his travel ban was lifted on April 3, 2013). The EP's envoys argued that the mission managed "to maintain its complete independence and impartiality, in a transparent and open manner engaging with all relevant actors in Ukraine and not allowing any side to use it instrumentally for its own purposes."[74]

> We believe this mission has demonstrated a capacity to deliver outcomes that are necessary for the upcoming strategic decisions in the relations between the European Union and Ukraine. We recognize that much work still needs to be done and that, as a privileged channel of communication, the mission can assist in making further progress.[75]

Speaking at a joint press conference, Martin Schulz said: "All EP political group leaders unanimously called the Cox-Kwaśniewski mission to Ukraine a success, endorsed its prolongation, and invited the mission to report back again at the end of September." The chamber's president also argued it was a good decision because "the monitoring mission has proved to be a powerful tool to engage with all segments of Ukrainian society: government, opposition, civil society, and the judiciary." Schulz emphasized the fact that the mission helped build mutual trust not only between the EU and Ukraine, but also in Ukraine itself, where the divisions between the government and the opposition ran deep. Finally, "the mission's reputation of impartiality and independence is a great asset to both the EU and to Ukraine, and it is part of a process of increasing engagement, which has to continue,"[76] argued Schulz.

In May, an unexpected piece of information indicated that the Vilnius summit—which was supposed to be held in six months—could be successful after all: Tymoshenko was soon to be released and allowed to undergo medical treatment in Germany. Kwaśniewski refused to comment on the revelations:

> We have been holding talks with the government, the opposition, and Yulia Tymoshenko. We have visited Ms. Tymoshenko with Pat Cox in Kharkiv, we have talked to the president, the prime minister and representative of the administration in Ukraine. All sorts of initiatives are proposed in such talks. I can't discuss any details because discretion is crucial for the mission's success.[77]

Kwaśniewski added, "Which proposals turn out to be realistic remains to be seen."[78] Speaking with the Ukrainian edition of *Forbes*, the deputy prosecutor general, Renat Kuzmin, confirmed that there was a possibility that Tymoshenko could be hospitalized abroad: "There is no legislation that specifically rules out such a solution, but it's not as easy as it seems. In order to make it happen, political decisions on an international level need to be made, but it is definitely possible."[79]

First of all, Tymoshenko would have to express her willingness to be hospitalized abroad. She might be allowed to leave the country after being granted a pardon. However, Lady Yu had been saying she would not ask for one under any circumstances, because it would be equal to "acknowledging the dictatorship."[80] Her lawyer shared the sentiment: "Only a person who committed a crime can ask for a pardon. Yulia Tymoshenko did not commit any crime."[81] In August 2013, her relatives also publicly stated that they would not request a pardon, because Yulia Tymoshenko did not wish to "ask for anything from this regime."[82] This approach was not making things any easier for Kwaśniewski and Cox, who had been lobbying her to seek a pardon. They wanted to determine whether she would be willing to address Yanukovych in a letter in this regard, but, as Kwaśniewski recalls, "she did not want to do it for a long time. And when she finally wrote a letter, it turned out it would have been better not to write anything because the contents were aggressive and offensive toward Yanukovych."[83] Kwaśniewski found a solution if Tymoshenko remained adamant and would not request a pardon: he and Cox would do it on her behalf.

On Thursday, October 3, the envoys arrived to Kharkiv to finalize talks with Lady Yu about her hospitalization in Germany and the pardon. On Friday, they met Yanukovych and handed over the request for amnesty. The letter read: "Our appeal comes at a time of strategic importance for EU-Ukraine relations. Addressing the issues of selective justice is one of the key requirements identified by the European Union's Foreign Affairs Council in December 2012."[84]

Speaking at a press conference, Serhiy Vlasenko said: "[The EP's envoys] authorized me to inform you that yesterday, in a meeting with Viktor Yanukovych concerning the decision on Tymoshenko's travel abroad, Cox and Kwaśniewski submitted the request for pardon of Yulia Tymoshenko."[85] Vlasenko also read Tymoshenko's statement, in which she declared: "Pat Cox and Aleksander Kwaśniewski are constantly negotiating with Viktor Yanukovych for my release. I am infinitely

II. The European Union's Special Envoy to Ukraine

thankful to them for that, as well as to all the world leaders who delegated them, issued them their mandate, and who support their work."[86]

> Pat Cox and Aleksander Kwaśniewski conveyed to me an offer to go to Germany for medical treatment. I publicly accept this offer. My departure abroad will not solve the problem completely, but I have faith that this step will diffuse the situation on the eve of the Eastern Partnership summit. I would like to declare loud and clear: my potential departure for Germany is not equal to emigration. I will never seek political asylum and will never hide in other countries. I will be actively involved in the process of liberating Ukraine.[87]

In the meantime, Party of Regions legislators argued that the president could not simply order Tymoshenko's release from prison. "He can do it under article 106, paragraph 27, of the Ukrainian constitution.... He can take a piece of paper, take a pen from his pocket, write 'I hereby pardon, and so on,' and it is done,"[88] Vlasenko retorted. He said that that was exactly how Lutsenko's case ensued. The precedent of the release of the former interior minister, for which Kwaśniewski fought, armed Tymoshenko's defendants with strong arguments. That was precisely what Kwaśniewski had in mind. Since Tymoshenko finally expressed her will to undergo hospitalization abroad and Yanukovych had the legal means to make it happen, as demonstrated by Lutsenko's case, the EU said, "check." There were two options left for Yanukovych. He could have folded or he could have bluffed and raised the stakes. He decided to go for the second solution.

A week after the visit to Kharkiv and Kyiv, it was time to present a report in Brussels. Half a year had passed since the previous presentation. Speaking at a meeting of the Conference of Presidents, Cox and Kwaśniewski underlined that the final report would be presented in the final days of their tenure and for now they wished to share a few crucial opinions "regarding the current state of affairs and the way forward."[89] As from June 2013, all trials and criminal investigations against Tymoshenko had been put on hold. She was being treated in the Kharkiv Hospital, by doctors from the Charité Clinique in Berlin. In June 2013, it was concluded that her condition required an immediate surgical intervention, but she refused to undergo a surgery in Ukraine because of her mistrust toward the government.

> We were mandated by the European Parliament to deal with the question of selective justice in Ukraine. The conditions for signature were set by the For-

eign Affairs Council of the EU, not by our mission. In our opinion, these conditions, especially as regards Yulia Tymoshenko, still remain to be fulfilled. After 16 months and 22 missions, we conclude at this point in time that further work is required to ensure compliance.[90]

Kwaśniewski and Cox argued that prolonging the mission's mandate would help find a solution acceptable for all the parties concerned, before the Council's decision on the future of the Association Agreement. They noted that given the approaching deadline, "we urge all parties in Ukraine, the EU institutions and its Member States to lend their focused and fullest support to the mission in order to secure the necessary conditions that would ensure success at the Eastern Partnership summit in Vilnius."[91] They also pointed out all the reforms successfully carried out by Ukraine:

> We have systematically encouraged the authorities and the opposition to work together in order to meet with key expectations by the EU especially in terms of standards of democracy and Rule of Law. Electoral legislation is being improved following the last parliamentary elections and a date for new elections in the five disputed constituencies has been set on 15 December 2013. The new Criminal Procedural Code is being implemented, significantly reducing the number of pre-trial detainees. Moreover, the Venice Commission has recently adopted mostly positive recommendations as regards further proposed reforms to the Judiciary and the Public Prosecutor's Office. These reforms, if conducted and implemented fully and in line with European standards, could significantly change the political and legal landscape in Ukraine, an improvement which is also much needed to attract the available foreign direct investment.[92]

Positive signals from Kyiv kept the dream alive. When Cox and Kwaśniewski conveyed in Brussels, deputy prime minister, Konstantin Hryshchenko, proclaimed that all the remaining roadblocks on the way to the EU-Ukraine agreement would be removed: "I believe that the report drafted by Aleksander Kwaśniewski and Pat Cox will be a milestone leading to resolving the problem of Yulia Tymoshenko. As President Kwaśniewski has already pointed out, the proposal will be satisfactory to our European partners and it will be carried out in accordance with the Ukrainian law."[93] The European Union still preferred results to promises. The Vilnius summit was going to take place in just a month, so the EU decided to send reinforcements to Ukraine.

"The time for bluffing is over on both sides now. It's time for action,"[94] said Radek Sikorski, summarizing the meeting with Yanukovych in which

II. The European Union's Special Envoy to Ukraine

he had taken part together with Carl Bildt on October 22. Sikorski underlined that "the time is running out and the risk that the agreement will not be signed is really high. I hope we succeed this time and that we won't have to wait for Ukraine for another 300 years."[95] Foreign ministers of Poland and Sweden were of the opinion that Ukraine still stood a chance of signing the Association Agreement during the upcoming Vilnius summit, but all the criteria would have to be met, including the resolution of the Tymoshenko case. Commenting on the EP's envoy's mission, Carl Bildt said: "We will not go into details, but what they report will be decisive. If there is a green light from Pat Cox and Alexander Kwaśniewski there will be a green light for Ukraine in Europe."[96]

Bad Signals, Black Thursday and the Vilnius Summit Fiasco

In early November, the prospects of the Association Agreement looked uncertain. The Eastern Partnership summit was scheduled for November 28–29 and each day, even each hour, mattered. On Wednesday, November 13, Cox and Kwaśniewski were to present their recommendations to the European Parliament, so that the European Council could make its decision the following Monday.

On November 7, Cox and Kwaśniewski held a series of meetings with leading politicians from the Party of Regions. According to the report by the *Ukrayinska Pravda* paper, based on a first-hand testimony of an observer who was present during the talks,[97] the special envoys spent the day traveling between the Verkhovna Rada and the Presidential Administration Building. This detailed account reveals Yanukovych's schemes and delaying tactics.

As reported by *Ukrayinska Pravda*, Cox and Kwaśniewski started the day with a meeting with Viktor Yanukovych. The EU's special envoys explained that Germany was not able to guarantee Tymoshenko's return to Ukraine after her treatment would be concluded. Berlin did not wish to take sides and by promising Yanukovych that Tymoshenko would be sent back to Ukraine, it would de facto confirm the former prime minister's guilt. They also confirmed that all the paperwork related to

Tymoshenko's departure would have to be finalized before the start of the Eastern Partnership summit in Vilnius. According to the *Ukrayinska Pravda's* source, Yanukovych listened to the envoys' words and did not voice any major concerns. Kwaśniewski and Cox underscored the importance of the Party of Region's position, which held a majority in the parliament. They inquired whether he could lobby the party's legislators in order to ensure success. Yanukovych promised he would promptly call the speaker of the Verkhovna Rada, Volodymyr Rybak, and the chairman of the Party of Regions, Oleksandr Yefremov, and request their assistance in adopting necessary legislative resolutions. When Cox and Kwaśniewski left the presidential palace and headed for the parliament, they seemed full of confidence.[98]

The Verkhovna Rada was less than a kilometer away so they got there in just a few minutes. Once there, Volodymyr Rybak assured them that Ukraine had set sail for the EU and no alternatives were on the table. Then, behind closed doors, Rybak held talks on the contents of the resolution on Tymoshenko's hospitalization abroad. Leaders of the opposition were also present. The meeting ended up in a complete fiasco. According to the opposition leaders, the representatives of the Party of Regions refused to vote on the draft motions for resolutions and suggested that a joint resolution should be drafted. That was not what Yanukovych had promised, therefore Cox, Kwaśniewski, and the opposition leaders headed for the office of Oleksandr Yefremov, where they hoped to clear up the misunderstanding.

When asked frankly whether the Party of Regions was willing to put the resolution to a vote within two days, Yefremov replied that no motion for resolution had been drafted and the working group, responsible for drafting one, had not convened yet. Cox and Kwaśniewski reminded him that time was running out and the resolution had to be adopted by November 14. According to *Ukrayinska Pravda*, the EP's envoys were distinctly confused when they heard Yefremov's response that it was not up to him, but up to the working group and that he was unaware when it was going to finalize its work. Cox and Kwaśniewski reportedly asked: "How is that possible? In every meeting, we were assured that the problem was pretty much solved and the only missing link was the parliament." Yefremov acted as if he was being insulted and complained that this was the first time the special envoys had taken

II. The European Union's Special Envoy to Ukraine

the time to meet with him. Kwaśniewski was not moved. "Each time we visited Ukraine, we met with representatives of the current administration, and this is the 25th time we have come here." "I get it, but I chair the largest party in the parliament—the Party of Regions—and this is the first time we've met," quipped Yefremov. Kwaśniewski hardly managed to hold his temper.

> Listen. We met with your party's chairman, Mykola Azarov, over twenty times. Seventeen times, with the founder of the party Viktor Yanukovych. They were the ones who told us who we should meet next. They said we should meet with Volodymyr Oliynyk, and so we did. Had they told us we should come and see you, we would have. And now it seems like they—together with Mr. Rybak, who is present here—promised one thing, but you're telling us something completely different!

Yefremov responded, "It was them who made the promises.... Have I ever made any promises to you? I have not. Have you ever met with me? You have not.... There are 172 legislators in my faction and I have to convince every single one of them." "But if there was any political will, the problem would be solved in a matter of hours," said Kwaśniewski. "That's not exactly the way things work. We are a democratic party and everyone is entitled to their opinion," Yefremov concluded with pride in his voice, only to get back to the same old story about all the faults of Tymoshenko. "Still, the case of Tymoshenko's hospitalization has to be resolved within three to four days. We are to present our report on November 14. The country's future is at stake," said Kwaśniewski. Yefremov remained indifferent: "We can understand it, but our voters believe she's a criminal."

Kwaśniewski addressed everyone present: "All right. Can anyone indicate a concrete date, when a draft of the joint motion for a resolution on the case of Tymoshenko will be ready?" To the amazement of Rybak and Yefremov, the opposition leaders announced they were prepared to vote for any of the proposals. Rybak repeated that the Party of Regions would support a resolution but it was difficult to determine exactly when, given that the working group had not convened yet. Kwaśniewski still insisted on getting a straight answer, "When will this happen? Can you do it next Tuesday?" "We don't know," said Yefremov. "Wednesday?" continued Kwaśniewski. "We cannot answer this question." Kwaśniewski lost his patience, "We get it now. It's simple: you're telling us that the Association Agreement with the EU will not be signed, is that right?" Representatives of the Party of Regions said again that it would depend on the working group's work.[99]

This spectacle, performed by the leaders of the Party of Regions, revealed the political pathology characteristic for Yanukovych's era: a widespread lack of professionalism, poor conduct when confronted with European politicians, and a willingness to make promises that no one intended to keep. Did Yanukovych and Yefremov play good cop/bad cop? Did Yanukovych call Yefremov as soon as Cox and Kwaśniewski left his office? According to the former president of Poland, the meeting at the Verkhovna Rada was just a show. Yanukovych didn't even have to call Yefremov: "Yanukovych preferred not to leave any traces. They acted like a bunch of gangsters: they knew what to do until further notice. Their behavior indicated the case was not supposed to concern them at that stage."[100]

> The Party of Regions found itself in two parallel universes. On one hand, before the summer, Yanukovych was doing his best (at least on a declarative level) to convince the Party of Regions to support an association with the EU. His address at the party congress, when he spoke about two priorities, was a significant development. Then there was the meeting of the party's leaders, where he supposedly made an appearance and said that the door was open and anyone who was against associating should just leave the room. No one—of course—left. Whether he was being sincere is a subject for another discussion, but the party got the message about the direction they were heading.[101]

Kwaśniewski returned to Ukraine four days later. He tried to sway the Party of Regions and argued for the adoption of the legislative resolution, but to no avail. Meeting Andriy Klyuyev, the Secretary of the National Security Council and Defense of Ukraine, did not prove to be helpful either. In the meantime, on November 13, the Conference of Presidents of the European Parliament extended the mandate of the mission until the time of the Vilnius Summit. Cox and Kwaśniewski arrived in Brussels directly from Kyiv and, for the third time, presented their report on the situation in Ukraine.

Following 26 missions to Ukraine, the special envoys noticed significant progress in terms of Ukraine's fulfillment of the EU's criteria. However, they also concluded: "We regret to observe that at this time we are not yet in the position to report full compliance." What was it that Ukraine did and did not manage to do? The legislation concerning

II. The European Union's Special Envoy to Ukraine

(Left to right) Pat Cox, Martin Schulz and Aleksander Kwaśniewski discuss the political situation in Ukraine. Brussels, November 13, 2013. © European Union 2013. Source: EP.

the public prosecutor general and the reform of the electoral legislation were adopted in the beginning of November. The second reading was scheduled to take place 9 days before the Eastern Partnership summit. Unfortunately, the case of Yulia Tymoshenko was much more problematic. According to Cox and Kwaśniewski:

> After several months of reflection and discussion of different options, the mission suggested the partial pardoning of Mrs. Yulia Tymoshenko as the most viable way to resolve the remaining problem of selective justice. This option would represent the minimum requirement capable of yielding the maximum effect, would depend solely on the authority and goodwill of the President of Ukraine, and would not involve delegating responsibility to other institutions and would not necessitate changing any existing legislation. However, President Viktor Yanukovych has indicated a preference for the alternative path of a special law that would permit treatment abroad of convicted persons on health and humanitarian grounds, including Mrs. Yulia Tymoshenko.[102]

In the last couple of weeks, a number of resolutions on Tymoshenko's hospitalization abroad were tabled in the Ukrainian parliament, but none of them were jointly accepted by the government and the opposition.

Speaking in the European Parliament, Kwaśniewski and Cox underlined the complete lack of trust in Kyiv and argued that if Vilnius ends up a fiasco, the opposition and the government would blame each other. Even though the Party of Regions constituted the working group, it did not table a motion for resolution. At the same time, it refused to adopt any of the legislative acts drafted by the opposition, despite the fact that President Yanukovych publicly declared, both to the Ukrainian media and in direct talks with heads of state and foreign ministers from the EU, that he would sign a resolution adopted by the Verkhovna Rada.

The findings presented by Cox and Kwaśniewski reminded the EP about the conditions that had to be met in order for the Association Agreement to be signed on November 29. The final parliamentary session, scheduled before the deadline, had the potential of tipping the scales. However, should it end up in a deadlock, there would be a lot of finger pointing. For this reason, Kwaśniewski and Cox reaffirmed that the "mission urges all parties involved to constructively use the short time available to reach a historic consensus that could result in a successful summit in Vilnius." The EU's Foreign Affairs Council was scheduled to meet in five days.

> At this time that it would be premature to conclude that compliance with the conditions set has been met or alternatively that such compliance still cannot be achieved. In our considered opinion the issues outstanding can be resolved by one means or another. What is critical is not the capacity to deliver a solution but rather the political will to do so. What is indispensable in the coming week is to find that political will, to act and to deliver.[103]

At a press conference held Thursday, Aleksander Kwaśniewski reiterated that the resolutions scheduled to be adopted by the Verkhovna Rada would be necessary for the Association Agreement to be signed. The former president of Poland expected this to happen on Tuesday, November 19. He pointed out that there was a high level of anxiety among Ukrainian parliamentarians and that a "multidimensional approach" was necessary to ensure that the preconditions, agreed upon a year earlier, would be fulfilled. Only then the Association Agreement could be signed in Vilnius. Trying to stay positive, Kwaśniewski said that he was confident that both President Yanukovych and the opposition strongly supported integration with Europe. At the same time, he underlined the psychological nature of the Tymoshenko case.

II. The European Union's Special Envoy to Ukraine

Numerous changes had been adopted in regard to the penal code but, despite this, there was still a lot of room for improvement: "Rome wasn't built in a day! In this case I should say: Kyiv was not built in a day!"[104]

On November 18, prior to the meeting of the EU's foreign ministers, Radek Sikorski said that the Vilnius summit was approaching "and it can still make history. We all know what the stakes are, including the stakes of today's talks." He had reminded the Ukrainian authorities on numerous occasions "not to do everything at the last minute. Unfortunately, they have waited till the last minute, hence the uncertainty about the outcome."[105] Three days later, everything became clear: the Association Agreement would not be signed.

On Thursday, November 21, one week ahead of the Eastern Partnership summit, the Ukrainian government communicated that it intended to stop preparations to sign the Association Agreement. Deputy Prime Minister Yuriy Boyko explained that Ukraine's decision was caused by the country's need to improve its deteriorated trade relations with Russia, as well as the EU's failure to offer adequate compensation for Ukraine's losses. He argued that these losses amounted to 30–40 billion hryvnia (roughly 30–40 million Euros). In order to deal with the problem, Ukraine proposed that a trilateral committee, including Ukraine, Russia, and the EU, should be created.[106] The Ukrainian government had obviously been working on an economic pretext to obstruct the agreement with the EU.

On Wednesday, a day before the deleterious decision was announced, Aleksander Kwaśniewski met with Štefan Füle in Kyiv. The EU Commissioner told him he had held a very difficult conversation with Azarov. The Ukrainian side argued that the Association Agreement was problematic because it complicated their trade relations with Russia. Kwaśniewski always thought that this absurd argument was cooked up by Moscow. After all, the DCFTA was initialed in March 2013 and its contents were not confidential. Quite the contrary—they were available online for everyone to see. If Kyiv was indeed willing to hold consultations, it had all the time necessary to voice its concerns, since 20 months had already passed. Nevertheless, Füle concluded he would try to clear things up in Brussels and left Ukraine with the intention of coming back to Kyiv before the Vilnius summit.

Having met with the commissioner, Kwaśniewski called his colleague Heinz Fischer, the president of Austria. He knew Yanukovych was on an official visit in Vienna and he hoped Fischer would try to convince him to get rid of the obstacles on the way to the Association Agreement. Fischer agreed to help. He had an engagement scheduled at the Opera House and that is where he intended to bring up the subject.

On Thursday morning, before the meeting with Prime Minister Azarov, Fischer called Kwaśniewski. "You got me in quite a mess!" said Fischer. After the opera performance was over, Yanukovych tormented his interlocutor with his four-hour-long Tymoshenko monologue, which featured the typical diatribe about her criminal nature. Back in Kyiv, a few hours after Fisher's phone call, Kwaśniewski met with Mykola Azarov, who had just left a cabinet meeting and apparently "looked like hell." "Ukraine is freezing its preparations to sign the Association Agreement," he told the former Polish president.

> We had a sad and dramatic conversation. I said (and I'm proud of this today): "You're making a historic mistake and you'll pay a steep price for it." I didn't have in mind the events that later took place on the Maidan. But the decision made by Yanukovych's team—even assuming there would be no Maidan—meant their European perspective would be put on hold for decades.[107]

Kwaśniewski broke the news to the Polish Press Agency and it went viral all over the world. At the same time, at the Hofburg Palace in Vienna, the presidents of Austria and Ukraine were holding a joint press conference. At one point, Yanukovych stated that the European Union was Kyiv's main objective. Suddenly, Heinz Fischer was handed a note with the information Kwaśniewski had shared with the Polish Press Agency. Yanukovych got a similar note. The surprised Austrian president pointed out that Ukraine was not going to sign the Association Agreement. Yanukovych began acting a bit disoriented. Standing right in front of a large, 18th century painting depicting Maria Theresa Habsburg (whose flushed cheeks matched those of Viktor Yanukovych), he argued that Ukraine would continue to follow its European path. "Even today, during my short stay in Vienna, the Austrian Parliament adopted legislation, which will help Ukraine fulfill the necessary criteria."[108]

The confused Heinz Fisher called Kwaśniewski and asked, "What

II. The European Union's Special Envoy to Ukraine

is going on here? Is it possible that the Ukrainian government made a decision without the president even knowing about it?" "Heinz, give me a break," replied Kwaśniewski. "It is absolutely not possible. In this country the prime minister can't even use the restroom without the president's permission."[109] Yanukovych was simply playing a game. It turned out to be quite effective, since some of the young Ukrainian officials with whom Kwaśniewski and Cox were working in Ukraine still hoped that Azarov was acting alone and keeping Yanukovych in dark. According to Kwaśniewski, Azarov used purely economic excuses to explain the government's decision: "He practically said that Ukraine was standing at the edge of a cliff. Both in terms of its production output, with certain industries cut in half, due to the Russian embargo, as well as in terms of sky-high gas prices, without any revenue. The government decided to take short-term steps instead of adopting long-term measures."[110]

Kwaśniewski concluded that the Association Agreement would be beneficial to Ukraine in the long run and apparently a deal was made between Azarov and Dmitry Medvedev in Petersburg, on November 20, meant to "enable Ukraine to catch its breath for a couple of months." Azarov also suggested that it would be good to hold negotiations in a trilateral framework, including the EU, Ukraine, and Russia. However, Kwaśniewski argued "the proposal was unrealistic because the EU speaks with partners who wish to sign an Association Agreement without the presence of third parties or other states, acting as chaperones or godfathers."[111]

Kwaśniewski had no delusions. The decision to freeze the negotiations was taken by Yanukovych:

> Part of the Euro-optimistic camp in Ukraine was hoping that since Yanukovych was on an official delegation in Vienna and the government was in Vilnius, the latter might have decided not to sign the deal without his knowledge. That is simply not true. The government, along with the Party of Regions, has been loyal to him. Even though the party has recently started to undergo a process of disintegration.[112]

Kwaśniewski admitted: "Ukraine is a country where the president's position is formidable. I am certain that without prior consultations with Yanukovych the government would not have taken any decision."[113]

> President Yanukovych's statements are indeed completely different than those made by Prime Minister Azarov. But given my experience with Ukraine, I

know that the government would not have made such a decision had it not consulted it with President Yanukovych. To me, it's beyond any doubt that it is a common position of both the government and the president.[114]

Half of the Ukrainian society wanted the agreement to be signed. Ironically, for the past few months, Yanukovych had been trying to convince the other half that it was the right thing to do. "When Yanukovych said he was going to pull back from signing the deal with the EU, I told him: 'you are making a big mistake,'" Kwaśniewski recalled.[115] The former president of Poland criticized the decision because of both political and technical reasons. First of all, the timing was bad due to the EU's political calendar. The Association Agreement had been drafted for a year and European elections were to be held in 2014, followed by the appointment of new European commissioners. Therefore, 2014 was problematic in terms of negotiations with Ukraine. On the other hand, Ukraine was to hold presidential elections in 2015. In consequence, "this pause may take a long while,"[116] argued Kwaśniewski. What did all this mean for Yulia Tymoshenko?

Kwaśniewski attended the Verkhovna Rada's session on that infamous Thursday. New electoral legislation, part of the preconditions for association, was adopted on that day. The nail-biting vote, of course, concerned the possibility of allowing inmates to undergo medical treatment abroad. Tymoshenko addressed all the opposition legislators in an open letter in which she appealed for their support of the resolution tabled by the Party of Regions. "Stop playing their games. Vote unanimously for any one of the Party of Regions' draft laws, regardless what is written in them. Do this for the sake of the Association Agreement." Tymoshenko admitted she was well aware that Yanukovych would use the legislation to "try to take me abroad in shackles during the signing of the Association Agreement and then after the signing return me to prison in those same shackles," but this was the price she was willing to pay.[117] The opposition followed Tymoshenko's plea, but the Party of Regions had its own plans.

All the laws that were supposed to enable Tymoshenko to undergo hospitalization abroad were voted down. Six different motions were put to a vote. The Party of Regions, as well as the Communists, abstained in each case. The opposition yelled "Disgrace!" "The masks have come off," concluded Arseniy Yatsenyuk. "President Yanukovych did not have the intention of signing the deal with the EU. Even his own party will

II. The European Union's Special Envoy to Ukraine

not support the act he tabled himself."[118] Kwaśniewski, who watched the entire spectacle sitting at the Verkhovna Rada's visitor's center, recalls:

> The Party of Regions was disciplined. But there was no discipline when it came to the vote on the case of Tymoshenko. They kept stalling even when the opposition was willing to compromise. Some of the resolutions proposed were completely absurd. One included a paragraph that Germany would guarantee that officials of the Ukrainian penitentiary would guard Tymoshenko's room. We even helped them draft a simple document, which was supposed to simply enable the former prime minister to go to Germany. Doctors would decide how to treat her, not the penitentiary personnel. Had Yanukovych agreed to these terms, it would have been done.[119]

The Ukrainian people, who watched the parliamentary session live, could have reached a similar conclusion. What happened in the Verkhovna Rada was a surprise. After all, Yanukovych declared he would sign any act adopted by the parliament, because he knew it was necessary for the agreement with the EU. Still, his party abstained. That meant he was lying.

On Thursday, Cox and Kwaśniewski issued a statement expressing their "deep disappointment at the unilateral decision of the Ukrainian Government," because "the time-out formula now decided by the Ukrainian authorities is not without clear downside risks, is likely to last for considerable time and the process, if and when renewed, will be complicated by the decision made today."[120]

The legislation reforming the prosecution was supposed to be put to a vote on Friday, but following the freezing of preparations for signing of the Association Agreement, the adoption of the new act was an open question.

> We will be present at the parliament tomorrow, but given today's decisions, we don't know what kind of a reaction to expect from the legislators, especially from the ruling party. Who knows, maybe the Party of Regions will come to the conclusion that since the agreement will not be signed, there's no need to adopt further legislation. After all, the legislation in question was part of the integration package and it was supported by the EU as a necessary step for modernization, for the reform of the judiciary, and for solidifying Ukraine's democratic institutions.[121]

On Friday, November 22, roughly two thousand people gathered at the Maidan of Independence. The Euromaidan was born.

Was Yanukovych playing the EU card from the very start, in order to gain leverage in his talks with Russia? Were the pro–EU signals and the blue camp's friendly rhetoric towards Brussels just a diversion aimed at getting a better gas deal from the Kremlin? According to Aleksander Kwaśniewski, Yanukovych "seemed to be serious" about his approach towards the EU.[122] Ukraine's president had confirmed this in his speech in the Verkhovna Rada, when he said that integration with the EU was a priority and economic modernization was necessary for fostering closer relations with Europe. According to Kwaśniewski, "He had the support of all parties in the parliament at the time. And there is no reason not to believe these statements."[123]

The Association Agreement was not only supported by almost all the political forces, but also—even more importantly—the Ukrainian society. At a September 2013 Yalta European Strategy meeting, Kwaśniewski was convinced that Ukraine had never been that close to the EU: "It's not a matter of years anymore; it's a matter of days, a matter of weeks. The Vilnius summit starts in roughly two months and you can finally be with the EU. Both sides share this huge responsibility."[124] The same month, Kwaśniewski concluded, "I have taken part in a great number of meetings and I know that the majority of the Ukrainian people want their country to be associated with the EU, where they see possibilities for their children."[125] The former president of Poland emphasized the fact that not only young people, living in the Western part of the country, favored association with the EU. The idea was supported by people in the East, representatives of the business world, and artists. "Will we sign the Association Agreement? I believe we will. But we still need to deal with a few difficulties."[126]

> I appreciate the fact that Ukraine made a politically risky decision and chose Europe. This was evident in the summer of 2013, when Russia, using various vindications, imposed its embargo on a number of Ukrainian goods. With this in mind, we need to appreciate the Ukrainian authorities, which decided to take this step and work towards this goal. I hope we will be able to celebrate together in Vilnius.[127]

But there were no celebrations. The Ukrainian people were completely disappointed during the Vilnius summit because, once again, they were let down by politicians driven by their desire to stay in power.

> President Yanukovych decided to take some time off from negotiating with the EU due to reasons of an economic nature and his prospects for the 2015 presi-

dential election. He did not consider the society's reaction in his calculations. After Yanukovych made the decision, I saw tears in my Ukrainian colleagues' eyes. Hope was indeed taken away from them. It turned out that the EU was an important goal to many of them.[128]

The upcoming 2015 presidential election was what concerned Yanukovych the most. Since his electoral base was more pro–Russian than pro–European, Kwaśniewski concluded he was afraid "he would lose his supporters and would not gain new voters, since those who favored Europe would not have voted for him anyway."[129] Yanukovych found himself in a tough spot. At that time, the former president of Poland did not see any way out for Yanukovych.[130] As an experienced mediator, Kwaśniewski believed that a common ground with the opposition should be found; however, finding it would not be easy, because the opposition demanded early presidential and parliamentary elections. In consequence, Kwaśniewski suggested that the European aspirations themselves should serve as a common ground, since it was the only thing those two camps shared: "All bets are off. The Association Agreement, as well as the DCFTA, were not signed in Vilnius, but we can still make it happen."[131]

By dropping out of the negotiations with the EU, Yanukovych sealed his own fate. Still, nobody expected he would end up the way he did in the cold days of early 2014. He had at his disposal all the means to suppress the Euromaidan. And he did just that. All the people killed by snipers' bullets had their lives taken by the security services controlled by the president. During the clashes between Berkut and the protesters, Aleksander Kwaśniewski spoke of Yanukovych's iron fist: "His position within the security apparatus is undeniably strong. The militia did not move into Maidan without his consent. The government makes no decisions without him either."[132] The Ukrainian society would not give up without a fight, though.

According to Kwaśniewski, Yanukovych did not expect Maidan to grow that strong and to last for that long: "I am confident that exhaustion was his game. He was hoping people would just go home. Well, he should have known better. After all, in 2004 people protested despite the harsh winter too."[133] From the very start, Yanukovych underestimated the public support for integration with the EU, even though roughly half of the Ukrainian society was in favor of it. It was partic-

Aleksander Kwaśniewski (right) moderates a panel during the annual YES conference. He is shown here with the president of Ukraine, Viktor Yanukovych. September 2012. © Yalta European Strategy 2012, photograph by Sergei Illin.

ularly important for young people. The question is: Did Yanukovych surround himself with poor advisors, was he simply out of touch with the society's sentiments, or did he lack a clear vision of Ukraine's future? Before his fall, Kwaśniewski described Yanukovych as follows:

> Yanukovych knows his way around Ukrainian politics very well, in good times and bad. After his defeat in the 2004 election, he didn't succumb to depression but in fact managed to stage a comeback in 2010. He is a tough man and a tough politician. His experiences have made him a suspicious person. Communication isn't his strong side. He's more of a technocrat. And his family has gained a lot of influence.[134]

Yanukovych often went to great lengths in trying to explain to Kwaśniewski the source of his fortune and his influence. In the book by Zbigniew Parafianowicz and Michał Potocki entitled *Wolves Are Above the Law: How Yanukovych Lost Ukraine*, Aleksander Kwaśniewski described the Ukrainian president in the following way:

> He is a wealthy man and he wanted to justify it somehow. In one of his stories he was a test-driver for BMW in Munich, where he supposedly spent a couple

II. The European Union's Special Envoy to Ukraine

years. To which I replied that he must be fluent in German. He changed the subject right away. His next story was even more ridiculous. He was trying to convince me and Cox that he became a billionaire by playing poker at the time the U.S.S.R. was collapsing. He also told us he scuba dived in the Black Sea, by the Crimean coast. He told us that he swam five kilometers underwater ... at once. Another time, it would be fifteen and then—twenty kilometers. He claimed he used a rocket, designed for that purpose, and it helped him stay in shape. He argued that scuba diving stimulated weight loss.... The problem was that his stories were all messed up. In order to be a good liar, you need to have a good memory. Yanukovych didn't.[135]

According to Kwaśniewski, in addition to being a pathological liar, Yanukovych lacked a clear, farsighted vision: "I got to know President Yanukovych quite well and I was struck by his indecisiveness: on one day, he was headed for Europe; on another, Russia was his destination. It was so typical of him."[136] Kwaśniewski came to the conclusion that "the Ukrainian leadership has no strategy, and that it only sees things in the short term, so as to survive the next few months."[137] Consequently, Yanukovych's team underestimated public opinion and thought that it was manipulated by outside forces.[138] "When he informed us that the agreement would not be signed, I knew there was going to be trouble. He did not expect it to get that big. He was caught off-guard. These sort of autocrats don't understand people, they live in ivory towers. He did not expect Maidan to become that huge and to endure all that time."[139]

The political crisis, which followed the breaking of the negotiations, revealed the true nature of Yanukovych, even though his decision was caused to a great extent by Russian pressure. For this reason, Kwaśniewski dismissed the notion that everything was staged from the start.[140] The president's camp changed its attitude in the summer of 2013, when Russia imposed an embargo on Ukraine. According to Kwaśniewski:

> Many lawmakers with ties to companies began applying more pressure on the ruling party. These are companies that sell products to the Russian market, so they begged Yanukovych and his party for help. They said that they were out of money and that people were losing their jobs. That was when Putin's meetings with Yanukovych began, and soon they became longer and longer.[141]

Contrary to the Ukrainian society's expectations regarding European integration, Yanukovych and the Party of Regions suddenly made a U-turn. According to Aleksander Kwaśniewski, "it is beyond any doubt that the enormous pressure, applied by the Russian Federation, turned out to be very effective."[142] The government justified its decision with the country's poor economic and fiscal situation. Putting a halt to the preparations to sign the Association Agreement was the price they agreed to pay in order to deal with Ukraine's short-term difficulties. However, the country's poor economic situation was no coincidence. It was caused by Russia. As argued by Aleksander Kwaśniewski:

> It seems to me that their intentions were sincere up until summer, when Russia started to apply pressure. Ukraine intended to sign the Association Agreement. After all, a broad range of legislation was reformed and I'd be the last to say it all meant nothing. Therefore, I'm of the opinion that the unparalleled pressure, exercised by Russia, was key. Moscow employed the entire range of tools it had at its disposal in Ukraine. And this is the result we get.[143]

Kyiv might have been sincere about its willingness to cooperate with the European Union, but "due to Russia's pressure, the political climate changed,"[144] argued Kwaśniewski. Following the Russian embargo imposed on Ukraine in the summer of 2013, exports of metallurgical products, machinery, cars, trucks, wagons, etc., were put on hold. The losses suffered by Ukraine's economy were overwhelming. Jobs were lost and salaries were not being paid. Kwaśniewski underlined the fact that "In its struggle over Ukraine, Russia employed very harsh, even ruthless, methods."[145] Gas prices were still high, even though they were being negotiated. Ukraine's economic overdependence on Russia made it easier for the Kremlin to exercise blackmail. According to Kwaśniewski, both sides were to blame for Ukraine's poor economic condition, since it wasted two decades it could have spent on reforms. However, the Russian embargo had a direct impact on the situation's deterioration and "Moscow is to blame for the economic difficulties Ukraine is facing today."[146] Kwaśniewski was of the opinion that everything was moving in the right direction and a breakthrough "was within arm's reach."[147] But all of a sudden,

> The situation changed, the talks got tougher, less sincere; we know there's something going on behind the scenes. It's the summer of 2013. Russia is waging its final campaign and imposes an embargo on Ukraine in order to prevent it from signing the Association Agreement. Certain industries suffer a 50% fall in output. Propaganda is being spread on a huge scale. The Association Agreement is being labeled as a calamity, leading to surging prices.[148]

II. The European Union's Special Envoy to Ukraine

Even though the embargo was a blow to Ukraine's economy, in September 2013, Kwaśniewski described it as a double-edged sword: on one hand, it's pushing EU member states even closer to Ukraine. On the other, it inspires a significant rise in support of the Association Agreement among the traditionally pro–Russian part of Ukraine's society.[149]

Kwaśniewski believed that Russia was making a big mistake because the embargo enraged even the Moscow-friendly and Russian-speaking part of Ukraine.[150] When the situation spiraled out of control and the Euromaidan standoff erupted, the former president of Poland reiterated, "Russia is also to blame for the situation in Ukraine. After all, it's Moscow's actions over the past couple of months that have led to it."[151] Should the EU also be blamed for setting up an inevitable confrontation between Ukraine and Moscow? Brussels could have expected that Putin would try to torpedo Ukraine's association with the EU.

Kwaśniewski was never convinced that this was the case because the European Union was not responsible for Ukraine's poor economic situation and the political crisis: "It's not like Europe is doing whatever it can to lure Ukraine into its orbit. Europe merely responded to the Ukrainian government's political decisions, first expressed by Yushchenko and then Yanukovych's administration: 'we wish to sign the Association Agreement with the EU.'"[152] Kwaśniewski reminded of the two priorities from Yanukovych's speech delivered in the Ukrainian parliament in September 2013. The first one concerned the Association Agreement and the DCFTA. The second one mentioned modernization, which could only be carried out in close cooperation with Europe. "Today, it's clear that those declarations were not entirely sincere (or maybe they changed due to the pressure from Russia). However, millions of Ukrainian people trusted those words."[153] They took to the Maidan and were desperate because "the nation felt cheated, it felt that it was stripped of its dignity," and "Russia is the cause of it."[154]

According to Kwaśniewski, it is also probable that the Kremlin was in possession of documents that could discredit Viktor Yanukovych, and used them as leverage to influence his decisions. "Russians might have blackmailed Yanukovych with documents containing details of his financial transactions. It might have been one of the reasons he decided not to sign the Association Agreement with the European Union."[155]

For me, the summer of 2013 is crucial for understanding what took place in Ukraine. I cannot prove it, but it's what my gut tells me, after we found ourselves in the middle of this whole ordeal. Putin invited Yanukovych to his villa in Sochi in the summer of 2013. They spent six or seven hours there. On a number of occasions, we asked Yanukovych what the conversation was about. We also asked Klyuyev about it. Normally, they would tell us how tough and steadfast Putin is, how difficult it is for them to overcome such obstacles. That's how they portrayed themselves in front of the West, claiming they have to struggle against Putin, but they are doing fine. It was different with the summer 2013 meeting, which they summed it up shortly: nothing new, business as usual. But it was obvious that there was something more to it and that something secretive must have happened. Call it a modern version of the Molotov-Ribbentrop pact. There was something they did not want to talk about. I have a feeling that even Yanukovych's close associates knew nothing about it. They also told me they had not been informed, but they were concerned that something had happened.[156]

Kwaśniewski argues that the Russian president must have made Yanukovych an offer he couldn't refuse:

Putin drafted a three point agenda for Yanukovych in that meeting. Point one: You don't sign the Association Agreement and get 15 billion of foreign aid from us (announced soon after), we lift the embargo and can discuss gas prices. Point two: We will not propose our own candidate in the March 2015 presidential election, nor will we support any of your contenders. We can even help you if necessary (Yanukovych cared about power, because it was necessary to uphold the system and the source of his income, all the wealth he had stolen. That was not possible without political power. To him, power was not only about power itself; it was about his sense of security. That's the way he saw things). Point three: If you have any problems understanding point one and point two, point three is as follows: we know where your money is and if you want the world to know how it got there and how much there is, be my guest.[157]

"From the very start, Tymoshenko knew Yanukovych would not sign the Association Agreement," recalled Kwaśniewski. She always argued he would be looking for any and all excuses, because of his numerous connections and interests in Russia. "When I thought about it later, in hindsight, 70–80 percent of her analyses were accurate." According to Kwaśniewski, the former prime minister was able to predict what would happen, thanks to her deep understanding of Yanukovych's mentality, of his people, and their political interests.

In the wake of Russia's ruthless economic and political aggression and Putin's personal blackmail, was the European Union able to do

II. The European Union's Special Envoy to Ukraine

something and lead to the signing of the Association Agreement in November 2013?

Aleksander Kwaśniewski's assessment of the EU's actions in this regard is rather critical. However, the former special envoy of the European Parliament is very realistic about the EU's strengths and weaknesses. On the one hand, Kwaśniewski believes that the Russian embargo, imposed on Ukrainian products in the summer of 2013 was "underestimated by the EU institutions."[158] On the other, part of the criticism toward the EU was incorrect, because "Europe is an extremely democratic construct, where decision-making is based on compromise," thus "the EU cannot act like Putin, who controls Russia's budget, issues orders, and those orders are carried out."[159] Kwaśniewski recognized the EU's lack of swift-response mechanisms in the face of a crisis, and pointed to other weaknesses; however:

> Blaming ourselves in the EU makes little sense, because the European Union is a democracy, which does not have its own divisions, its own army and cannot resort to methods typical for dictatorships and authoritarian regimes. We can mediate, we can negotiate, we can try to convince, or provide financial assistance and cooperate on an economic basis. That is the arsenal at the disposal of the European Union.[160]

In consequence, Kwaśniewski's heaviest criticism, not only regarding the EU, but also the International Monetary Fund, concerns financial aspects. The European Union may not have its own divisions, but it does have financial instruments at its disposal. Unfortunately, the EU/IMF offer was "not good enough to say it could provide sufficient assistance in those difficult days, which could make up for the losses triggered by Russian sanctions. No such offer was on the table."[161] But even if there had been a tangible European offer, it would not have necessarily led to the signing of the Association Agreement. Two days before the Vilnius summit, Kwaśniewski concluded: "Had the European Union really considered what the consequences of Russia's pressure might be, it is possible the current situation would be completely different, but we can't be certain."[162] When asked if the situation would have been different, had the IMF and the EU offered a better deal to Yanukovych, Kwaśniewski stated:

> It's a difficult guess. One thing I know for certain: Russia would not have given up its influence in Ukraine, even if the IMF's offer had been better. What we

are dealing with is a conflict of a geostrategic nature. Ukraine is an extremely important partner from Russia's point of view. It wants Ukraine to be part of its own structures: the Eurasian Union and the Customs Union.[163]

It is evident that Brussels underestimated Russia's determination to prevent Ukraine from signing the free trade agreement with the European Union. "Indeed, Brussels was being naïve. For Putin, Ukraine is a very important factor, possibly the most important one. He could not have his Eurasian Union without it. The West underestimated the level of Russia's determination, but it is also underestimating the developments taking place in Kyiv."[164] Kwaśniewski argues that it was not right to limit the talks with Ukraine to legal reforms and forget about the ordeal, which was taking place in the background, and brought about the unfortunate turn of events. "I am not saying it could have been prevented. My point is, we should have made it more difficult for Yanukovych to flip the table by—for instance—speeding up the signing of the agreement and, optionally, discussing financial issues before that."[165] Unfortunately, while the failed Eastern Partnership summit was approaching, no serious talks were being held, because Ukraine did not express its desire for negotiations. On the other hand, the EU and the West as a whole had not prepared an economic package, which it "would be able to propose in order to help Ukraine make up for the losses caused by the Russian embargo."[166] The EU and the IMF's actions proved to be too little, too late:

> In my opinion, they wasted an important window of opportunity, which was open from the summer, when it all started, until the Vilnius summit, scheduled for November. For at least three or four months, the talks were focused on general issues and the long-term benefits of the Association Agreement. Those arguments were correct. After all, Ukrainians are well aware of the fact that the deal would be highly beneficial in a 10–15 year perspective.[167]

But nobody was going to consider the long-term benefits of the Association Agreement. Had Ukraine's budget run dry, there would have been no money for gas and households would have been left out in the cold without heating. The offer on short-term relief was overdue, because it was easy to predict what the Russian pressure would look like. Kwaśniewski argued, "we know what to expect of Russia and we know what methods it employs. It doesn't take a genius to figure

II. The European Union's Special Envoy to Ukraine

out that Russia always uses the same means." When it comes to the economy, the EU and the IMF could have responded in a much more sufficient way, "because the government is held accountable for what tomorrow brings."[168] The EU failed to deliver a resolute response in the summer. "As soon as Russia launched its campaign, Brussels should have created a swift-response plan. Words were said, declarations were made, but no action was taken. It might have also been beneficial to try to engage Moscow in order to persuade it not to employ this kind of method."[169]

The financial aid package for Ukraine was ready, but the conditions were very difficult. The IMF claimed it would provide the credit if the prices of energy would not go up. According to Kwaśniewski,

> It was impossible to implement this kind of change just one year ahead of the elections. On the other hand, the IMF was not open to negotiate this matter. At the same time, it's so easy for the Russians to provide aid to Ukraine. After all, they just need to lift the embargo, which they imposed in the summer, and Kyiv will be able to see the results right away. Russia can also lower gas prices, which will allow Ukraine to catch its breath. These are all actions, based on accounting tricks. For Europe, it's much more difficult, because it requires actual money.[170]

No government would commit political suicide by raising gas prices one year ahead of elections. However, as argued by Kwaśniewski, "if they had agreed to a gradual increase of prices, and had it been acceptable to the IMF, we would have been able to talk money. Say, a dozen or so billion to be pumped into the Ukrainian system."[171] On the other hand, Kwaśniewski understood why the EU and the IMF were being so cautious. After all, "they did not wish to pump the money into an economy, which had not been reformed, and see it being wasted." At the same time, the Azarov government did not want to agree to the preconditions, which "were not bad and they would have to be met sooner or later."[172] Ukraine was not determined enough, because the IMF had prepared a credit package worth a dozen or so billion dollars. In consequence, blaming the European Union for not being able to offer financial aid overnight, ignoring all procedures, is practically equal to criticizing democracy. "The key to solving these problems is in Ukraine's hands and only the Ukrainian authorities can be held accountable."[173]

The Ukrainian Tiananmen: Euromaidan and Bloody Tuesday

Aleksander Kwaśniewski believed that the decision that Yanukovych made shortly before the EU summit in Vilnius, "namely to rebuff Brussels, came as a surprise," and the fact that he completely disregarded society's opinion, and didn't attempt to explain anything to his people, reveals that he "apparently believed that it wouldn't make that much difference to the public."[174] But it did. More and more people started to gather on the Maidan to demand that the Ukrainian government sign the Association Agreement.

In the final days of November, the heads of Poland and Germany's diplomacy issued a joint statement on Ukraine:

> The peaceful demonstrations, taking place in Kyiv and other Ukrainian cities, are the living proof of Ukrainian citizens' willingness to move their country closer to the European Union. We share this sentiment and we would like to declare our commitment to the Ukrainian nation, which could be—and still can be—the main beneficiary of the offer of close political and economic cooperation presented by the European Union. The offer of concluding the Association Agreement still stands. It requires the Ukrainian leadership to express political will and determination, as well as substantial progress in accordance with the rules established in December 2012.[175]

The EU institutions were also trying to exercise initiative, which was mostly exemplified by Catherine Ashton's belated actions. During her visit to Ukraine, which took place from December 10–11, 2013, the High Representative held several meetings with President Yanukovych, representatives of the opposition, and NGOs. Like other politicians and diplomats, she appealed for dialogue and non-use of force against the protesters. Yanukovych promised he would find a solution to the crisis within 24 hours.[176] But the crisis accelerated and the pressure on the regime kept rising. The pro–European and anti-government fever was spreading across the country.

By the end of January, the anti–Yanukovych demonstrations were not limited to the Maidan. They also took place in Ivano-Frankivsk, Odessa, and Sumy. On January 23, a couple thousand people blocked the way to an administration building in Zhytomyr. In Lviv, Rivne, Ternopil, and Cherkasy, protesters took over local administrative agen-

II. The European Union's Special Envoy to Ukraine

cies, which were subject to the president. Apart from demanding the signing of the Association Agreement and calling for European integration, protesters began demanding for Yanukovych to step down. It seemed unrealistic, because Yanukovych had been, more or less, democratically elected. Only the president had the power to organize early elections and only the parliament had the right to impeach Yanukovych. In consequence, Aleksander Kwaśniewski believed that the opposition should seize the opportunity, and "not allow being blamed for avoiding dialogue because, today, the opposition that says 'we do not wish to negotiate,' accepts the responsibility for this whole ordeal."[177]

Round-table talks are usually held between parties that do not trust each other: between "the authorities, whose conscience is far from clean and the opposition, which holds a book of grudges against the government."[178] The situation was much more complicated in 2004, during the Orange Revolution: "Now Yanukovych has a legal mandate as president, and the government has a legitimate parliamentary majority. But Ukrainians are divided over the question of whether the country should form closer ties with the EU. A majority is in favor of closer ties, 15 to 20 percent support a union with Russia and the rest have no opinion."[179] That is why Kwaśniewski believed that dialogue might have led to change. In 2013, he said:

> In my opinion, it is naive to believe that the political situation in Ukraine can be changed though radical declarations, even by masses in the streets. It's impossible. If the Ukrainian people want to change their situation, if they want to overcome the political crisis, if they want to sign the Association Agreement, they need to engage in dialogue.[180]

Kwaśniewski understood Yulia Tymoshenko's position, when she was calling for bringing down the government, because she was being held in a penal colony and did not trust Yanukovych. However, he did not believe that a long-lasting movement, operating across the entire country, could be created in 2013.[181] The political situation was completely different:

> Given that Yanukovych is a democratically-elected president, and the legitimate parliamentary majority supports the government—which is not without meaning for Western Europe—I would advise the opposition to make reasonable demands and to engage in dialogue with the authorities. I'm saying this despite my understanding for Yulia Tymoshenko's attitude.[182]

What did Kwaśniewski mean by "reasonable" demands? First and foremost, the opposition could present a precondition. It could agree to hold talks once the militia and military forces were pulled out of Kyiv and the people responsible for assaulting students on the night of November 30 were brought to justice. Then, the fate of the Association Agreement would have to be discussed: "If President Yanukovych tells Catherine Ashton he wants to sign the agreement, Commissioner Barroso should deliver the documents to the Verkhovna Rada as soon as possible, even tomorrow!"[183] The second issue concerned the country's political development through a creation of a compromise government. This government, comprised of both the parliamentary majority and the parliamentary minority, would be responsible for stabilizing the economy. It would also have to hold fair elections in 2015, which would basically determine the future of Ukraine's foreign policy.[184] Brussels could not call for a political coup because it considered Yanukovych to be a democratically-elected president of Ukraine. So what could the West do? The possibility of imposing sanctions was suddenly on the table.

In the wake of the regime's increasingly harsh actions, which led to the deterioration of the situation of human rights, the European Union started to ponder how it could effectively influence the Ukrainian authorities. Kwaśniewski argued, "sanctions are practically a one-time weapon. We should hold the big club in reserve and let the Ukrainian authorities be aware of such a prospect. And they are aware."[185] However, sanctions should be treated as a last resort, since they may not deliver the desired effect. "By imposing sanctions, we admit that we are helpless."[186] It was better to seek other solutions at that stage.

Kwaśniewski tried to persuade European politicians to maintain open channels of communication with both sides of the dispute. He argued that they should not give up the mediating position, despite their affinities for the democratic side, because "it's impossible to mediate and take sides at the same time."[187] It is necessary to be acknowledged by both. In consequence, Kwaśniewski emphasized that the dialogue should be continued and that putting an end to the political crisis was in Yanukovych's best interest. After all, the economic situation of Ukraine was dramatic, as it was at risk of going bankrupt. In 2014 in Davos, the former president of Poland said:

II. The European Union's Special Envoy to Ukraine

> We need to appeal on a political level and demand that aid does not come to a halt and that we return to the negotiating table. Nonetheless, we are aware of the fact that appeals don't necessarily get the job done and, therefore, I believe the Ukrainian authorities should be made aware of the instruments—such as personal sanctions—that the EU has at its disposal.[188]

Kwaśniewski admitted that he did not know whether sanctions would bring about the desired effect, but they could play an important part in certain circles. What happened on the Maidan was something more than a dispute between the authorities and the opposition: "It also reflects the civil society's expectations, and the civil society does not consider the opposition its most desired partner either."[189]

The streets of Kyiv were filled with mistrust and suspicion. The opposition leaders were not in charge of the Maidan, it was the other way around. Consequently, when party leaders were negotiating with Yanukovych, they had to report their actions to the Maidan masses and adjust them according to the crowd's reaction. The increasingly confrontational attitude and rhetoric of Vitali Klitschko was a perfect example. Following failed talks with the president, Klitschko addressed the Maidan and called him a liar: "Today it's just a few cities, tomorrow we'll be stronger. We will put up new barricades. Maidan will keep on spreading for as long as they don't start taking us seriously. All of Ukraine shall rise! Yesterday, I announced that no Ukrainian citizen will cooperate with this government and everyone will protest. We can see the results today. Action is being taken. The entire country shall protest."[190] Yanukovych found himself in a corner.

On January 25, during his talks with the opposition, Yanukovych proposed that detainees be released and all protesters offered amnesty. He also suggested that a working group for constitutional reform be created in order to amend the controversial legislative act of January 16, which limited civil liberties and the right to protest. He also made another offer: Yatsenyuk would become prime minister and Klitschko a deputy prime minister. Was this an opportunity ... or a trap?

In either case, the opposition declined and Klitschko argued that early elections were a non-negotiable demand: "We will not respond to provocations." A few days later, activists clashed with the militia in Dnipropetrovsk and Zaporizhia. More and more administrative buildings across the entire country came under control of the protesters.

This sparked concerns over the prospect of a state of emergency. In consequence, on January 27, Catherine Ashton warned the Ukrainian authorities against adopting such a drastic measure. According to the EU's High Representative, this would only make things worse and would not benefit anyone.[191]

On January 28, Viktor Yanukovych accepted Prime Minister Mykola Azarov's resignation. Aleksander Kwaśniewski had the opportunity to speak with Azarov, who told him that his decision to step down was supposed to enable compromise. The former president of Poland considered it a step in the right direction, but he did not expect it would be able to resolve the conflict.[192] The decision should have been made much earlier, especially given that the resignation of the government was among the top demands formulated by the Maidan: "Had [Yanukovych] agreed to this from the outset, it would have been possible to avoid escalations."[193] Still, Kwaśniewski believed that Azarov's resignation could pave the way to a compromise.[194]

On January 28, during an extraordinary session of the Verkhovna Rada, most of the radical legislation that had been adopted on January 16 was rescinded. Despite this, a heated debate erupted over the legislation granting amnesty to the protesters. The resolutions proposed by the Party of Regions allowed more protests at the Maidan Square, but it also required protesters to abandon public administration buildings. The legislation drafted by the opposition, calling for unconditional amnesty for all demonstrators, was not even put to a vote. In consequence, the opposition boycotted the session and the act that was adopted.

On the following day, the first president of independent Ukraine, Leonid Kravchuk, delivered a speech in the Verkhovna Rada. Speaking also on behalf of Leonid Kuchma, who was present in the parliament, Kravchuk argued that the crisis could only be overcome through cooperation between the government and the opposition. He also said that any constitutional changes should be adopted exclusively by the parliament, not by the courts. Despite the open debate, which also seemed to be constructive, the threat of the use of force was still looming large. On the same day, Radek Sikorski concluded: "Ukraine is looking at the following scenarios: good, bad, very bad, and apocalyptic. According to my sources, security services are still being mobilized in Ukraine.

II. The European Union's Special Envoy to Ukraine

The troops' salaries have been raised and equipment is being distributed. The situation is extremely tense. A state of emergency is still an option."[195]

"When I spoke with Yanukovych, I was concerned that he would be capable of opening fire on people," said Kwaśniewski.[196] Even though the threat of the state of emergency was still real, in the final days of January, Kwaśniewski noted, "The power structures in Ukraine have been disintegrating on such a scale that carving out an operation of that magnitude seems progressively unlikely. That's a good thing."[197] This did not change the fact that the situation was still "very unstable" and that things could get out of control at any time. "We are facing a tragedy," concluded Kwaśniewski. "Such a terrible scenario would have unimaginable consequences."[198] It was increasingly more evident that Yanukovych and the Party of Regions were losing control.

In the last days of January, the split within the Party of Regions was beginning to be increasingly apparent. Yanukovych reportedly threatened his party's legislators in the Verkhovna Rada. The split was a typical occurrence in the face of such a crisis and it demonstrated the "disintegration process within the ruling camp."[199] For that reason, the president's visit to the parliament "was caused by his fear of losing the majority. He was afraid he had lost a couple dozen lawmakers from the Party of Regions and wanted to discipline, intimidate, and blackmail them."[200] Kwaśniewski was of the opinion that the disintegration of power concerned oligarchs, but it also took place on an institutional level: in the military, the militia, and the judiciary. The people who—until recently—were willing to follow the government's orders were now becoming concerned over maintaining "a guise of neutrality, to be able to present documents in the future, after everything's changed. So that they would be able to say: 'Hey, I supported you, I was on the winning team.'"[201]

Meanwhile, the opposition's demands were becoming bolder. At a rally on February 2, it announced that a new parliamentary majority would be formed and the previous constitution, adopted in 2004, would be restored. Yuriy Lutsenko went as far as saying that the new majority would include lawmakers from the Party of Regions. But Yanukovych was not giving up. He was willing to shed blood.

On Tuesday, February 18, dramatic clashes between the demonstrators and the Berkut forces erupted. The debate on the restoration of the 2004 constitution was scheduled for the same day but, in the end, it did not take place. The previous day, leaders of the opposition were in Berlin where they met with Angela Merkel. They tried persuading her to impose sanctions on Yanukovych. That same day, Aleksander Kwaśniewski met with German President Joachim Gauck. "My talks with Chancellor Angela Merkel's advisors, right before the visit of the opposition leaders, included multiple scenarios. Unfortunately, what happened on Tuesday was a likely scenario."[202]

While in Berlin, Kwaśniewski argued that Yanukovych was not willing to compromise because he knew it would deprive him of power and that was unacceptable. "Things can easily get out of hand. We are dealing with growing radicalism and the disintegration of power structures."[203] Despite the violence on the Maidan, the protesters were fighting for a free and democratic Ukraine, which is why Kwaśniewski argued that these political developments constituted a harbinger of a blooming civil society. Therefore, the EU should be involved in supporting Ukraine's democratic development and its European aspirations. He underlined that Europe's goals should include putting an end to the violence, followed by assistance in creating democratic institutions.[204]

As the world was watching footage of riot police using sniper bullets in the streets of Kyiv, Russian broadcasters focused their reporting on alleged fascists and Bandera followers. Meanwhile, Yanukovych delivered his presidential proclamation, arguing that—despite the opinion of his advisors—he did not wish to resort to violence. He met with Arseniy Yatsenyuk and Vitali Klitschko again, but to no avail. Yanukovych was not willing to meet the opposition's demands and the opposition claimed that the president demanded that the protestors leave the Maidan. On February 19, the Ukrainian Ministry of Health announced that 25 people had been killed.

"President Yanukovych should have proposed a reasonable solution. Instead, his solution was Berkut's assault on demonstrators and dead bodies in the streets," noted Kwaśniewski.[205] Yanukovych "obviously has blood on his hands. He understands the gravity of the situation and, in a way, has no way out."[206] He was not willing to compromise in any way because he wanted to hold on to his power and money in order to secure his own future, no matter the price:

II. The European Union's Special Envoy to Ukraine

> There's basically no way out for the authorities. There's already blood on their hands. It makes no difference if the number of casualties goes up to 25 or 70. From a legal standpoint, those who ordered Berkut's onslaught are responsible. The authorities have no room to maneuver and no exit out, so they feel that they have to fight. And I know they will fight, because I know these people.[207]

On the other hand, the opposition had several problems of its own: it did not have much of a plan, its influence over the activists was fading, and there was nobody with whom they could negotiate. Meanwhile, calling for additional street protests could have led to more people being killed and shifted part of the blame on the opposition itself. Tensions were constantly rising, which led Kwaśniewski to conclude: "The country is out of control. It will start drifting. It will cease to perform its basic functions and we are already dealing with a deep economic crisis."[208]

Kwaśniewski considered "the worst case scenario as the most probable one," because the government did not want to back off and Kyiv's streets were burning: "After all this time, the people are simply tired and frustrated, so they have become radicalized. The people on the Maidan Square are growing angrier and it's only getting worse."[209] In late January, Kwaśniewski suggested a way out of the tense situation:

> I would opt for creating something we might call a government of national unity, or a national emergency government, because the situation is dramatic. Not necessarily with a leader of the opposition at the helm. Someone with authority who could guarantee good governance until the time fair presidential election is held, which would also be that person's responsibility. The question is: is there anyone in Ukraine who matches this criteria? I believe not many people would qualify, to be honest, very few would, but in the end, there has to be someone capable of getting this done.[210]

In Berlin, Kwaśniewski discussed four key actions the EU should undertake, together with the United States, in order to provide Ukraine with assistance. First of all, the EU and the U.S. should condemn any kind of violent acts committed by the regime, but also by any radicals. Second of all, the parties concerned should be encouraged to engage in dialogue and negotiations. Thirdly, "we need to make it clear to Mr. Yanukovych that he is responsible for this situation, and this conflict, and that we expect him to come up with solutions," because that is what governments do. Finally, Europe and the United States should support the unity of the opposition.[211]

In the meantime, a war was being fought in the center of Kyiv. Following each day of bloody fights, and the growing number of casualties inflicted by snipers' bullets, the prospects of a national unity government became unimaginable. The Maidan would not agree for the country to be ruled—possibly in a coalition—by those who they considered murderers. In consequence, saving people's lives required external help.

On Wednesday evening, February 19, the foreign ministers of Poland, France, and Germany arrived to Kyiv in order to broker a compromise agreement, which could prevent more casualties. Throughout all of Thursday, meetings with Yanukovych were being postponed one after another, and people kept dying in the streets. Radek Sikorski posted on his Twitter account a number of photographs depicting smoke surrounding the presidential palace. He also tweeted about the explosions and gunshots coming from various directions. In the evening, the talks finally began. As reported by Sikorski, it felt like being in the middle of the Apocalypse. He and his entourage entered the presidential building together with snipers—the very same people who fired shots at the people on the Maidan Square.[212]

"We only have one night," commented Kwaśniewski. "We are trying to buy more time. Every hour without casualties matters. It may not be a lot, but it's better than nothing."[213] Nobody knew how far the desperate Yanukovych was willing to go. Kwaśniewski said: "I'm afraid that the most probable scenarios are bad, even terrible. But we cannot afford to lose hope. We have to keep trying and give it our best to stop the violence and, ultimately, restore dialogue."[214]

The talks, which started at the office of Yanukovych on Thursday night, lasted until Friday morning. The first point agreed upon was the restoration of the 2004 constitution. The proposal of creating a government of national unity also had Yanukovych's approval. Finally, early presidential election would be held by the end of the year, even though initially Yanukovych did not even want to discuss this issue. The last point was a concession Kwaśniewski did not expect (just two days earlier he said that organizing a 2015 presidential election would "potentially defuse the situation"[215]). However, it was not certain whether the opposition and the Maidan would accept the agreement.

II. The European Union's Special Envoy to Ukraine

The negotiations on Friday were extremely difficult. Cameras registered Radek Sikorski warning representatives of the opposition that they had to sign the agreement "or you will all be dead."[216] The opposition finally agreed, but "the most tense and dramatic time was the Friday morning, when there was a risk of the agreement being thrown out the window."[217] They had to convince the Maidan it was the right thing to do. Vitali Klitschko asked Radek Sikorski and Frank-Walter Steinmeier to meet with the Maidan Council, which was distrustful of any deals with Yanukovych. "Do not underestimate the power of the government. Do not make the same mistake that Solidarity did [in Poland] in December 1981. The government has firearms at its disposal," warned Sikorski.[218] The Maidan was finally convinced and the vote took place: 34 out of 36 votes were cast in favor of the agreement.[219] After a few hours, in the presence of foreign ministers of Poland and Germany, Yanukovych and the opposition signed the agreement.

Sikorski faced criticism in Poland for allegedly imposing on the Ukrainian opposition the agreement with Yanukovych. Kwaśniewski did not see it that way: "I heard Radek Sikorski reportedly said, 'If you don't support this deal you'll have martial law, you'll have the army. You will all be dead.' I am not sure if that was the case, but there is one thing I do know for sure: the threat of a civil war was the alternative. Civil wars are bloody and disastrous to the economy and the state. Many innocent people die in the process."[220] The former president of Poland spoke highly of Sikorski's mission: "Minister Sikorski's determination, and his ability to get the Weimar Triangle together, helped secure the ceasefire and the agreement. It's definitely an achievement. Were his words too harsh? Under certain circumstances, you have to get emotional; you have to demonstrate that too much is at stake. The desired effect was reached."[221] Resoluteness was necessary: "It's all about the tension. The goal was reached. Sikorski's words were harsh, but under certain circumstances, there's a place for emotions to take over."[222] Moreover, "the criticism directed towards Minister Sikorski holds no merit. The level of tensions during those talks justifies the arguments he used."[223]

Given that Yanukovych had broken his share of promises, it was uncertain whether the deal would be respected. Nobody knew what to expect of the Maidan either, which led Kwaśniewski to suggest it would be a good thing to treat the agreement "as a strong basis for conflict resolution and, most importantly, for putting an end to the violence on both sides."[224] There were no guarantees that this would work. After the agreement was signed, Sikorski had to convince representatives of the Maidan to accept the contents of the deal. It was not an easy task. The regime was despised to the extent that Vitali Klitschko had to explain himself in front of the crowd as to why he shook Yanukovych's hand.

Despite what seemed like an insurmountable obstacle, Kwaśniewski came to the conclusion that the opposition should accept the terms. The agreement was going to be a hard pill to swallow because people could hardly hold their tempers and the radicalization of the Maidan was understandable since their "family members and friends were being killed."[225] But civil war would be even more disastrous.

> How can anyone trust bloody Yanukovych who is pleading now for a peace agreement? I believe the only way to go about it is to sign it, and to maintain the EU triangle: Radek Sikorski, Laurent Fabius, and Frank-Walter Steinmeier. This is the EU's achievement, but the credit also goes to the Weimer Triangle, which was able to achieve something tangible for the first time in many years. That is why the ministers' presence is necessary. They have to be there during the next couple of hours. And they need to visit frequently in the days to come in order to guarantee that the terms of the agreement are respected.[226]

Sikorski did express his willingness to return to Ukraine and assist in the process of the implementation of the deal. It turned out not to be necessary. Events unfolded more rapidly than anyone could have expected.

Yanukovych Escapes: Why Didn't Putin Predict the Euromaidan?

> We are looking at ten months of uncertainty, because the presidential election will only take place three months ahead of the constitutional schedule. The Maidan does not wish to spend ten more months with this president. For the Maidan, he is fundamentally unacceptable. In consequence, it does not matter if it's a matter of ten, four, or two months. The problem won't go away.[227]

A few days before Yanukovych signed the agreement with the opposition, Kwaśniewski said, "I believe that until the time of the 2015

II. The European Union's Special Envoy to Ukraine

presidential election we will be dealing with a permanent crisis. We'll be hearing both good and bad news, without any substantial changes."[228] He also argued: "Yanukovych, along with his posse, do not have another choice. They have to either surrender immediately and find a safe place to hide, or they have to fight. For them, power equals personal safety. I expect trouble."[229] Contrary to these words, Yanukovych was suddenly out of the equation. He surrendered … and fled.

Yanukovych left Kyiv for Kharkiv on Friday, February 21. The Verkhovna Rada adopted a resolution on Yulia Tymoshenko's release and the former prime minister was finally set free. On Saturday, 328 legislators voted in favor of the dismissal of Viktor Yanukovych. The adopted legislative act stated that the president had left his post and was responsible for the deaths of more than 80 protesters and police officers.[230] Tymoshenko made an appearance on the Maidan Square in the evening.

Sitting in a wheelchair, she expressed her gratitude to the demonstrators, whose actions led to her release. She said that the first thing she wanted to do was to touch the barricades where "our boys and girls" spilled their blood. She spoke of sniper bullets hitting hearts of activists. She appealed to the people not to leave the Maidan until all the demands have been met and tried to get a sense of the crowd's emotions and reactions. "Don't ever forgive!" she shouted. "And Yanukovych should stand trial before Maidan," she added. The crowd roared.

But such a trial was unlikely to take place. Yanukovych knew there was no reason for him to go back and that he should not expect a warm welcome. Especially after the public had seen his residence in Mezhyhirya. The "museum of corruption," as it was soon called, was tangible proof of the president and his family's criminal activities. Security personnel had abandoned the residence and its compounds, just as they abandoned public administration buildings before. Pictures of Ukrainians strolling around the 135-hectare presidential residence, which included golf courses, artificial lakes, tennis courts, and private hunting woods, hit the news around the world. Interestingly enough, that was where Yanukovych went hunting right after he returned from the failed Vilnius summit. On November 30, when Berkut clubbed demonstrators at the Maidan Square and attacked them with tear gas, the president was hunting wild boars.[231]

The African ostriches, which were walking around the private zoo in Mezhyhirya, might not have been concerned with the ordeal, but the Ukrainian people found the residence outrageous. Many of them went there directly from the barricade-infested Maidan. Their faces were still black from the smoke of burning tires. The visitors had the privilege to see Yanukovych's collections of paintings, religious icons, and dozens of cars and motorcycles. They also discovered the president's preference for marble, gold toilets, and doors made of Lebanese cedar ($64,000 apiece).[232] He also had a soft spot for music, or at least for the sight of expensive musical instruments. The hallway featured a white Steinway & Sons piano, which was worth 77,200 GBP. It was a replica of John Lennon's birthday gift to Yoko Ono from 1971, which featured in the music video of the song "Imagine," where Lennon suggested people should imagine a world with no possessions.[233] Such a world was obviously unimaginable for Yanukovych.

Commenting on the Ukrainian president's preference for luxury, Aleksander Kwaśniewski said: "Luxurious life is typical for all despots. Yanukovych had gone through difficult times: his family was poor and he served time in prison. He wanted to be as rich as the oligarchs. Now, mix this with a complete lack of taste and you end up with a result such as the Mezhyhirya residence."[234]

The footage of the residence angered the Ukrainian public opinion even further, but nobody was really surprised. Ukrainians were accustomed to the fact (not to say that they were fine with it) that oligarchs exploited their country, where business and politics were two sides of the same coin. According to Aleksander Kwaśniewski, the problem is caused by a misperception of what power and governance are about.

> There is a mental division between Ukraine and Europe. For us, democracy is a goal of its own, and political power serves as a tool that we use to achieve it. In Ukraine, in Russia, political power is the ultimate value, not democracy. In consequence, if democracy can be beneficial, it's embraced. If not, it's rejected. Democracy, authoritarianism, semi-authoritarianism, or any other system is acceptable. The political elites might have been democratically elected, but there is no attachment to democracy as a value of its own.[235]

Yanukovych did not value democracy at all. When democratic decisions did not serve his purpose anymore, he decided to escape. The question remains: was it his own decision?

II. The European Union's Special Envoy to Ukraine

The events of the night of February 21 and 22 are intriguing. Right after the agreement was signed, Yanukovych left Kyiv and departed for Kharkiv in the dark of the night. Party of Regions representatives from eastern and southern districts held a meeting in that city and Yanukovych had announced earlier he would participate in the gathering. He could not expect anything positive out of Kyiv, since the security personnel had left administrative buildings (the reasons for their actions remain unclear). The situation was perplexing: the agreement, by some viewed as beneficial for Yanukovych, was signed and acknowledged by the opposition and a majority of Maidan representatives. But Yanukovych decided to flee from Kyiv and Berkut troops left the premises they were supposed to protect. Why this all happened remains unclear. In an interview, Radek Sikorski reported his conversation with Leonid Kozhara, who was the foreign minister at that time. According to Kozhara, once members of the special forces were no longer legally authorized to use firearms, they became concerned over their own safety and decided to return to their barracks. Another theory argues that the pace of the regime's collapse led the security personnel to the decision to abandon the president.[236]

Kwaśniewski is of the opinion that Yanukovych's decision to escape from Kyiv one day after he signed the agreement with Sikorski and Steinmeier is not logical—unless someone else was involved. "I believe Putin instructed Yanukovych to flee." The decision could not have been taken overnight because Yanukovych had a moving-house operation going on. Documents were being destroyed, money was being collected.[237]

Arseniy Yatsenyuk's assessment of these mysterious developments falls along the lines of Kwaśniewski's theory. He argued that the sudden withdrawal of security forces from governmental premises was not caused by Yanukovych's panic attack. It could have been staged to look that way, but it was really a trap for the opposition: "They wanted the crowd to set the parliament and the presidential palace on fire," claimed Yatsenyuk.[238] The authorities were hoping the protesters would destroy the public buildings when Yanukovych left Kyiv. It would have given him a perfect excuse to restore order with force and drown the "putsch" in blood. According to Radek Sikorski, over the phone, Putin was trying to talk Yanukovych into taking firm measures.[239] The opposition did not fall into the trap. But it seems like Putin had a plan B: triggering total chaos in Eastern Ukraine.

Aleksander Kwaśniewski believes Yanukovych should have anticipated that the decision not to sign the Association Agreement would lead to street protests. He should have also expected the protests to focus on the Association Agreement on the first day and to target Yanukovych and his corrupt regime in the days to follow. "The fact that Yanukovych did not see it coming is not that surprising, since he's quite limited intellectually. But Putin's inability to anticipate such a turn of events can lead to two conclusions. Conclusion one: he really does not understand Ukraine, but I find this hard to believe. Conclusion two: he found this scenario convenient."[240]

Kwaśniewski points to two elements of Putin's policy, which are easy to comprehend. Putin's conversations with Yanukovych, which took place in the summer of 2013, make perfect sense because Putin was pursuing his plan of incorporating Ukraine into the Eurasian Union. That is why economic and personal blackmail seemed to be a logical tool from the Kremlin's point of view. However, it is surprising that Putin did not take any precautions in regard to the demonstrations in Ukraine. "If someone wanted to do so, it would have been very easy to take the appropriate precautions," says Kwaśniewski. "All it would have taken was heavy construction equipment in the middle of Khreshchatyk Street and an excuse that road or sewage works were underway. All of a sudden, the biggest square is out of the picture, and organizing large-scale demonstrations on other squares would not have been that easy."[241] This brings us to the following conclusion.

Moscow had constantly accused politicians from Brussels, CIA agents, and fascist militias trained in Warsaw and Vilnius for the eruption of the Euromaidan. According to the official version circulated by the Kremlin, the demonstrations were not spontaneous; they were planned in the West. But Kwaśniewski has a conspiracy theory of his own, one that is a reversed version of Moscow's theory. The scenario featuring demonstrations, street clashes, and the brutal suppression of the Euromaidan was beneficial to some. "It seems to me it suited them because it would destabilize Ukraine to the point of inertia."[242] That is why causing total chaos in Kyiv was Putin's game plan. As it turns out,

II. The European Union's Special Envoy to Ukraine

Kwaśniewski was right. One year after the escape of Yanukovych, Putin admitted to his role in these developments.

In an interview featured in the film *Crimea: The Return to the Homeland,* screened by the national TV broadcaster Rossiya-1 in March 2015, Putin revealed the details of the operation carried out on the night of February 22 and 23, 2014. The mission's main objective was to "save the life of the president of Ukraine." According to Putin's own testimony, Yanukovych was facing the prospect of being physically eliminated by the opposition, which was planning to ambush his convoy. For that reason, the Russian president ordered his security services to save Yanukovych "via land, sea, and air routes." Spetsnaz helicopters evacuated and transported him to Crimea and then to Russia. Putin was in charge throughout the entire operation: "We finished at approximately seven in the morning," said the Russian president. "Right before parting with my four colleagues, I told them: 'The developments in Ukraine leave us no choice but to start preparations of Crimea's reunification with Russia.'"

* * *

On February 24, Aleksander Kwaśniewski and Pat Cox issued a statement on the situation in Ukraine.

> As the country is living through the most remarkable historic changes in its modern history; we would like to express to the people of Ukraine our admiration, our support and our encouragement.
>
> In 2012 and 2013, we made 27 visits to Ukraine aimed at helping Ukraine overcome the obstacles on its pathway to the Association Agreement with the European Union and to find a solution to cases of selective justice including that of Yulia Tymoshenko. We are extremely pleased to welcome her freedom.
>
> We wish to pay our deepest respects to all who have died during the past few weeks and to offer our sincere condolences to all families and relatives of the Maidan's victims. Major political changes are taking place in Ukraine as a result of the extraordinary mobilization of the Ukrainian people fighting for a better future and a more democratic and European Ukraine.
>
> These achievements have come at a great cost to Ukraine. Too many have been killed due to the failure of the previous administration to listen to citizens' calls for change. Justice is necessary, fair Justice, in line with Ukraine's international commitments. Revenge would be to repeat the mistakes of the past.
>
> The large mobilization in Kyiv and in many other cities must have regard to

those many Ukrainians who today are worried about their future and that of their country. The next government of Ukraine must work for the future of all Ukrainians without exception to ensure stability, to guarantee the unity of the country and to pave the way for transformation.

Key to avoid disappointing the high expectations of all Ukrainians will be the effective fight against corruption and cronyism which poisons Ukraine's politics and political class, as well as real reform of the judicial and electoral systems to ensure a truly democratic future for Ukraine.

The international community and in particular the European Union urgently must support Ukraine in preserving its territorial integrity and in facilitating in all ways possible the country's passage to greater democracy, justice and prosperity. The EU must also strive to develop a positive and constructive engagement with Russia on Ukraine's regional relations.[243]

Kwaśniewski underlined that improving the terrible financial situation and preparing the May 25 elections should be among the new government's priorities. "Both tasks seem to be possible as long as the European promise of short- and long-term financial aid is fulfilled."[244] Kwaśniewski concluded that the EU's assistance would be necessary to bring the country back from the brink of an economic collapse and allow the new Ukrainian government to attempt to face Russian pressure and tackle corruption and the existing social inequalities. According to Kwaśniewski, Ukrainian society was the country's biggest hope, because it was becoming increasingly conscious of the chances provided by a European perspective and was determined to make use of this opportunity.[245] Considering the willpower and sacrifice of the people on the Maidan Square, Kwaśniewski argued Maidan activists should be "implanted" into Ukraine's social and political life, so that a few of their leaders enter the new government.[246] The former president of Poland reiterated his opinion that Ukrainian politics "are in need of young blood. The Maidan fortress created internal structures and new elites, in a similar fashion to the early days of Solidarity."[247] The question remained: were the old elites, who used their wealth to control Ukraine, prepared for this change?

Ukraine's oligarchs were very alarmed by the developing events on the Euromaidan. Yanukovych's cronies feared the prospect of European and American sanctions, which would affect them directly. Kwaśniewski argued they were afraid of a "revolutionary scenario," because if a real revolution were to spread across Kyiv and other Ukrainian cities, it would be highly undesirable "from their economic point of view, given

II. The European Union's Special Envoy to Ukraine

their security and influence.... Sooner or later, revolutions always target the wealthy and, given my knowledge of that region's history, oligarchs had to take this into account."[248]

Kwaśniewski considers the oligarch's role in Ukrainian politics a complex matter because "several Ukrainian fortunes have shady sources, but they are important for the country's future."[249] Oligarchs will not simply vanish and they play a part in the power structures. Still, they can potentially help protect Ukraine and assist its European integration. Kwaśniewski argues: "the oligarchy is more enthusiastic about European integration than any other group in Ukraine."[250] Why? According to Aleksander Kwaśniewski, Ukrainian oligarchs long desired to become part of "the civilized business world" and, therefore, they favor the European option. They have had enough of "wild capitalism," they want to travel and invest overseas and they want their fortunes to be protected by the law. But economic integration with the EU was an expensive investment and the Russian embargo cost them millions, if not billions in losses.[251] Among the oligarchs who were hit hard by the Russian embargo was the seventh richest person in Ukraine,[252] Petro Poroshenko, "the Chocolate King."

Poroshenko does not consider himself an oligarch. "I am not an oligarch because an oligarch is a person who uses state power to enrich themselves. I was in the opposition the whole time."[253] His company, Roshen, was not targeted by the Russian sanitary inspector general by pure coincidence. In July 2013, Russia banned Roshen's products, whose imports generated income of $40 million in 2012 alone.[254]

Kwaśniewski had high hopes for Petro Poroshenko and he suggested in February 2014 that the Chocolate King would make a good prime minister.[255] Firstly, he was esteemed among the opposition and was present at the Euromaidan throughout the entire time. He also took part in the Orange Revolution in 2004. It would be a "very good decision," because Poroshenko "enjoys a great deal of credibility among the people of the Maidan, he was with them from the start and provided financial assistance. He is very rich."[256] On the other hand, he knew how to cooperate with the Party of Regions and even joined Azarov's government while briefly serving as the minister for foreign affairs. Moreover, Poroshenko has wide political experience, "he's a moderate politician, not a radical."[257] Kwaśniewski had his views on who was the right man to lead the country but insisted: "we cannot make any suggestions, those decisions have to be taken by the Ukrainian people."[258]

A credible president, who has room to maneuver, will be the bedrock of Ukraine's stability, argued Kwaśniewski. He was of the opinion that a new president should start his tenure by carrying out three objectives: build a wide government coalition, including members from the East and the Party of Regions, "to counter the argument that everything revolves around Western Ukraine"; demilitarize several groups supporting Maidan, "because there are too many of them in Ukraine and they interfere with the country's daily business"; and engage in dialogue with Russia.[259]

Kwaśniewski's well-intentioned recommendations did not stand the test of time. In the coming months, the Party of Regions collapsed and, while Russia continued to interfere with Ukraine's "daily business" more than anyone else, the Maidan demilitarized itself because those who carried weapons joined the volunteer battalions and left for the eastern front. In terms of dialogue, Kyiv did indeed engage in dialogue with Moscow, but it was essentially a dialogue with an aggressor.

Yulia Tymoshenko's Release as a Condition for the Signing of the Association Agreement

"I believe that we gave more than a hundred percent with Pat Cox," Aleksander Kwaśniewski noted two days prior to the failed Eastern Partnership summit. "We were extremely focused on our efforts; we held a mandate, which concerned three aspects of legislative reforms, the electoral legislation and—for lack of a better term—political prisoners. We managed to free two of them and we were close to accomplishing our mission and freeing Yulia Tymoshenko."[260] They were close indeed, but the main objective, which was also the driving force of the mission, was not brought to fruition. On the other hand, the European Union might have made a mistake by rendering the release of Yulia Tymoshenko a precondition for the signing of the Association Agreement.

When Kwaśniewski was offered to participate in the mission, he managed to convince Martin Schulz to widen its scope. "It seemed like

II. The European Union's Special Envoy to Ukraine

a "mission impossible" to me and I concluded that we may not be able to achieve anything if we only focus on the case of Yulia Tymoshenko. We should seize the opportunity and pursue other goals, such as judicial reforms." Even though the mandate did not cover free trade issues, the mission focused on economic aspects.[261]

Kwaśniewski pointed out that the release of prominent political prisoners, including the former acting defense minister and the former minister of the interior, was a significant achievement. It was also supposed to be a useful tool in their game with Yanukovych: "We wanted a precedent. We wanted to be able to say: 'Listen up, don't hide behind law and legislation, because you have already disregarded the law when it was necessary to do so.'" It was evident that Yanukovych did not want to set Tymoshenko free, but "the case of Lutsenko proved that the game with Yanukovych was not pointless."[262]

Progress was visible in various fields. Reforms of the rules on criminal procedure had been drafted and the parliament came close to adopting a new act governing the prosecution. "We pressed for a reform of the public prosecutor's office, which still operates on the basis of the Soviet model."[263] "We had hoped that our perseverance, our openness, and all our time would enable us to remove the obstacles standing in the way of the Association Agreement with the European Union."[264] But the deal was not signed in November 2013. "The most frustrating thing is the fact that we were so close. Both the legal and political preconditions the mission was focused on, meaning reforms of the judiciary and the electoral law, as well as the case of Yulia Tymoshenko, were either accomplished or close to being accomplished."[265]

It is clear today that the continued imprisonment of Yulia Tymoshenko provided Yanukovych with a sort of alibi. The Russian embargo (and, quite possibly, personal blackmail) brought him down to his knees, but the fact that Tymoshenko was being detained allowed him to construct a different narrative, in which he could argue, "I can't just set Tymoshenko free, because we have an independent judiciary. I cannot pressure the courts. The EU does not respect the Ukrainian legal system and is willing to sacrifice its relations with Ukraine for the sake of a single politician, who is rightfully facing charges." That was how he wanted to spin the story, though most Ukrainians saw right through him.

For many months, representatives of the Party of Regions used the aforementioned argument during their visits to Brussels. According to the Yanukovych regime, the gas agreement signed by Tymoshenko with Russia led to significant losses in Ukraine's budget. The regime claimed Tymoshenko had abused power, was a criminal, and should serve time in prison. For European politicians, her imprisonment was unjust and even if the gas deal put Ukraine at a disadvantage, the consequences should be political: Tymoshenko should be punished by her voters, not by the president.

Right before the Vilnius summit, Kwaśniewski pointed out that the EU had formulated three preconditions, which had to be met before the Association Agreement could be signed. The conditions included: legal reforms, electoral reforms, and judicial reforms. The third case, which was related to the problem of selective justice, was basically a call to resolve the case to Yulia Tymoshenko, which was the reason the mission was created in the first place. Kwaśniewski highlighted the fact that "significant progress" had been made in terms of legal reforms because new regulations, pertaining to various aspects of the judiciary and the rule of law in Ukraine, had been adopted.[266]

According to the former president of Poland, the EU was sincere about its willingness to sign the Association Agreement, because it took note of the acceleration of the pace of Ukrainian reforms and its authorities' pragmatic approach. The Association Agreement was complete by the time Tymoshenko was sentenced and imprisoned. Thus, Ukraine's European integration was taken hostage by the case of Yulia Tymoshenko. When inquired whether the release of the former prime minister was an appropriate prerequisite to the signing of the Association Agreement from the EU's point of view, Kwaśniewski said:

> Cox and I were asked to find a solution to the case, so that the Association Agreement could be signed. This could also have been a partial pardon, and a reduction of her prison sentence to two years. Then Yanukovych himself proposed allowing her to leave the country for medical treatment. But his supporters wanted her to serve the full sentence.[267]

Yanukovych was presented with a dilemma: he had to choose between setting free a formidable political opponent in order to meet the EU's condition or keeping the former prime minister locked up to save face among his supporters. "To a certain point, it seemed like he

II. The European Union's Special Envoy to Ukraine

wanted to find a way out of this situation. On the one hand, he hated Tymoshenko and was scared of her as a potential political rival. On the other, he wanted to appease the West."[268] But since he did not want to release her, he tried to defame her in front of Western leaders.

According to Aleksander Kwaśniewski, bringing the case of Tymoshenko to a head by the EU was irrational from today's perspective: "Maybe focusing on it was a mistake." But at the same time, the EU is "an organization based on values."[269] In December 2013, Kwaśniewski told Germany weekly *Der Spiegel*,

> At an earlier point, it might have been possible to convince them to allow Tymoshenko to leave the country for an operation. Yanukovych wouldn't have lost face, but he would have demonstrated that he was capable of a humanitarian gesture. After all, it was a question of medical treatment and not Tymoshenko's rehabilitation. Continuing to keep her imprisoned was far more costly, politically speaking.[270]

In the mission's early days, Kwaśniewski was of the opinion that this adamant approach to the case of Tymoshenko, presented by Germany's Chancellor Angela Merkel, was not a mistake, but was a bit overemphasized. Kwaśniewski had known Tymoshenko since the Orange Revolution in 2004. "I knew things weren't completely black and white and that she was neither crystal clear, nor outright bad, as Yanukovych attempted to portray her." But for as long as there was a chance to set her free, "we had to work toward that goal, even if it meant taking Yanukovych's lies at face value."[271]

> For as long as Tymoshenko's case was being discussed, it was the right thing to do. For as long as we argued she had to be released, it was the right thing to do. But making her release a compulsory prerequisite to the signing of the Association Agreement was when we went too far. Crossing that line was a mistake, but we managed to fix this thanks to Tymoshenko herself, to put it bluntly.[272]

The bottom line was that it was necessary for Tymoshenko to receive medical treatment abroad. Had Yanukovych agreed to this, it most likely would have been good enough for the EU to agree to sign the Association Agreement. The European People's Party (EPP) was most unremitting about the release of the former prime minister, and considered this a necessary precondition. Since the party Batkivshchyna was a member of the European Christian Democrat political family, Tymoshenko received a great deal of support from her allies in Brussels. Throughout the entire duration of the mission, Kwaśniewski could sense the EPP's unyielding attitude that there would be no second-guessing about the "decisive role of Tymoshenko's case."[273]

An EPP press release dated October 15, 2013, entitled *EPP Group wants Cox/Kwaśniewski mission to now focus on freeing Tymoshenko* reads:

> The EPP Group wants to enable the signing of the Association Agreement. Two of the three requirements for the Agreement, the reform of the judiciary and the electoral law, are on the way to being solved within an acceptable timeframe. The question of selective justice could be solved in a fitting manner on the basis of the Cox-Kwaśniewski proposals, with a view to the signing of the Agreement.[274]

Cordial relations between Batkivshchyna lawmakers (most of whom were former ministers of Tymoshenko's cabinet) and the political parties from the EPP guaranteed that the EU would not forget the precondition of Tymoshenko's release from prison. The case of the former prime minister was constantly being brought up by her associates, who were very familiar with the political corridors of Brussels and the offices of the most prominent Members of the European Parliament. However, when Tymoshenko appealed to European leaders not to let the Association Agreement be taken hostage by her situation, she made a decision not to connect the repressions she was facing with Ukraine's European future. Kwaśniewski considered this an important gesture:

> Tymoshenko showed great character. The so-called "Tymoshenko issue" was resolved by Tymoshenko herself, right before the Vilnius summit. It was her sovereign decision, and she authorized us to convey this message to Chancellor Merkel and other leaders, that the Association Agreement should be signed regardless of her situation and what her fate might be.[275]

The former president of Poland believed that this gesture was of great importance because it enabled the EU to get out of the corner in which it found itself when Brussels made Tymoshenko's release a precondition for Ukraine's European integration. The fact that the European Union made this a prerequisite was "probably too drastic and it limited our maneuverability,"[276] said Kwaśniewski. On the other hand, no one could have expected that the case of Yulia Tymoshenko would trigger a mission, which would turn into a game of chicken with Yanukovych. And

II. The European Union's Special Envoy to Ukraine

it was the Ukrainian president who swerved right before the head-on collision with the EU.

The tragedy that took place in Kyiv and other cities most likely helped ensure Tymoshenko's wellbeing. During the time of the violent clashes on the Maidan, Kwaśniewski concluded: "It's a paradox, but what has been going on in Ukraine guarantees Tymoshenko's safety. That's because should anything happen to her, or should anything bad happen in Kharkiv, where she's being held in isolation, the temperature on the Maidan would rise even higher and it could lead to a revolution."[277]

The Euromaidan managed to finish what the Cox-Kwaśniewski mission started. Even Yulia Tymoshenko admitted she was grateful to those who participated in the mass protests in Kyiv for her freedom. But it cannot be ruled out that Kwaśniewski and Cox should be given credit for saving her life.

Kwaśniewski's frequent visits to Ukraine, his political and diplomatic input, as well as the media attention they attracted, guaranteed the safety of the former prime minister. Since it was certain that her case would not only be followed by Ukrainians, but also by the international public opinion, it was necessary to present the conditions of her prison cell in a positive light. The cell had undergone maintenance ("euro-remodeling")[278] in order to meet European standards. However, the footage of bruised Tymoshenko and reports indicating that the lights in her room never went out and that she did not receive proper medical treatment shocked international observers. Surveillance equipment was hidden in shower rooms, in the toilet, her cell, as well as the rooms where Tymoshenko received treatment. "What do you do with those tapes? Do you watch them by yourself or in the company of your amused friends?" read Tymoshenko's letter to Yanukovych, dated October 2012.[279]

The mission undertaken by the European Parliament's special envoys had a direct impact on the conditions under which Yanukovych's public enemy number one was being held. The Cox-Kwaśniewski report, presented on April 18, 2013, in Strasburg, noted that the former prime minister was being hospitalized under the surveillance of only female guards and that video surveillance was not being used. Moreover, German doctors of the Charité Clinique supervised her treatment.

Visitors were able to see her more frequently and her access to her daughter and lawyers was no longer restricted as it had been previously. Despite visible improvements of the conditions of Lady Yu's imprisonment, Kwaśniewski believes that Yanukovych still wanted to monitor all of her conversations. "Tymoshenko was probably being eavesdropped until the day she was set free. I believe that the content of our conversations reached Yanukovych and some kind of sophisticated surveillance was being used. But I cannot prove my suspicions."[280]

Despite the fact that Tymoshenko was a political prisoner and was mistreated, Kwaśniewski's recollections also include a humane dimension of this sad story:

> There was a director who went by the name Anafasiyev, but people called him the *glavnyy vrach* (head doctor). He was an incredible person. He had gone through hell. They transferred his hospital to a prison cell. Even our visits interfered with his regular work duties, but he would always conduct himself in a kind, professional manner. He was the sort of Russian who would help others if he found himself in a Siberian labor camp. Luckily, these kinds of people still exist, otherwise our civilization would already be a thing of the past. I can't help but think of him with a sentimental attachment. He represented a kind of remarkable Russian, Soviet intelligentsia: modest, cultured, open-minded, and humble. He was the *glavnyy vrach* with a strong moral backbone.[281]

Kwaśniewski recalled that the mission was everything that has been characteristic of politics for centuries: "It was almost Shakespearean. The meetings with Yanukovych, the meetings with Tymoshenko and the suspense, which only kept rising."[282] The final act took place on February 22, 2014. Sitting in a wheelchair with tears in her eyes, Tymoshenko addressed the Maidan masses. At the same time, Yanukovych was fleeing to Russia. Just as Iago devised a plan to destroy Othello, Ukraine's president wanted to eliminate his political rival, Yulia Tymoshenko. Luckily, his schemes were not as sophisticated. His fate was sealed: in January 2015, an international arrest warrant was issued for Viktor Yanukovych.

Was he aware of the risks and consequences? "I don't think he was," said Kwaśniewski. "Yanukovych did not understand the West and the notion of the rule of law. He did not expect that he would cause such a storm and that he would spend the following two years being mostly absorbed with the Tymoshenko case."[283] The former president

II. The European Union's Special Envoy to Ukraine

of Poland also emphasized the importance of the idea of gender solidarity. This tends to be overlooked, but—to some extent—world leaders did not forget about Lady Yu because of female leaders.

After she was arrested, two of the most powerful women in the world decided to support her: Hillary Clinton and Angela Merkel. If Yanukovych expected the case to die down over time, he could not have been more wrong. Kwaśniewski tried to convince him there would be no going back to business-as-usual for as long as Tymoshenko remained locked up. "I remember well the many times that we met, and I look forward to the day when we can meet again," former U.S. Secretary of State Condoleezza Rice said in her letter of support to Tymoshenko. "Please know that until then, I will think of you and pray for your health and release,"[284] she added.

Kwaśniewski: "I tried to explain to him: 'You're making a big mistake. You have to understand that this is the only way they can proceed. They can't say they are not concerned with the fate of their colleague, the former prime minister. Especially since there aren't that many female prime ministers around.'"[285] Unfortunately, these arguments had little impact. They were beyond his comprehension.

Yanukovych's strategy derived from the way of thinking typical for gangsters from Donetsk: any potential threat should be dealt with by the use of force. Unlike Western states, Ukraine was fertile ground for this kind of approach to settling political scores. Aleksander Kwaśniewski noted the sharp contrast between political rivalries in democratic countries and in Ukraine:

> If Tymoshenko faced these kinds of charges in the European political realm, she would be in serious trouble. In a democracy, any politician would be simply handicapped by these sorts of allegations and it would be more beneficial [for a political rival] to keep him or her exposed to the public, rather than imprisoning her. But this approach derives from attachment to democracy and the rule of law, which was not Yanukovych's strong side.[286]

Kwaśniewski is of the opinion that up to a certain point, Yanukovych wanted to find a way out of the Tymoshenko ordeal (even though, concurrently, he hoped to convince the West she was a bad person). Moreover, the charges against her were not based on solid arguments and did not lead to a conviction, which could potentially turn the Western public opinion against Tymoshenko. Yanukovych's scheme to portray her as a common criminal, instead of the "Ukrainian version of Nelson Mandela,"[287] did not come to fruition.

That is why Yanukovych attempted to blame Tymoshenko for the murder of Yevhen Shcherban, a Ukrainian parliamentarian, who was shot dead, together with his wife, at the Donetsk airport in 1996. In April 2012, the deceased legislator's son and member of the Donetsk oblast council of the Party of Regions—Ruslan Shcherban—wrote a letter to the U.S. Ambassador to Ukraine. In his correspondence, he argued that several Western politicians "are protecting murderers from justice, as this is the only way to describe the ultimatum, concerning the release of Tymoshenko, being constantly presented to the Ukrainian authorities."[288] Kwaśniewski claims the accusations were preposterous, because the murder of Shcherban was a typical case of a Donetsk clan assassination and Tymoshenko had never belonged to any of these groups. "I explained to him that if they dig up the case of Shcherban's murder and Tymoshenko gets a good lawyer, the truth about the Donetsk clan will see the light of day. Throughout the 1990's alone, at the time 'wild capitalism' was being built, five thousand people died as a result of assassinations, suicides, and car accidents."[289]

At one point Yanukovych told Kwaśniewski that his administration was getting close to being able to announce where overseas Tymoshenko had hid her fortune. In the end, Yanukovych didn't follow through. Why? Kwaśniewski believed that the news never made headlines for two reasons: either there was no money or the money was deposited in the very same banks where Yanukovych and his cronies kept their own dirty money. Moreover, the transfers were most likely being carried out by the same people and the same firms. "Yanukovych's team came to the conclusion that if they start digging up Tymoshenko's money, all hell will break loose."[290] Eventually, Yanukovych got a taste of his own medicine: his accounts were frozen and he ended up on sanction lists. All the while, Tymoshenko was getting ready for a comeback, but her political resurrection did not look the way she had expected.

Considering the former Orange Revolution leader's political comeback, Kwaśniewski took note that Ukrainians, the young generation in particular, were looking for new faces in politics. In consequence, they turned toward the Maidan leaders. The palpable electoral fatigue affected the entire political class. The former president of Poland said Tymoshenko

II. The European Union's Special Envoy to Ukraine

"arrived on the Maidan convinced she would be welcomed as both a victim and a sign of hope. People did see her as a victim; they expressed a great deal of compassion. But at the same time, she was totally rejected as a symbol of hope."[291]

> She must have imagined she would receive a savior's welcome. It turned out people didn't forget about what transpired following the Orange Revolution. I got the impression from a great number of Ukrainians that they were glad Tymoshenko had been released. But at the same time, they were not looking forward to her political comeback. It's a good thing she decided to undergo medical treatment in Germany. She will have enough time to define her new role in Ukrainian politics.[292]

Kwaśniewski attended the presidential inauguration of Petro Poroshenko in June 2014. Yulia Tymoshenko was also present at the ceremony. After it was concluded, she embraced Pat Cox and the former president of Poland and said: "Today, I know you were the only people who really cared about my release." Kwaśniewski claims her statement was not that far from the truth. People from Tymoshenko's political circle were simply afraid of her. In consequence, not all of her entourage was wholeheartedly involved in the rescue mission.[293] Lady Yu, the "Orange Princess," the symbol of Yanukovych's political repression, was no longer needed.

* * *

At the end of January 2014, Aleksander Kwaśniewski said he did not rule out the possibility of extending his mission and that he would make himself available, should that be the request of the European Parliament. "Our mission was discreet; we do not hold any official positions. Therefore, we will carry on if necessary. We have maintained an open line of communication with the opposition, the government, and Martin Schulz. We are ready if the need arises."[294] Kwaśniewski concluded that the time for intensifying the efforts of EU's official structures had come, but the decision had to be made by European leaders: "The European Union can no longer be limited to moral support, it has to be prepared to take concrete steps, to offer financial aid to Ukraine."[295]

"We can say that Pat Cox and my mission has come to an end," said

Kwaśniewski in front of the Verkhovna Rada in June 2014. "Ukraine is going to sign the Association Agreement and Miss Tymoshenko is free and she was in the parliament earlier today. Therefore, the mission has been accomplished, even though there were difficulties we had to deal with. We will, of course, continue to support Ukraine and its independence with Mr. Cox."[296]

Three months later, speaking at the Yalta European Strategy conference in Kyiv, Martin Schulz said:

> During my first mandate I launched a special mediation mission headed by Presidents Pat Cox and Alexander Kwaśniewski, who are here with us today, and I can only pay tribute to their stamina and dedication. They went to Ukraine on 27 missions involving 150 working days, spending more time with each other than their wives. Their rich experience and deep expertise they have acquired could prove invaluable to Ukraine in the future as well.[297]

III

"Russia Won't Stop": The Russian Factor in the Disintegration of Ukraine

Peter the Great, Catherine the Great, Joseph Stalin ... Vladimir Putin?

Aleksander Kwaśniewski repeatedly emphasized the fact that Ukraine is the most important piece of Vladimir Putin's geopolitical puzzle. He called it the Eurasian Union, and the project is essentially a refurbished formula for a Russia-led superpower. In consequence, Putin "will definitely not stop." However, he has to consider the remarkable level of social resistance and "the determination demonstrated by Ukrainian people on the snow-covered and freezing Maidan. It proves that the incorporation of Ukraine or even extending Russian influence within Ukraine's borders cannot be carried out the way he initially intended."[1] Moreover, Kwaśniewski argued: "The key is the will of the people, the will of the nation." He also said that if Ukrainians could decide whether to join the free trade area with Russia or to sign the Association Agreement, "most of them would choose the West."[2]

But the decision to integrate with the democratic West would stand in the way of Putin's plans to recreate Russia's empire. He would like as many former Soviet republics and former member states of the Russian empire on board as possible. Despite the fact that he "knows that some of them, such as the Baltic republics, are out of the equation. On the other hand, wealthy countries, such as Azerbaijan, can afford autonomy. That is why he will target weaker countries, which are dependent on Russia's energy supplies, with historical, linguistic, and cultural ties to Russia. Ukraine will come under fierce pressure."[3] From the Kremlin's point of view, there is only one option for Ukraine: economic and political integration through the customs union, as designed by Moscow. In consequence, "Russia will employ any means it has at its disposal. It will exercise hard and soft power in order to prevent Ukraine from getting closer to Europe and from signing the Association Agreement. Russian influence stretches from the state administration to the media; Russians can also use their fleet."[4] In addition, Putin is a patient man. In order to restore the Russian empire—argues Kwaśniewski—Putin needs all of Ukraine. Such a task cannot be completed within a few months. It will take years: "The Eurasian Union is already operating and it can be joined by Ukraine in a month, in a year, or even in five years. According to Putin, the West is going through an identity crisis and it's weak because of its economic problems and the lack of leadership. Time is on Putin's side."[5]

Ukraine is a key component of Putin's Eurasian Union because other partners are concerned about Russia's dominating position. According to Kwaśniewski, Kazakhstan is concerned about the political aspects of the customs union, "which comes as no surprise. After all, a country of 16 million is to associate with a country of 140 million. On top of that, a couple million people out of the 16 million are Russian."[6] Putin's offer to join the Eurasian Union was basically addressed to all of Central Asia, including Turkmenistan. Moreover, "Armenia will most likely join in, but not necessarily Azerbaijan, because its economy is strong enough to afford sovereignty. Georgia will surely experience pressure, especially given the new political situation. It's difficult to say where Moldova fits in. Russia may just ignore it. But Ukraine is the most important piece of the puzzle."[7]

In consequence, "Russia will do whatever it takes to bring Ukraine into its sphere of influence."[8] Bearing in mind that Ukraine had been granted an observer status in the Eurasian Union, Kwaśniewski believed that the entire European diplomacy knew that upgrading Ukraine to a fully-fledged member of the customs union was part of Putin's grand strategy.[9] The former president of Poland argued that the Eurasian Union would be created even without Ukraine's participation, although it would not be as grand. "Ukraine is a top priority, which leads Russia to employ its entire arsenal, which ranges from the embargo to propaganda and the offensive of Russian media."[10] Putin considers it "a task of historic proportions,"[11] because he "wishes to repeat the achievements of Peter the Great, Catherine the Great, and Joseph Stalin. All of them managed to create a superpower and this is what he has been dreaming of. For us this isn't any reason to get angry, but rather, to draw proper conclusions."[12]

For Russia, contemporary Ukraine is more than just an important political and economic piece of the geopolitical puzzle. It is also the origin of the empire and part of "the same cultural entity."[13] Aleksander Kwaśniewski points out an ambiguity in Russia's attitude toward Ukraine. On the one hand, it sees it as the former Kievan Rus, the cradle of Russia's statehood. On the other, Ukraine is perceived as a periphery, a remote area, which is not entitled to the respect it would otherwise enjoy, based on its place in history:

> This makes me think of Kiselev's political talk show on Russian television, where I used to feature in the days of the Orange Revolution. The anchor told me that the Russian people would never be able to accept two things. One: Crimea—the place where they used to spend their vacation as children, pioneers, parents, and veterans—is no longer part of their country (as we know, Khrushchev gave Crimea to Ukraine in 1954). Two: that FC Dynamo Kyiv—the 34-time champion of the U.S.S.R., which won the European Cup—is a foreign soccer club. It may just be a story, but it illustrates a mental barrier, reinforced with Russia's sense of superiority and the Russian people's contempt toward Ukrainians.[14]

This superiority complex contributed to the support of Putin's takeover of Crimea and caused the eruption of euphoria in the streets of Moscow, which followed the annexation of the peninsula by the Russian Federation. After all, for a lot of Russians, this was not a big deal: Crimea simply returned where it belonged in the first place.

The Anschluss of Crimea

Speaking about the situation in Crimea at the end of February 2014, Aleksander Kwaśniewski noted that Russia had a vast range of options at its disposal: "Moscow is able to mobilize Crimea's Russian population and to organize a secessionist referendum; Russian troops are deployed in Sevastopol; and Russia's influence in Ukraine's governmental institutions and the media is remarkable."[15]

Kwaśniewski's assessment of the Kremlin's strategy was on the mark. On February 27, troops of armed militants took over the parliament and the building of the local Autonomous Republic of Crimea. Soon after, troops consisting of soldiers without military insignia took over the runway of the Belbek Airport in Sevastopol (the largest military airport in Crimea), and civilian airports in Sevastopol and Simferopol. The soldiers were well equipped and looked like members of special forces. Even though their uniforms had no military insignia, they claimed to be part of Russian-speaking self defense forces in Crimea.

On the day the "little green men" started taking over public administration buildings, Aleksander Kwaśniewski was in Vilnius, where he attended the commemoration of the 20th anniversary of the treaty between Poland and Lithuania.[16] While discussing Polish-Lithuanian relations, the former president argued that the developments in Ukraine shed a different light on the issue of the Lithuanian minority in Poland and the Polish minority in Lithuania:

> We need to set a good example for Ukraine, for Crimea, for everyone, who lives in a place where the issue of ethnic minorities is more problematic than it is here. We live in dangerous times. For the past dozen or so years, we were convinced that our region was safe and stable and that nothing bad could happen to us. The recent developments in Ukraine should be a wake-up call.[17]

The likelihood of an escalation was caused by the Russian parliament's March 1 decision to authorize Vladimir Putin to use force in Ukraine.[18] In his op-ed, published by the Polish newspaper *Gazeta Wyborcza*, Aleksander Kwaśniewski concluded that Crimea was not the endgame. "We have heard what representatives of the Russian Federation have said: it's about Ukraine. Definitely about the eastern part of Ukraine, but maybe even all of it."[19] The former president of Poland added that the rhetoric supporting Putin's decision was extremely aggressive and it resembled the Soviet Union's scariest tunes. "It sounded like a track from the past. I'm afraid it's not just a negotiating method, but a serious plan for Ukraine."[20] Kwaśniewski argued that the international community should make it clear that Russia "has no legal, political, or moral right to treat a sovereign country this way. It's simply unacceptable."[21] In addition, "Ukraine wishes to choose its own future and it seems like it will choose Europe. But Russia is doing whatever

III. "Russia Won't Stop"

it can—through both economic and military means—to anchor this country within its sphere of influence."[22]

At that time, Kwaśniewski argued, "We should prepare for the worst" and "take this threat seriously and react swiftly. The war hasn't started yet, but it can start anytime."[23] In case Russia resorted to aggression, sanctions should be imposed immediately in order to make the Kremlin realize that Western threats cannot be taken lightly:

> What we should be wary of are opinions such as the one expressed by a Russian legislator; he said he had spent a long time in the Council of Europe and that Russia should not be concerned with world opinion. After all, the international community made some commotion about Chechnya and South Ossetia, but it didn't last long. I believe they need to be proven wrong regarding their perception that the West can only talk the talk, but will never walk the walk.[24]

"Look at the former Soviet republics," the laid-back Russian president argued at an extraordinary press conference at his Novo Ogaryovo residence, situated near Moscow. "You can go to a store and buy a uniform. Were these Russian soldiers? No, they're very well-trained self-defense forces.[25] Kwaśniewski underscored that Putin's appearance was part of Russia's omnipresent propaganda and, although it's hard to assess to what extent Russian politicians started believing their own lies, the Russian president was well aware that these were not self-defense forces given that they were using Russian military vehicles.[26]

On the night of March 16 into the morning of March 17, an ecstatic crowd gathered at the Lenin Square in Simferopol to celebrate their "return" to Russia after the Sunday referendum. Fireworks lit up the sky, their colors reflected in the scattered empty vodka bottles. The navy orchestra performed Soviet songs on a stage submerged in Russia's tricolor flag. The partygoers weren't concerned that Ukrainians and Crimean Tatars boycotted the referendum and the international community deemed it a farce. By the time the hungover attendants of the Lenin Square festivities woke up on Tuesday, they were already in Russia.

Two days after the referendum, Vladimir Putin spoke in front of the Russian parliament and declared it legally binding. He proclaimed that it fulfilled democratic criteria and met international standards. Opening his speech, Putin proclaimed that 96 percent of the voters (with an 82 percent voter turnout) supported Russia's annexation of

Crimea. What followed that statement was a typical presentation of the Kremlin's version of history. The Russian president said, "literally everything is saturated with common history and common sense of dignity" in Crimea:

> The ancient city of Chersonesus, where Prince Vladimir was baptized lies here. His spiritual decision of converting to Orthodoxy determined the common cultural, axiological, and civilizational foundations of the Russian, Ukrainian, and Belarusian people. Russian soldiers are buried in Crimea. It is their heroism that put Crimea under Russia's jurisdiction. Crimea is also home to Sevastopol, the legendary city, the city of a great destiny, the stronghold and the bastion of Russia's Black Sea Fleet.[27]

Putin added that Crimea would also remain an inseparable part of Russia in the people's hearts and minds. Allowing the Crimean Autonomy to become part of Ukraine was a historic mistake: "After the revolution, the Bolsheviks, for a number of reasons—may God judge them—added large sections of the historical South of Russia to the Republic of Ukraine. This was done with no consideration for the ethnic make-up of the population, and today these areas form the southeast of Ukraine. Then, in 1954, a decision was made to transfer Crimean Region to Ukraine, along with Sevastopol, despite the fact that it was a federal city." According to Putin, Khrushchev was responsible, and his motives should be judged by historians. The people of Crimea complained in 1991 that they were "handed over like a sack of potatoes."[28]

As argued by the Russian president, the Euromaidan and the regime change that followed were nothing other than a coup, organized by people who "resorted to terror, murder, and riots. Nationalists, neo–Nazis, Russophobes, and anti–Semites executed this coup. Today, it is those kind of people who call the shots in Ukraine." According to Putin, Russia respects the brotherly nation of Ukraine, therefore "just as it has been for centuries, [Crimea] will be a home to all the peoples living there. What it will never be and do is follow in Bandera's footsteps!" The Russian president listed all the injustice and humiliation suffered by the Russian people in the wake of the collapse of the Soviet Union and added he understood Ukrainian people well:

> I understand why Ukrainian people wanted change. They have had enough of the authorities in power during the years of Ukraine's independence. Presi-

III. "Russia Won't Stop"

dents, prime ministers, and parliamentarians changed, but their attitude to the country and its people remained the same. They milked the country, fought among themselves for power, assets, and cash flows and did not care much about the ordinary people.... I would like to reiterate that I understand those who came out on Maidan with peaceful slogans against corruption, inefficient state management, and poverty.[29]

Commenting on Putin's address and his remarks regarding corruption and poverty in Ukraine, Kwaśniewski concluded that everything the Russian president said might as well be said about Russia, because "many of the problems, which led to the Maidan's eruption, or maybe even all of them, are present in the Russian Federation."[30] In Kwaśniewski's assessment, Putin's speech was a demonstration of force, infested with propaganda and nationalistic sentiments. That's risky, because "once you've let the nationalistic genie out of the bottle, it spreads despair. I know that the vast majority of the Russian people are happy with Putin, but the price may be steep. Both for them, but also—most importantly—for the entire region. That's what I'm primarily concerned about."[31]

> All this is taking place with a lot of over-confidence, even impudence, in the background. And it needs to be dealt with. We can't just let it be, because history knows many cases such as this one. Certain countries hosted the Olympics, only to carry out an Anschluss shortly after. And it did not happen a thousand years ago. It happened only a couple dozen years ago. If the Olympic Games were supposed to show us the new face of Russia, the annexation of Crimea showed us Russia's old face. The one we know from the past, the one we have every reason to fear.[32]

Kwaśniewski notes that the annexation of Crimea was intentionally organized and its execution was carried out perfectly, along with elements of propaganda: "The annexation challenges international law and contradicts Russia's international obligations, such as the Budapest Memorandum of 1994."[33]

On January 14, 1994, the United States, Ukraine, and Russia signed a trilateral statement, which obliged Kyiv to dismantle its nuclear arsenal within two years: "all SS-24s on the territory of Ukraine will be deactivated within ten months by having their warheads removed" and that the nuclear warheads from RS-18 (SS-19) and RS-22 (SS-24) missiles would be transferred to Russia.[34] In November 1994, the President of the United States, Bill Clinton, and Ukrainian President, Leonid

Kuchma, signed the Charter of American-Ukrainian Partnership, Friendship and Cooperation. And in December 1994, Ukraine signed the Memorandum on Security Assurances in Connection With Ukraine's Accession to the Treaty on the Non-Proliferation of Nuclear Weapons. This document became known as the Budapest Memorandum. Under this agreement, the United States, Russia, and Britain gave Ukraine security assurance and recognized its territorial integrity.[35]

Ukraine voluntarily signed away its nuclear arsenal only three years after it declared independence. It was praised internationally as a responsible and predictable stakeholder and a country willing to cooperate with both the U.S. and Russia. Twenty years later, after Crimea was annexed by the Russian Federation, the guarantees of the Budapest Memorandum turned out to be an empty promise. In 2014, neither the United States, nor the U.K. felt obliged to keep their side of the deal because the document did not precisely describe what kind of actions should be taken in case of a violation of Ukraine's territorial integrity. After Putin's takeover of the Crimean peninsula, a wide range of mental gymnastics were performed in to order to excuse the West from any obligations and responsibility. One argument against American and British involvement argued that the security guarantees of the Budapest Memorandum were only binding in case of a nuclear war. One can imagine how reassuring this must have sounded to the Ukrainian people: should a nuclear warhead fired on Ukraine cause a nuclear holocaust, Washington and London will come and save the day.

What is Aleksander Kwaśniewski's take on this controversial point? "For me, the security guarantees of the Budapest Memorandum go beyond a nuclear conflict. It includes passages on Ukraine's territorial integrity. The problem is that in 1994, no one expected that one of the signatories of the document would pose a security threat to Ukraine in the future."[36]

Did the West lose face? To answer that question it is helpful to look back on a piece entitled "Ukraine's Decision to Join the NPT," by Sherman W. Garnett, which appeared in *Arms Control Today* almost 20 years before the annexation of Crimea. In 1995, Garnett wrote:

> And the security assurances imply that the United States will play a role in addressing future Ukrainian security concerns, possibly even including Crimea and the division of the Black Sea Fleet. These commitments are not

III. "Russia Won't Stop"

the same as the security guarantees the United States has with NATO or other treaty partners. Yet they cannot be empty promises either. At least, they cannot be if the United States and other Western countries understand the stakes involved in the success of the Ukrainian state—not simply for nuclear disarmament but for regional security and stability in a critical and potentially explosive part of the world.[37]

It is difficult, however, to expect that one of the signatories (Russia) would consider its actions a violation of Ukraine's territorial integrity, since it never really agreed with the loss of the peninsula in the first place. In his "annexation speech," Putin underlined that nobody expected the Crimean territory to leave Russia when it was ceded to Ukraine in the 20th century: "Back then, it was impossible to imagine that Ukraine and Russia may split up and become two separate states. However, this has happened. Unfortunately, what seemed impossible became a reality. The USSR fell apart."[38]

Putin wants to rebuild the empire that collapsed in 1991 and he will not be asking Ukraine for its opinion. Crimea will not quench his thirst. Kwaśniewski does not believe that "[Putin] fulfilled his dreams by annexing Crimea, because the restoration of a new Russian super empire is his endgame. In order to achieve this goal, he needs all of Ukraine, not just the Crimean Peninsula."[39] He started with Eastern Ukraine and did it all, of course, to save the "downtrodden" Russian-speaking people of the Donbas.

Hybrid Warfare and Separatism: Russian Terrorists in the Donbas

Russia was stationing 40 thousand troops by the Ukrainian border throughout the first half of 2014, but these troops did not lead the invasion. On the contrary, no invasion took place at all. Moscow did not fight a traditional war against Ukraine. It employed hybrid warfare instead. The strategic objective of destroying the enemy did not change. But the offensive took more time and included unconventional means, such as special forces (Spetsnaz with no national insignia), terrorism, cyber attacks, as well as trade and economic warfare. The employment of these kinds of tools facilitates an ambivalence in the international community. Those who choose not to believe what is happening in Ukraine can simply repeat the slogans of Putin's news channel Russia Today (which reaches 600 million viewers worldwide) that Russia is not a side in the conflict. This is exactly what took place during the time of the Crimean Peninsula operation, and that was merely the first phase of the Kremlin's hybrid war. The second stage spread across Eastern Ukraine.

After Crimea had been annexed, the separatist forces operating in the east consolidated and were more daring in terms of their demands for autonomy and their military actions. At the end of March, two thousand people took to the streets of Donbas and demonstrated, calling for greater autonomy and Yanukovych's return to power. They shouted: "Crimea, Russia, Donbas!" Demonstrations were also organized in Kharkiv, Luhansk, and Odessa, where—apart from greater autonomy—an enhanced status for the Russian language was demanded. In the meantime, following negotiations with the German foreign minister, Russia agreed to create a six-month OSCE observation mission in Eastern Ukraine, but not in Crimea, which—according to the Kremlin—was already part of Russia.

Aleksander Kwaśniewski advocated the notion of an Organization for Security and Co-operation in Europe (OSCE) observation mission in early February. He said that addressing the OSCE in order to convene a conference with the participation of the U.S., EU, Ukraine, and Russia, was among the ideas discussed by various experts. The former president of Poland argued that Russians should be sitting at the negotiating table, because "they are partially responsible for everything that's been going on in Eastern Ukraine," and a ceasefire could be enforced.[40] Moreover, OSCE observers have to be present on the ground, because "they can put an end to the wave of propaganda that is being used to brainwash people."[41]

The pace of the destabilization of the eastern part of Ukraine increased in April 2014. That is when pro–Russian demonstrators took over administrative buildings in Donetsk and proclaimed the creation of the Donetsk Republic. They also called on President Putin to dispatch "peace troops" to Ukraine's eastern border. They prepared for a potential police intervention and raised barricades made out of tires. Groups of separatists surrounded the building of Ukraine's Security

III. "Russia Won't Stop"

Service and made their way into the armories. The following days saw demonstrations in Sloviansk and Kramatorsk. In mid April, Ukrainian forces also launched their anti-terrorist operation in order to take back the buildings controlled by the separatists. Following negotiations with the participation of Ukraine, the U.S., and the EU in Geneva, anti-terrorist activities were put to a halt because Easter was approaching. According to the Geneva accords, the OSCE mission was supposed to assist Ukrainian authorities in the de-escalation of the conflict. Among the conditions agreed upon by the sides (by Russia, among others), was the obligation to abandon administrative buildings by the separatist forces. In the meantime, Ukrainian authorities presented photographs depicting members of the so-called self-defense forces present in both Crimea and Eastern Ukraine. Russian military intelligence (GRU) officers were among them.

The Kremlin also raised the stakes by conducting military exercises at the Ukrainian border in late April. The helplessness of the international community, as well as the futility of the Geneva accords, were confirmed when OSCE observers were captured by separatists in Sloviansk. The United States appealed to Russia to influence the separatists in order to release the hostages. Moscow assured it would do whatever it could to free them and blamed Ukraine, arguing it did not provide security for the OSCE observers. At the same time, "little green men" wearing the same kind of uniforms as those who took over Crimea consolidated their positions in subsequent eastern Ukrainian cities.

Everyone knew that the separatists were controlled by Moscow. Secretary of State John Kerry made it clear in an in-camera meeting of the Trilateral Commission in Washington: "Intel is producing taped conversations of intelligence operatives taking their orders from Moscow and everybody can tell the difference in the accents, in the idioms, in the language. We know exactly who's giving those orders, we know where they are coming from."[42]

* * *

Having met Putin on numerous occasions, Aleksander Kwaśniewski believes that he is determined to regain Russian's imperial status and to make history as one of imperial Russia's great leaders. Putin despises Mikhail Gorbachev and Boris Yeltsin and blames them for the collapse of the Soviet Union. Understanding the psychological side of Putin's motives is key to comprehending Russia's aggression in Ukraine.[43]

Putin finds the spontaneous nature of the Maidan social movement hard to accept. That is why the Euromaidan's activists are portrayed as puppets of the U.S. and the EU. The Russian president even accused Poland of training "fascists" and "Bandera followers." According to the Kremlin, Eurasia is the only choice Ukraine can make. Aleksander Kwaśniewski, on the other hand, believes that the EU should not be thinking in a zero sum game terms, like Russia. Ukraine's integration with the European Union cannot lead to the severance of the country's ties with its neighbor:

> It should not be a "take it or leave it" alternative, meaning that Ukraine has to choose between the EU and Russia. It is not possible due to several reasons: its geography, culture, language, tradition, and economic ties. Ukraine needs good relations with Russia. Ukraine should pursue a balanced position between Russia and the EU, with a clear vision of its own future.[44]

It is, however, difficult to speak about cordial relations between the two, bearing in mind Russia's aggression against Ukraine. The annexation of Crimea and Russia's sponsorship of terrorism in the self-proclaimed republics of Donetsk and Luhansk solidified Ukraine's independent spirit and its sense of sovereignty: "Many people in Ukraine, including Russia-friendly people, felt humiliated. Russia underestimates the value of Ukraine's independence for a greater part of its society. It is strong enough to justify all the difficulties the Ukrainian nation has been going through."[45] In consequence, "paradoxically, Putin's actions in Crimea may work to Kyiv's benefit in the long run."[46]

The question remains: how much longer can Ukraine stand up to Russia's hybrid warfare? Kwaśniewski is of the opinion that such a war cannot be planned ad hoc. It has to derive from a meticulously prepared doctrine: "You can't mobilize these kind of forces in a day or two." Everything was planned well in advance.[47]

Putin's plans for Ukraine are common knowledge. It remains to be seen whether the transatlantic community will be able to respond in an effective manner.

IV

The West's Strategy

> *We stand against having a military organization meddling in our backyard, next to our homeland or in the territories that are historically ours. I just cannot imagine visiting NATO sailors in Sevastopol, ... Most of them are fine lads, by the way. But rather let them visit us in Sevastopol than the other way around.*[1]
>
> —Vladimir Putin

Finlandization: The Sinatra Doctrine Is Not for Ukraine

When asked about the future of the Brezhnev Doctrine in October 1989, the spokesman of the Soviet Ministry of Foreign Affairs, Gennadi Gerasimov, replied: "You know the Frank Sinatra song 'My Way'? ... We now have the Sinatra doctrine."[2] What he meant by that was that Poland, Hungary, and the other countries from the Soviet bloc would be able to do things their own way as Sinatra used to sing in his famous song. And this was exactly what they did when they joined NATO in the late 1990s. Soon after, other Central and Eastern European states followed suit, including the three former Soviet republics of Lithuania, Latvia and Estonia.

Official diplomatic relations between NATO and Ukraine were established right after it proclaimed independence and joined the Euro-Atlantic Partnership Council. In doing so, Leonid Kuchma was effectively balancing between the East and the West. In May 1995, Kuchma stated that if he had enough time after visiting the European Union, he would "definitely visit NATO headquarters" and that "no country has the right to veto that NATO's doors should be open to any country.

Ukraine included ... we must really try to expand cooperation including with NATO."[3] In March 1997, Yuriy Scherbak, the Ukrainian ambassador to the U.S., stated in Washington that as NATO moves eastward, free access should be granted to all countries that meet the alliance's criteria. Closer relations were also ascertained at the Madrid Summit in July. There, the NATO-Ukraine Charter on a Distinctive Partnership established the NATO-Ukraine Commission (NUC), which held its inaugural meeting in Brussels in mid–October. Its task was to point out areas for consultation and cooperation.

The ever-changing nature of the Kuchma administration's political priorities, as well as his tendency to use NATO as a bargaining chip in Kyiv's relations with Moscow, did not prevent the mutual relations from deepening. Ukraine's cooperation with NATO was taken to a new level in November 2002 with the NATO-Ukraine Action Plan, which was aimed to deepen and broaden their contacts. The Plan set out specific objectives that covered political, economic, security, defense, military, legal, and information issues, which were included in Annual Target Plans. In these Annual Target Plans (considered positive methods to meet NATO requirements and a prerequisite to a potential Membership Action Plan), Ukraine set its own targets for the internal activities and actions that it will pursue in cooperation with NATO. This may have seemed like an important step forward, but the Action Plan was adopted at the time when Ukraine's relations with NATO faced tremendous difficulties. Their dealings were extremely strained by reports of the alleged sale of the Kolchuga passive sensor and the murder of Georgiy Gongadze.

Ukraine's NATO dreams were revived by the Orange Revolution and pro–Western declarations made by Yulia Tymoshenko and Viktor Yushchenko. During his visit to Brussels in February 2006, Yushchenko announced Ukraine's readiness to ratify a Membership Action Plan (MAP). One month later, he signed a decree, which created a committee dedicated to preparing Ukraine for NATO membership. Furthermore, Ukraine's cooperation with the alliance was not severed after the "pro–Russian" Viktor Yanukovych was sworn in. In 2011 in Odessa, Ukrainian and American soldiers conducted military exercises called Sea Breeze. Ironically, Yanukovych agreed to these exercises with the Americans, although they had been cancelled in 2006 and 2009, during

IV. The West's Strategy

Yushchenko's time in office. Nevertheless, in 2010, Yanukovych pushed through legislation on Ukraine's neutral status, in order to cater to Vladimir Putin. It's noteworthy that the Verkhovna Rada revoked this legislation in 2014.

The war in Eastern Ukraine and the incorporation of Crimea by Putin's military reinvigorated the discussion on the future of Europe's security architecture and Ukraine's role in it. "Finlandization" features among the frequently proposed solutions. This term is defined in various ways, but it comes down to the premise that the international community would adhere to a common, informal understanding on Ukraine's limited sovereignty (mainly in terms of foreign policy) in regards to Russia.

Zbigniew Brzezinski was one proponent of Ukraine's Finlandization. He believes, "In addition to being tough-minded on Ukraine and Russia, we ought to at the same time, be willing to negotiate seriously an outcome that they and we can live with. And this is why the Finnish model, I think, is very relevant here."[4] Brzezinski was of the opinion that Ukraine should enjoy normal and peaceful relations with Russia, like Finland—not a NATO member state—did. In consequence, he argued in 2014:

> Obama should convey clearly to Russian President Vladimir Putin that the United States is prepared to use its influence to ensure that a truly independent and territorially undivided Ukraine pursues policies toward Russia similar to those so effectively practiced by Finland: mutually respectful neighbors, wide-ranging economic relations with both Russia and the European Union, but no participation in any military alliance viewed by Moscow as directed at itself—while also expanding its European connectivity. The Finnish model may be the ideal example for Ukraine, the European Union and Russia.[5]

Brzezinski emphasized the importance of Ukraine's development through integration with Europe, eventually leading to the country's EU membership. Therefore, "it should be made clear that Ukraine does not seek, and the West does not contemplate, Ukrainian membership in NATO. It is reasonable for Russia to feel uncomfortable about that prospect."[6]

As argued by Andrew Wilson, the Finnish security model is viable when international conflicts are resolved peacefully and the interests of regional and global competitors are taken into consideration. However, "Ukraine is not Finland! Ukraine stands at the crossroads and it has to choose between democratic, European development and the Eurasian authoritarian model. Under these circumstances, talk of a 'Finlandization' of domestic affairs, defense of state sovereignty, and Ukraine's participation in international security structures is hardly possible!"[7]

Critics of the doctrine of Finlandization point out that the term itself has negative connotations and has been rejected by the Finnish people due to being *passé*.[8] Moreover, a more insightful study of Finland's Cold War experiences reveals the steep price of their alleged neutrality. In reality, Finnish politicians (including Urho Kekkonen, who was president from 1956 to 1982 and was the only Western leader awarded the Lenin Peace Prize) manipulated public opinion with the Soviet threat in order to remain in power. Even though the situation in Finland was better than it was in the Warsaw Pact states, the Soviets were still able to apply political pressure and influence the country's internal affairs. In addition, there was both formal and informal censorship, with the goal of facilitating cordial relations with the Soviet Union.[9]

Applying the Finnish model is based on the assumption that in return for neutrality—meaning not joining NATO—Russia will let Kyiv maintain its sovereignty and Ukraine will be able to develop into a stable, democratic, and prosperous state. However, the likelihood of such a scenario seems to be unlikely, given that the existence of a free and democratic Ukraine is a threat to Putin's corrupt and authoritarian Russia. In consequence, "the Kremlin will seek nothing less than the collapse of democracy in Ukraine."[10] Besides, it was Ukraine's European aspiration, not its willingness to join NATO, which sparked the crisis.[11] And the European Union is by no means a military alliance. It is based on the foundation of a common market and high democratic and human rights standards. Putin finds all these values terrifying.

Analogies have been drawn between the history of Finno-Russo relations and the war in Ukraine. The former president of the World Bank, Paul Wolfowitz, argues that "it is possible that Ukraine could do for Putin what Finland did several years ago for Joseph Stalin and demonstrate that people willing to fight for their independence are not people you should tangle with."[12] The example set by the so-called

IV. The West's Strategy

cyborgs—the soldiers who defended the Donetsk Airport during the 240-day siege of pro–Russian terrorists—proves that Ukrainians are ready to fight for their independence. In this case, should the West step up and provide military equipment to Ukraine?

Zbigniew Brzezinski pointed out: "we lost thousands and thousands of young Americans in Vietnam. Where did the Vietnamese get the weapons with which they killed our soldiers? Think about that. The Russians didn't hesitate."[13] He argued that if NATO member states do not provide weapons to Ukraine, it will send "signals to Putin that he can militarily escalate as he wishes in order to destabilize Ukraine altogether."[14] Kwaśniewski's position on this matter is more circumspect.

"In order to maintain its sovereignty, Ukraine needs a capable military, and its army is in terrible shape. It requires equipment and modernization. Russia and Belarus will not provide what is necessary. I believe that NATO member states cannot afford to say no," says the former president of Poland.[15] However, "the idea of arming Ukraine so that it could fight Russia makes no sense. It's also immoral. First of all, it's a war they cannot possibly win. Secondly, the number of casualties would be sky-high and it simply would not lead us anywhere."[16] For this reason, Kwaśniewski believes, "we should not arm Ukraine, so that it could fight a war against Russia," however:

> a framework for arms sales to Ukraine is necessary. Ukraine is a sovereign state and, as such, it cannot go on without an army. It's a matter of independence. Ukraine needs a well-equipped and well-trained army, which will be able to cooperate with NATO's forces in various capacities. The problem with Ukraine's army is that today it practically does not exist. It only exists on paper.[17]

If this is the case, can the Ukrainian people even dare to dream about joining NATO?

Aleksander Kwaśniewski argues that articulating NATO membership as Poland's top priority proved to be very helpful. The road to the alliance was not easy, especially in the early 1990s, when neither the president, nor the military supported the idea.

> Lech Wałęsa was not overly supportive at that time, when he came up with the concept of a "NATO II." And the military was simply terrified with the prospect of joining the alliance. No significant progress was made in the early 1990's, but—what is very important—the popular idea of neutrality, of a kind

of "Finlandization" was rejected. It would have been highly disadvantageous to us. We would have found ourselves in a grey area, somewhere between Russia and Europe, with a united Germany [to the West].[18]

Since Poland rejected Finlandization to its advantage, is Ukraine bound to accept it? Aleksander Kwaśniewski seems to agree with this position:

> NATO is not even being discussed now. We're talking about the EU. The question remains: Is Ukraine prepared to sign the Association Agreement and has it done its homework? It took Poland 13 years. It may be 15 to 20 years in Ukraine's case. If it gets the job done, if a mental transformation follows, the Finnish model may prove to be a viable solution. But it's a long and bumpy road.[19]

In 2008, Kwaśniewski argued: "Russian plans can be significantly limited by Ukraine and Georgia's accession into NATO, not by a missile defense system. This is crucial for our security. Ukraine in NATO is the most effective additional security guarantee we can get."[20] Over a decade earlier, in 1997, he said: "Poland is a proponent of NATO's expansion. We can imagine a European security architecture composed of all Central Europe, including the Baltic States, Romania, and Bulgaria. If other countries—such as Ukraine—wish to join in, we are certain that it would benefit Europe's security."[21]

During the meeting with Bill Clinton at the Castle Square in Warsaw, on July 10, 1997, Aleksander Kwaśniewski concluded that the invitation extended to Poland, the Czech Republic, and Hungary at the NATO summit in Madrid was of "historic" significance, because it put an end to the Yalta order, i.e., the division of Europe as agreed upon by Franklin D. Roosevelt, Winston Churchill, and Joseph Stalin in February 1945.[22] Ironically, 17 years after Kwaśniewski's declaration about the end of the "Yalta order," which was the embodiment of spheres of influence, Yalta was taken over by the Kremlin. And it does not seem like it will return to Ukraine anytime soon. Putin wishes to put an end to the international order that was created in 1991, when the United States was the sole victorious superpower of the Cold War. It was at that time, argues the Russian president, that Americans "began to believe in their uniqueness, that they were chosen and that they have the right to determine the fate of the world, because they are always right."[23] According to his interpretation of history, the disappearance

IV. The West's Strategy

of the bipolar system rid the world of stability. Putin wants to bring it back.

According to the narrative of the Kremlin, two mutually reinforcing motives need to be taken into account. First, the West humiliated Russia throughout the 1990s, at a time when it was weak. Second, the West took advantage of this moment of weakness and proceeded with NATO's expansion, despite its earlier obligations. Speaking of those "difficult" years, Putin inquired: "What about the Russian state? What will you do, Russia? You kept your head down, swallowed the disgrace and came to terms with it. Our county's situation was so difficult that we were simply not able to protect its interests."[24] Putin made similar arguments at the Munich security conference in 2007:

> I think it is obvious that NATO expansion does not have any relation with the modernization of the Alliance itself or with ensuring security in Europe. On the contrary, it represents a serious provocation that reduces the level of mutual trust. And we have the right to ask: against whom is this expansion intended? And what happened to the assurances our western partners made after the dissolution of the Warsaw Pact?[25]

Seven years later, Putin was at it again. This time, his speech was focused on the annexation of Crimea: "We were being lied to, decisions were being taken behind our backs, and we were being presented with a fait accompli. Such was the case with NATO's expansion and the deployment of military infrastructure along our borders. It was always the same old story: 'It does not concern you.' It's easy to say that it doesn't."[26]

In reality, NATO member states never made such promises to Russia, which was confirmed by Mikhail Gorbachev himself. When inquired by the Russian media about his decision not to push for concrete promises in writing (most importantly about the promises made by Secretary of State James Baker that NATO would not move eastward), Gorbachev replied:

> The topic of "NATO expansion" was not discussed at all, and it wasn't brought up in those years. I say this with full responsibility. Not a single Eastern European country raised the issue, not even after the Warsaw Pact was terminated in 1991. Western leaders didn't bring it up, either. Another issue we brought up was discussed: making sure that NATO's military structures would not advance and that additional armed forces from the alliance would not be deployed on the territory of the then-GDR after German reunification. Baker's statement was made in that context, mentioned in our question.[27]

Nevertheless, Gorbachev added he had always argued that NATO's expansion would be "a big mistake from the very beginning. It was definitely a violation of the spirit of the statements and assurances made to us in 1990."[28]

According to the former U.S. ambassador to Ukraine, Steven Pifer, who served as deputy director at the Soviet Desk of the State Department, nobody really took NATO's eastward expansion seriously in 1990.[29] It changed mostly because countries such as Poland made it clear that they wanted to join the North Atlantic Alliance. There was also a common understanding—although not shared by everyone—that a democratic state, prepared to fulfill the requirements and willing to be a NATO member state, could submit an application. Since the latest expansion, this sentiment has been losing support. The opinion that not every state has the right to join the alliance has been gaining ground. This trend was among the subjects discussed in 2014 by the German newspaper *Der Spiegel* and Henry Kissinger.

> **Kissinger**: But I don't think it's a law of nature that every state must have the right to be an ally in the framework of NATO. You and I know that NATO will never vote unanimously for the entry of Ukraine.
>
> **Spiegel**: But we cannot tell the Ukrainians that they are not free to decide their own future.
>
> **Kissinger**: Why not?[30]

The increasingly common position contradicts what Aleksander Kwaśniewski said in 1996, in the NATO's headquarters in Brussels, when he argued that Poland's accession was something more than fulfillment of its people's aspirations:

> It is also an element of the natural evolution of Western civilization. It is a necessary step, also from the West's point of view, toward building Europe's future as the continent of cooperation, dialogue, and security. It is not our intention to demarcate new divisions in Europe. On the contrary—we wish to overcome the divisions, which still exist. NATO's enlargement will bring about the proliferation of security and stability. It will solidify democracy. It is a positive thing that the historic process of the continent's unification puts an end to the traditional way of thinking about its affairs. The origins of this way of thinking go back to the days of the Cold War.[31]

Less than a decade after these words were said, Europe was less secure and increasingly unstable, as Putin managed to sabotage the historic process of the continent's unification and to deepen the divisions between the alliance's member states.

IV. The West's Strategy

Less Means More: The Future of Ukraine-NATO Relations

The lack of unity among NATO member states was exposed at the April 2008 summit in Bucharest, when Ukraine and Georgia's bids for the Membership Action Plan (MAP) were rejected. Taking note of the divisions over the two former Soviet republics, Moscow took advantage of the situation in order to prevent them from getting closer to NATO. Just two weeks after the summit, Russia upped the pressure on Tbilisi,[32] and the war between Russia and Georgia started in August. The Kremlin thus successfully hindered Georgia's NATO aspirations. Similarly, it is hard to imagine the North Atlantic Alliance's willingness to extend an invitation to Ukraine while it's fighting a war with Russia and part of its territory is occupied. Checkmate? Not necessarily.

In his analysis of the NATO summit in Bucharest and the Russo-Georgian armed conflict in the book *A Little War That Shook the World*, Ronald D. Asmus concluded, "Sometimes, in strategy, as in life, less can be more," and asks, "What was it that Tbilisi needed most—strong political statements of support, or real engagement on the ground and substantive cooperation?"[33] A similar question should be asked today: What does Kyiv want from NATO?

In an op-ed for *The Hill*, Aleksander Kwaśniewski argued that although Ukraine is "not a member, it is a de facto part of the security umbrella provided by NATO." Given Russia's dedication to regain its super power status through the customs union, Ukraine's geopolitical significance for Europe cannot be overlooked. Amiable relations between Ukraine and the EU can potentially benefit the West in terms of energy security and traditional security. "Ukraine is a critically important energy transit route for Russian gas to much of Europe. It also has its own as-yet-undeveloped shale gas reserves, which Chevron and Shell are beginning to explore,"[34] argues the former president of Poland.

Kwaśniewski is of the opinion that "Ukraine can be a source of stability and security in the region, a non–NATO nation that nevertheless cooperates with NATO and provides a counterweight to growing Russian regional power." Ukraine's enormous potential for Europe's security is an opportunity that cannot be missed. It does not mean, however, that Russia is to be regarded as an enemy, given its deep historical ties with Ukraine. In consequence, "for it to prosper, for this nation of 47 million to reach its potential, it must maintain a productive, mutually beneficial relationship with Russia."

> Ukraine is a natural buffer with Russia, and its willingness to work with NATO not only helps enhance NATO's security umbrella over the continent but also reassures Russia that NATO's expansion does not threaten Moscow. Its ability to act as a bridge between Russia and the European Union also enables cooperation between the two, especially in areas where their interests overlap.[35]

In 2014, Aleksander Kwaśniewski argued that NATO's reaction to the situation in Ukraine was appropriate, because political measures should be employed first, followed by economic measures, with the measures at NATO's disposal being considered a last resort.[36] The alliance was analyzing the situation and holding internal discussions. Because the matter in question was very complicated, it needed to be investigated thoroughly, in order to select appropriate tools.[37] The crisis in Ukraine will not go off the radar anytime soon and NATO's position needs to be adjusted in accordance with ongoing developments. Still, moderation is the key: "The situation is sensitive. A single reckless statement or decision can lead to escalation. But I am confident that NATO will return to close cooperation with Ukraine and Georgia soon. However, it has to be prepared for the worst-case scenario, regarding the developments in Ukraine."[38]

Kwaśniewski considers a variety of potential scenarios and none of them is perfect. Two new versions of Transnistria emerge. According to the negative scenario, Russia maintains the status quo, because it is exhausting for Ukraine and its people. The positive scenario sees Russia willing to take a step back and negotiate due to economic difficulties. Kwaśniewski argues that the West should agree to hold talks under such circumstances. Among the conditions would be the disarmament of the separatist forces and Russia's agreement to quit financing them. Kyiv would guarantee extensive autonomy to the Eastern regions, and Moscow would not question them being part of Ukraine.[39]

Subsequently, fair elections, monitored by international observers, should take place. "I am sure that the new government would be pro–Russian," says Kwaśniewski. On the other hand, it would be a win-win

IV. The West's Strategy

situation. The Ukrainian authorities would manage to maintain the territorial integrity of Eastern Ukraine and Moscow would be able to influence the developments on the ground. This scenario poses a few questions. The most important one regards financial matters, namely the expenses necessary to rebuild what has been destroyed during wartime. Kwaśniewski argues that dealing with financial aspects is much easier for Russia, since it can provide assistance along the lines of lifting existing embargos. So, all Russia has to do to start playing a constructive role is stop playing an unconstructive one. But the problem is much more complicated from the Western point of view, since actual financial help needs to be found.[40] In other words, Russia can help by not causing trouble, whereas the U.S. and the EU have to fork over their taxpayers' money.

Today, the future of Ukraine depends on sustainable financing of basic reforms, necessary to modernize the country. According to Kwaśniewski, Ukraine needs $25 billion a year in order to get back on its feet.[41] "There's a lot Europe can do, both in economic and political terms. We are not as helpless as we would sometimes like to believe. Obviously, we will not resort to military means, because that is not the way the Western world works. But economic and political means are surely within reach."[42]

That is why Kwaśniewski believes that the EU should strongly cooperate with the United States.

In February 2014, when the Kremlin conducted its Crimea operation, Barack Obama said that the U.S., along with its European allies, supports the right of self-determination of the Ukrainian people. He also expressed his concern over Russia's actions in Crimea: Any sort of breach of Ukraine's sovereignty would be highly destabilizing. It is not in Ukraine, Russia, or the EU's interest. President Obama said this would equal breaking Russia's obligation to respect Ukraine's independence and its territorial integrity. Moreover, he argued it would be against international law and said that there would be consequences to any kind of military intervention.[43]

Speaking with *The New York Times* in June 2014, Kwaśniewski said: "What we most need to hear from President Obama is what to do with Ukraine, how to deal with this new Russia. We are not interested in a confrontation with the Russians. We are not interested in

Cold War II. But we will have a difficult time getting through the next four or five months without very clear and very determined American leadership."[44]

Since the early days of the crisis in Ukraine, Kwaśniewski advocated further engagement of the U.S. In February 2014, when Yanukovych's fate was still unknown and it seemed like early presidential election might be held, Kwaśniewski argued that the European mission should be continued or even upgraded to a level involving heads of states. He also suggested a solution, which would enable the U.S. to get involved:

> I will tell the Americans that the document everyone has forgotten about is still valid. In 1994, the presidents of Russia, the U.S., and Ukraine signed an agreement on Ukraine's denuclearization. The security guarantees of Ukraine's sovereignty and stability are of grave importance. The agreement can be used as a basis for the creation of a joint U.S.-Europe-Russia group, which would monitor the developments on the ground. It would also make sure the deal is being respected and provide assistance, should tensions reemerge.[45]

Epilogue: In the Center of the Whirlwind

The mission has been accomplished, but it took blood and sacrifice for this to happen.
—Aleksander Kwaśniewski

The level of hostility and frustration was enormously high and all it took was a single spark. The spark, which started the fire, was the decision not to sign the Association Agreement.
—Aleksander Kwaśniewski

One month ahead of the Vilnius summit, Kwaśniewski argued the signing of the Association Agreement and the free trade agreement would be a pivotal moment, which would define Ukraine's future and its strategic decisions for decades to come.[1] The signing of the Association Agreement with the European Union at the Eastern Partnership summit was supposed to make history, in a similar fashion as the referendum on independence of 1991. The fact that over 90 percent of voters residing in Ukraine voted for independence was not only shocking to Russia, it surprised many Ukrainians too. After several years had passed, Aleksander Kwaśniewski asked Mikhail Gorbachev what he had expected would happen at the time. Gorbachev responded that he thought the result would be very close, around 45 percent versus 55 percent, but the option of remaining part of the new version of the U.S.S.R.—the Commonwealth of Independent States—would prevail. Kwaśniewski asked Leonid Kravchuk the same question. Kravchuk expected the same proportions, but in favor of Ukraine's independence.[2]

According to Aleksander Kwaśniewski, Ukraine has been confirming its strength as an independent and sovereign state since the 1991 referendum. Over two decades later, Ukrainian identity has proven to be "deep-rooted even in the areas where you wouldn't expect it to be."[3] The former president of Poland is correct to point out that Ukraine's statehood does not have a long history, even though generations of Ukrainian people had dreamt about it.[4] Both Gorbachev and Kuchma underestimated the people's will in 1991. Viktor Yanukovych made a similar mistake at the turn of 2013. He failed to understand that with Ukrainian identity taking root, a European identity was beginning to blossom.

Just as Yulia Tymoshenko became a hostage of Viktor Yanukovych, the process of Ukraine's European integrations was taken hostage by the case of the former prime minister. Initially, Yanukovych might have had good intentions in this regard. However, his meeting with Vladimir Putin in Sochi in the summer of 2013 changed everything, and he began to play Tymoshenko's case to his advantage, argues Kwaśniewski. His goal was to spark the EU's refusal to sign the Association Agreement. The Ukrainian president knew exactly what kind of game he was playing, and it was called "stalling."

According to Aleksander Kwaśniewski, Yanukovych was convinced that the case of Yulia Tymoshenko was so well known to Europe that it would retreat from its desire to sign the Association Agreement: "From his point of view, it would be a perfect scenario. He would be able to say: 'I want to sign it, they don't.' Why are they willing to tie the fate of Ukraine, a nation of almost 50 million, with the fate of a common thief and criminal?"[5] But the EU did not fall for it and Tymoshenko said the deal should be signed no matter what happens to her. Yanukovych realized he had lost at his own game. The EU had not taken the decision to postpone the signing ceremony until the former prime minister was released. Instead, it was the Party of Regions that decided to stop the necessary preparations on the eve of the Eastern Partnership summit in Vilnius. This decision was the source of the Maidan protests. Yanukovych disregarded the opinions of the Ukrainian people from the start and this led to his defeat.

* * *

Following another day of difficult negotiations, on the plane returning from Kyiv to Vienna, Kwaśniewski said to Pat Cox: "Have you noticed something peculiar? We have held so many talks and no one ever tried to ask us about a PR angle, how to communicate with society, with the outside world. In Europe, PR-related issues would take 90 percent of the time." Cox agreed that this was an unusual thing. Kwaśniewski believes it was one of the main sources of the developments that followed.

> Yanukovych and Azarov did not communicate with the public at all. The Ukrainian people—Yanukovych's supporters in particular—were not informed why he decided to sign the agreement and why he changed his mind. When it comes to the part of the public, which dreamed of joining Europe and was fed up with Yanukovych and corruption, there was hope that our presence, our mission would sustain the chance of success. But the hope was cut short abruptly.[6]

Kwaśniewski's mission kept alive the Ukrainian people's expectations for reforms and integration with the EU. For those who wished to imagine their future in the EU, it was a light at the end of the tunnel. In the summer of 2012, it seemed like everything was lost, but the EU, which is not famous for flexibility and swift decision-making, found a way to keep the door open for Ukraine. For the next 18 months, Kwaśniewski fought to make sure it stayed open.

Pat Cox often described the mission as "unorthodox" and Kwaśniewski pointed out that its formula went beyond traditional diplomacy. The decision of the president of the European Parliament and the prime minister of the Ukrainian government constituted the mission's legal basis. "In the wake of the frozen EU-Ukraine relationship, we were regarded by both sides as the only guys who can get something done."[7]

Aleksander Kwaśniewski recalled that his cooperation with Cox was very constructive and said that a Pole will always find common ground with an Irishman. It was an interesting experience for both of them. The former President of Poland was very familiar with Ukraine, given his 20-year-long experience in that field, whereas Cox had visited the country for the first time as the EU's special envoy. His fresh approach turned out to be highly beneficial: "I might have gotten used to certain things that still amazed Pat. That way, we were able to define the country's real problems." Kwaśniewski describes Cox as a fully-fledged democrat, true to his principles, who enjoys life, meeting people, networking, and exploring the world.[8] It seems fair to say that that is something they have in common.

According to a prominent Ukrainian foreign affairs scholar, "Kwaśniewski understands Ukraine. He knows our sayings and is familiar with things, which you normally need to explain to foreigners."[9] Such characteristics guarantee efficiency—especially in Ukraine—but can potentially be a source of controversy. Kwaśniewski is well connected in the Ukrainian political, diplomatic and business realms. But in Ukraine, one individual can be simultaneously active in all three domains, which makes the country different from Western democracies. Kwaśniewski has faced criticism in Poland due to such connections.

In mid May 2014, *BuzzFeed* published a piece on Vice President Joe Biden's son, Hunter Biden, who was on the board of directors of Burisma Holdings, Ukraine's largest independent oil and gas producer.[10] The owner, Mykola Zlochevsky, was Minister of Ecology and Natural Resources in Mykola Azarov's government between 2010 and 2012. The article also reported that Aleksander Kwaśniewski had served on the board since January 2014.

Moreover, it was pointed out that a team of American advisors from Burisma conducted lobbying efforts in the United States. Apart from Hunter Biden, former advisor to John Kerry, Devon Archer, was another member of Burisma's board. Burisma also employed David Leiter, who headed Kerry's office when he served as Secretary of State, in May 2014.[11]

The story focused on the question of whether there was a conflict of interest, given Joe Biden's publicly expressed support for Ukraine in its struggle for energy security, which was hampered by the Kremlin. At the same time, Biden's son served as an advisor to the company focused in exploring Ukraine's energy resources. Interestingly enough, Moscow did not consider this to be problematic, which may reveal something about the potential source of the story.

The Russian government's spokesman, Dmitry Peskov, argued in his commentary for *BuzzFeed* that Russia did not regard Biden's activities as a conflict of interest and added: "as everyone knows, there's no gas in Ukraine. The gas in Ukraine is Russian."[12] The article was obviously supposed to damage Biden's reputation. Joe Biden had been supportive of Ukraine, visited Kyiv on numerous occasions, and attended

Epilogue

Petro Poroshenko's presidential inauguration. The article caused collateral damage that also hit Kwaśniewski because Poland was in midst of a European Parliament election campaign.

Had it not been for Kwaśniewski's support of several political candidates, the story would have lost momentum, just as it did in the United States. However, when these revelations hit the news, several Polish politicians, both from the right and the left, saw an opportunity to exploit it. "Kwaśniewski works for Yanukovych's man," echoed the main theme.

In his own defense, Kwaśniewski argued that his support for Burisma, a independent company that has been exploring natural gas in Ukraine since 2002 and was important for "Ukraine's energy security vis-à-vis Russia"[13] and "for strategic reasons, we should assist Ukrainian companies, which explore natural gas and will also explore shale gas, because it is crucial for this country's future, which is currently under threat."[14] Secondly, referring to Zlochevsky as "Yanukovych's man" lacks merit, because "he was dismissed for being too independent and was replaced with a man loyal to Yanukovych."[15] Moreover, "he had been critical of Yanukovych's policies."[16] When inquired about money, Kwaśniewski said: "Of course there is money, but involvement with a company such as Burisma benefits Ukraine's independence." During the two years of the mission's intense work in Ukraine, he got to know Zlochevsky quite well, and it was clear to him that his motives in business and for Ukraine's future path were pro–European. "And I will always work with pro–European people."[17] Given that he makes an easy target, Kwaśniewski's approach is bound to draw criticism in the future.

* * *

Between June 2012 and November 2013, Aleksander Kwaśniewski held 21 meetings with opposition leaders, 16 deliberations with EU ambassadors in Kyiv, six meetings with 18 different NGOs, and four consultations with former presidents of Ukraine. He also held 68 telephone conversations with both the opposition and government representatives. His mission included 75 days in Ukraine and 19 in Brussels and Strasbourg.

The mission might have been exhausting, but Kwaśniewski under-

Epilogue

lined that, above all, it was "exciting." The former president of Poland couldn't help but feel helpless during the summit in Vilnius, but everything he had worked for soon came to fruition. Yulia Tymoshenko was released and Ukraine signed the Association Agreement.[18] Speaking about his experiences, Kwaśniewski said that he found himself right in the epicenter of the storm. From today's perspective, it is clear that the real storm had yet to hit Ukraine. The Euromaidan, the Heavenly Hundred, the annexation of Crimea, the war against separatist forces and Russia in Eastern Ukraine. Will the storm ever settle?

Kwaśniewski claims the crisis will be a lasting one and there are no quick solutions to it.[19] On the other hand, Putin's actions will strengthen Ukraine's national identity in the long run. It is a process that has been taking place for years, but Russian aggression accelerated it. Ukraine is no longer a distant place for Europeans, even those from Western parts of the continent. "It only brings Ukraine closer to Europe and Europe to Ukraine. That does not mean we are to expect immediate results. Russia will do anything to delay the process and that's something we need to be prepared for."[20]

Putin's goal is to convince everyone, including the people with anti–Russian views, that Ukraine has no choice but to accommodate Moscow's demands. In the wake of the war with Russia, the Ukrainian identity is getting stronger, although, argues Kwaśniewski, "imagine a complete economic disaster and households without heating. This is Putin's endgame. He hopes people get exhausted to the point that they decide to agree to Russia's terms. This is his plan."[21]

Kwaśniewski argues that Putin underestimated the scale of anti–Russian sentiments in Ukraine that he would have to face. In consequence, the Kremlin can no longer rely on military means: "It is no longer viable. They know that such a move in Kyiv would cause an uprising, and that would be horrifying." But they can use other tools: "natural gas, crude oil, embargos, propaganda, money, the fifth column, and other means, which will allow them to destabilize the country up to the point that it spins out of control."[22]

"Putin wants all of Ukraine," says Kwaśniewski "and he wants to get it by destabilizing the Ukrainian state." The question is: Will he succeed?

It will not be an easy task. In November 2014, Kwaśniewski described the Ukrainian people as "a proud nation, which does not take kindly

Epilogue

to those who humiliate it."[23] It will be crucial how far the U.S. and the EU are willing to go to help Ukraine. The former special envoy believes that the level of unity presented by the Western world exceeded Putin's expectations. He was convinced the West would be divided and the sanctions would not be that severe. The Russian president did not expect oil prices to drop that rapidly either. "Will it change Putin's policy, or will it only modify it?" asks Kwaśniewski. Only to answer his own question: "I'm afraid it won't change. It may force him to take more time, give up certain methods, he will seek compromise when necessary, but it will only be a game."[24] Time will tell if the West falls for it.

Saying goodbye to Pat Cox, Aleksander Kwaśniewski tried to convince his Irish friend to write a book. "It should start like this: 'When I arrived in Ukraine, I knew nothing about it. I'm about to conclude my 27th visit and I have spent 75 days in this country. And I can tell you that I still don't know what's going to happen.'"[25]

Nobody does. "The situation is complicated and dynamic. There is little reason to be optimistic. But we need to keep trying as long as there is hope," says Kwaśniewski. His Ukrainian mission is not over yet.

Chapter Notes

Introduction

1. Christian Neef and Jan Puhl, "SPIEGEL Interview with Poland's Kaczynski: 'We Are Very Vigilant When it Comes to the German-Russian Relationship,'" *SPIEGEL ONLINE*, March 6, 2006, accessed April 3, 2014, http://www.spiegel.de/international/spiegel/spiegel-interview-with-poland-s-kaczynski-we-are-very-vigilant-when-it-comes-to-the-german-russian-relationship-a-404675.html.
2. Krzysztof Burnetko, "*Krajobraz po sąsiedzkiej rewolucji*," *Tygodnik Powszechny*, January 16, 2005.
3. Michał Kacewicz and Michał Krzymowski, "Aleksander Kwaśniewski: Inna liga," *Newsweek.pl*, January 23, 2013, accessed August 19, 2014, http://polska.newsweek.pl/aleksander-kwasniewski-inna-liga,100582,1,1.html.
4. "Full transcript of the Atlantic Council's Third Annual Bronislaw Geremek Lecture, delivered by former President Aleksander Kwaśniewski and former National Security Advisor General Jim Jones," *Atlantic Council*, February 28, 2013, accessed February 10, 2014, http://www.atlanticcouncil.org/news/transcripts/transcript-2013-annual-bronislaw-geremek-lecture.
5. Author's interview with Aleksander Kwaśniewski, Warsaw, December 16, 2014.
6. Pat Cox and Aleksander Kwaśniewski, *Mission update on 18 April 2013, Strasbourg*, European Parliament Monitoring Mission to Ukraine.
7. Author's interview with Aleksander Kwaśniewski, Warsaw, December 16, 2014.
8. "Cox, Kwaśniewski to monitor Tymoshenko appeal on behalf of EP," *European Parliament/The President*, June 6, 2012, accessed June 14, 2012, http://www.europarl.europa.eu/the-president/en/press/press_release_speeches/press_release/2012/2012-june/html/cox-kwasniewski-to-monitor-tymoshenko-appeal-on-behalf-of-ep.
9. Marcin Wojciechowski, "Prezydent Kwaśniewski o swojej ukraińskiej misji," *Gazeta Wyborcza*, June 14, 2012, accessed May 6, 2014, http://wyborcza.pl/1,76842,11928861,Prezydent_Kwasniewski_o_swojej_ukrainskiej_misji.html?as=2.
10. Aleksander Kwaśniewski, *Integration of Ukraine with the EU*, European Parliament's conference, October 15, 2013.
11. Martin Schulz, "Speech at the Yalta European Strategy—YES conference," *European Parliament/The President*, September 12, 2014, September 20, 2014, http://www.europarl.europa.eu/the-president/en/press/press_release_speeches/speeches/speeches-2014/speeches-2014-september/html/speech-at-the-yalta-european-strategy-yes-conference.
12. Jan Puhl and Christian Neef, "'Brussels Was Naïve,' Ex Polish Leader on Failed Ukraine Talks," *SPIEGEL ONLINE*, December 9, 2013, accessed October 12, 2013, http://www.spiegel.de/international/europe/spiegel-interview-with-aleksander-kwasniewski-on-ukraine-talks-a-937964.html.
13. Ростислав Хотин, "Александр Квасневський: Росія робить величезну помилку, тиснучи на горду Україну," *УНІАН*, November 14, 2013, accessed September 9, 2014, http://www.unian.ua/politics/851883-aleksandr-kvasnevskiy-rosiya-robit-velicheznu-pomilku-tisnuchi-na-gordu-ukrajinu.html.
14. "ТОП-10 лобістів України у світі," *Інститут Світової Політики*, accessed February 5, 2014, http://iwp.org.ua/ukr/public/976.html.
15. "Ukraina na trudnej drodze do Eu-

ropy. Aleksander Kwaśniewski gościem Salonu InMitte," *Ambasada Rzeczypospolitej w Berlinie*, February 18, 2014, accessed March 17, 2014, http://www.berlin.msz.gov.pl/pl/aktualnosci/tytul_strony_2.

16. Krzysztof Burnetko, "*Krajobraz po sąsiedzkiej rewolucji*."

17. "Ukraina na trudnej drodze do Europy. Aleksander Kwaśniewski gościem Salonu InMitte."

18. Renata Grochal, "Kwaśniewski: Tusk jako prezydent Unii nie ucieknie od problemu Ukrainy," *Wyborcza.pl*, October 30, 2014, accessed November 10, 2014, http://wyborcza.pl/1,76842,16886925,Kwasniewski_Tusk_jako_prezydent_Unii_nie_ucieknie.html.

19. "Ukraina na trudnej drodze do Europy. Aleksander Kwaśniewski gościem Salonu InMitte."

20. "Sygnały dnia," *Polskie Radio*, January 14, 2005.

21. Jan Puhl and Christian Neef, "'Brussels Was Naïve,' Ex Polish Leader on Failed Ukraine Talks."

22. Małgorzata Nocuń, "Nie skreślajmy Ukrainy," *Nowa Europa Wschodnia*, October 23, 2012, accessed June 3, 2014, http://www.new.org.pl/1062,post.html.

Chapter I

1. Katarzyna Glazer, *Polska Agencja Prasowa*, November 18, 2005, accessed January 11, 2015, http://www.prezydent.pl/archiwum/archiwum-strony-lecha-kaczynskiego/import/archiwum-wywiadow-krajowych/rok-2005/listopad-2005-r-/polska-agencja-prasowa-18-listopada-2005-r-/.

2. Ростислав Хотин, "Александр Квасневський: Росія робить величезну помилку, тиснучи на горду Україну," *УНІАН*, November 14, 2013, accessed September 9, 2014, http://www.unian.ua/politics/851883-aleksandr-kvasnevskiy-rosiya-robit-veliczeznu-pomilku-tisnuchi-na-gordu-ukrajinu.html.

3. Aleksander Kwaśniewski, *Integration of Ukraine with the EU*, European Parliament's conference, October 15, 2013.

4. "Closing remarks: Aleksander Kwaśniewski," 9th Yalta Annual Meeting, *Yalta European Strategy*, accessed October 7, 2014, http://yes-ukraine.org/en/photo-and-video/video/drugiy-den-roboti-9-yi-yaltinskoyi-shchorichnoyi-zustrichi/zaklyuchne-slovo-aleksandr-kvasnyevskiy.

5. "Full transcript of the Atlantic Council's Third Annual Bronislaw Geremek Lecture, delivered by former President Aleksander Kwaśniewski and former National Security Advisor General Jim Jones."

6. "Kwaśniewski: Unia Europejska powinna być otwarta dla Ukrainy," *Jedynka—Polskie Radio*, February 16, 2014, accessed February 17, 2014, http://www.polskieradio.pl/7/477/Artykul/1052516,Kwasniewski-Unia-Europejska-powinna-byc-otwarta-dla-Ukrainy.

7. Aleksander Kwaśniewski, *Integration of Ukraine with the EU*, European Parliament's conference, October 15, 2013.

8. Joshua Keating, "Former Polish president: U.S.-EU ties 'too weak,'" *Foreign Policy*, March 1, 2013, accessed October 3, 2014, http://blog.foreignpolicy.com/posts/2013/03/01/former_polish_president_us_eu_ties_too_weak.

9. "Closing remarks: Aleksander Kwaśniewski," 9th Yalta Annual Meeting, *Yalta European Strategy*, accessed October 7, 2014, http://yes-ukraine.org/en/photo-and-video/video/drugiy-den-roboti-9-yi-yaltinskoyi-shchorichnoyi-zustrichi/zaklyuchne-slovo-aleksandr-kvasnyevskiy.

10. Renata Grochal, "Kwaśniewski: Zazdroszczę Tuskowi," *Wyborcza.pl*, September 9, 2014, accessed September 9, 2014, http://wyborcza.pl/politykaekstra/1,140681,16614668,Kwasniewski_Zazdroszcze_Tuskowi.html#TRrelSST.

11. *Ibid*.

12. Brian Wheeler and Alex Hunt, "Brexit: All you need to know about the UK leaving the EU," *BBC News*, October 2, 2016, accessed October 10, 2016, http://www.bbc.com/news/uk-politics-32810887.

13. Mike Bird and Georgi Kantchev, "Pound Plunges on U.K. Vote to Leave the European Union," *The Wall Street Journal*, June 24, 2016, http://www.wsj.com/articles/u-k-pound-jumps-after-brexit-polls-close-1466718460.

14. "Aleksander Kwaśniewski: to koniec Wielkiej Brytanii," *Wirtualna Polska*, June 24, 2016, accessed October 10, 2016, http://wiadomosci.wp.pl/kat,1342,title,Aleksander-Kwasniewski-to-koniec-Wielkiej-Brytanii,wid,18394120,wiadomosc.html?ticaid=117d89.

Notes—Chapter I

15. "Kwaśniewski: większe emocje wzbudza we mnie Brexit niż mecz z Niemcami," *Kropka nad i*, TVN24, June 15, 2016, accessed October 10, 2016, http://www.tvn24.pl/wiadomosci-z-kraju,3/brexit-aleksander-kwasniewski-o-skutkach-kropkanad-i,652915.html.

16. "Aleksander Kwaśniewski: Dramatyczna obłuda Brytyjczyków," *Rzeczpospolita*, June 24, 2016, accessed October 10, 2016, http://www.rp.pl/Brexit/160629475-Aleksander-Kwasniewski-Dramatyczna-obluda-Brytyjczykow.html#ap-1.

17. "Kwaśniewski: większe emocje wzbudza we mnie Brexit niż mecz z Niemcami," *Kropka nad i*, TVN24, June 15, 2016, accessed October 10, 2016, http://www.tvn24.pl/wiadomosci-z-kraju,3/brexit-aleksander-kwasniewski-o-skutkach-kropkanad-i,652915.html.

18. "Aleksander Kwaśniewski: to koniec Wielkiej Brytanii," *Wirtualna Polska*, June 24, 2016, accessed October 10, 2016, http://wiadomosci.wp.pl/kat,1342,title,Aleksander-Kwasniewski-to-koniec-Wielkiej-Brytanii,wid,18394120,wiadomosc.html?ticaid=117d89.

19. "Kwaśniewski przewiduje 'szok i chaos' po Brexicie. 'I w tym chaosie można się pogubić,'" *Fakty po Faktach*, June 24, 2016, accessed October 12, 2016, http://faktypofaktach.tvn24.pl/fakty-po-faktach-kwasniewski-przewiduje-szok-i-chaos-po-brexicie,655737.html.

20. Ibid.

21. "Aleksander Kwaśniewski: to koniec Wielkiej Brytanii," *Wirtualna Polska*, June 24, 2016, accessed October 10, 2016, http://wiadomosci.wp.pl/kat,1342,title,Aleksander-Kwasniewski-to-koniec-Wielkiej-Brytanii,wid,18394120,wiadomosc.html?ticaid=117d89.

22. "Co Brexit oznacza dla Polski? Kwaśniewski: Weszliśmy w okres szoku, chaosu i nieprzewidywalności," *Wprost.pl*, June 24, 2016, accessed October 11, 2016, https://www.wprost.pl/swiat/10012309/Co-Brexit-oznacza-dla-Polski-Kwasniewski-Weszlismy-w-okres-szoku-chaosu-i-nieprzewidywalnosci.html.

23. Jan Puhl and Christian Neef, "'Brussels Was Naïve,' Ex Polish Leader on Failed Ukraine Talks."

24. Aleksander Kwaśniewski, *Integration of Ukraine with the EU*, European Parliament's conference, October 15, 2013.

25. Małgorzata Nocuń, "Nie skreślajmy Ukrainy," *Nowa Europa Wschodnia*, October 23, 2012, accessed June 3, 2014, http://www.new.org.pl/1062,post.html.

26. Piotr Najsztub, "Za Ukrainę!" *Wprost* 16 (2013).

27. Aleksander Kwaśniewski, *Integration of Ukraine with the EU*, European Parliament's conference, October 15, 2013.

28. Piotr Najsztub, "Za Ukrainę!" *Wprost* 16 (2013).

29. Aleksander Kwaśniewski, *Integration of Ukraine with the EU*, European Parliament's conference, October 15, 2013.

30. Ibid.

31. Piotr Markiewicz, "Putin będzie się starał pozyskać słabe kraje. Ukraina będzie szarpana," *TOK FM*, November 27, 2013, accessed November 29, 2013, http://www.tokfm.pl/Tokfm/1,103087,15030741,_Putin_bedzie_sie_staral_pozyskac_slabe_kraje_Ukraina.html.

32. Małgorzata Nocuń, "Nie skreślajmy Ukrainy," *Nowa Europa Wschodnia*, October 23, 2012, accessed June 3, 2014, http://www.new.org.pl/1062,post.html.

33. "EU Position in World," *European Commission*, accessed June 5, 2014, http://ec.europa.eu/trade/policy/eu-position-in-world-trade/.

34. Zbigniew Brzeziński, *Strategic Vision: America and the Crisis for Global Power* (New York: Basic Books, 2012), 54.

35. Ibid., 36.

36. "Kwaśniewski: Unia Europejska powinna być otwarta dla Ukrainy," *Jedynka—Polskie Radio*, February 16, 2014, accessed February 17, 2014, http://www.polskieradio.pl/7/477/Artykul/1052516,Kwasniewski-Unia-Europejska-powinna-byc-otwarta-dla-Ukrainy.

37. Aleksander Kwaśniewski, *Integration of Ukraine with the EU*, European Parliament's conference, October 15, 2013.

38. Małgorzata Nocuń, "Nie skreślajmy Ukrainy," *Nowa Europa Wschodnia*, October 23, 2012, accessed June 3, 2014, http://www.new.org.pl/1062,post.html.

39. Ibid.

40. Aleksander Kwaśniewski, *Integration of Ukraine with the EU*, European Parliament's conference, October 15, 2013.

41. Jan Puhl and Christian Neef, "'Brussels Was Naïve,' Ex Polish Leader on Failed Ukraine Talks."

42. Ростислав Хотин, "Александр

Notes—Chapter I

Квасневський: Росія робить величезну помилку, тиснучи на горду Україну," *УНІАН*, November 14, 2013, accessed September 9, 2014, http://www.unian.ua/politics/851883-aleksandr-kvasnevskiy-rosiya-robit-velicheznu-pomilku-tisnuchi-na-gordu-ukrajinu.html.

43. *Fakty po faktach*, TVN 24, February 19, 2014.

44. Kwaśniewski: "pomarańczowa rewolucja" to wielki sukces, *Wirtualna Polska*, November 22, 2005, accessed October 21, 2014, http://wiadomosci.wp.pl/kat,13 42,title,Kwasniewski-pomaranczowa-rewolucja-to-wielki-sukces,wid,8095189,wiadomosc.html.

45. *Polska Agencja Prasowa*, January 25, 2005.

46. William Schneider, "Ukraine's 'Orange Revolution,'" *National Journal* 50 (2004).

47. "Rozmowy albo czołgi," *Gazeta Wyborcza*, November 25, 2004.

48. TVN24, November 23, 2004.

49. Ibid.

50. *Suma zdarzeń według Jacka Żakowskiego*, TVP 1, November 28, 2004.

51. Marcin Bosacki and Marcin Wojciechowski, "Kulisy rewolucji ukraińskiej," *Gazeta Wyborcza*, April 3, 2005.

52. Marek Ostrowski and Adam Kremiński, "Misja kijowska," *Polityka* 51 (2004), 36–39.

53. Marcin Bosacki and Marcin Wojciechowski, "Kulisy rewolucji ukraińskiej," *Gazeta Wyborcza*, April 3, 2005.

54. Marek Ostrowski and Adam Kremiński, "Misja kijowska," *Polityka* 51 (2004), 36–39.

55. Ibid.

56. Polskie Radio, January 1, 2005.

57. Krzysztof Burnetko, "Krajobraz po sąsiedzkiej rewolucji," *Tygodnik Powszechny*, January 16, 2005.

58. Bartosz Węglarczyk, "Prezydent Kwaśniewski: kto użyje siły, ten przegra," *Gazeta Wyborcza*, December 3, 2004, accessed January 13, 2014, http://wyborcza.pl/1,76842,2426358.html.

59. Wilson, *Ukraine's Orange Revolution*, 136.

60. Ibid.

61. Steven Pifer, "European Mediators and Ukraine's Orange Revolution," *Problems of Post-Communism* 6 (2007): 33.

62. Krzysztof Burnetko, "Krajobraz po sąsiedzkiej rewolucji," *Tygodnik Powszechny*, January 16, 2005.

63. Marcin Bosacki and Marcin Wojciechowski, "Kulisy rewolucji ukraińskiej," *Gazeta Wyborcza*, April 3, 2005.

64. *Wygraliśmy przyszłość: przemówienia, wywiady, dokumenty (wybór)*, 10 lat prezydentury Aleksandra Kwaśniewskiego (Warsaw: Amicus Europea, 2008), 24–25.

65. Steven Pifer, "European Mediators and Ukraine's Orange Revolution," *Problems of Post-Communism* 6 (2007): 33.

66. Ibid.

67. Karol Grünberg and Bolesław Sprengel, *Trudne sąsiedztwo: stosunki polsko-ukraińskie w X–XX wieku* (Warsaw: Książka i Wiedza, 2005), 762.

68. Grünberg and Sprengel, *Trudne sąsiedztwo*, 763.

69. Wilson, *Ukraine's Orange Revolution*, 53.

70. See Martin Streetly, "Jane's Radar and Electronic Warfare Systems 2008–2009," *Jane's Information Group*, Surrey 2006, 341.

71. Maciej Olchawa, *Imperialna rozgrywka: Ukraina w geopolitycznej strategii Stanów Zjednoczonych* (Krakow: Arcana, 2009), 82.

72. "Diplomatic snub? Say it in French," CNN.com, November 22, 2002, accessed October 21, 2014, http://edition.cnn.com/2002/WORLD/europe/11/22/nato.language/index.html.

73. Piotr Bajor, "Ukraina: polityczne salony od kuchni," *Nowa Europa Wschodnia* 3–4 (2016): 195.

74. Wilson, *Ukraine's Orange Revolution*, 136.

75. Andrew Wilson, *The Ukrainians: Unexpected Nation* (New Haven: Yale University Press, 2002) 192–200.

76. Andrzej Brzeziecki and Małgorzata Nocuń, "Kwaśniewski też był komunistą," *Tygodnik Powszechny*, January 30, 2005.

77. *Suma zdarzeń według Jacka Żakowskiego*, TVP 1, November 28, 2004.

78. Krzysztof Burnetko, "Krajobraz po sąsiedzkiej rewolucji," *Tygodnik Powszechny*, January 16, 2005.

79. Renata Grochal, "Kwaśniewski: Zazdroszczę Tuskowi," *Wyborcza.pl*, September 9, 2014, accessed September 9, 2014, http://wyborcza.pl/politykaekstra/1,140681,16614668,Kwasniewski_Zazdroszcze_Tuskowi.html#TRrelSST.

Notes—Chapter II

80. Renata Grochal, "Kwaśniewski: Nie pojechałbym dziś do Moskwy," *Wyborcza.pl*, May 13, 2014, accessed July 7, 2014, http://wyborcza.pl/politykaekstra/1,137934,15955837,Kwasniewski_Nie_pojechalbym_dzis_do_Moskwy.html.

Chapter II

1. *Fakty po faktach*, TVN 24, February 19, 2014.
2. "EU Ministers Urge Ukraine to Stop Bluffing on Tymoshenko," *Voice of America*, October 22, 2013, accessed October 7, 2014, http://www.voanews.com/content/reu-eu-ministers-urge-ukraine-to-stop-bluffing-on-tymoshenko/1774905.html.
3. Małgorzata Nocuń, "Nie skreślajmy Ukrainy," *Nowa Europa Wschodnia*, October 23, 2012, accessed June 3, 2014, http://www.new.org.pl/1062,post.html.
4. Lutz Hoffmann and Felicitas Möllers, *Ukraine on the Road to Europe* (Heidelberg: Physica-Verlag HD, 2001), 68.
5. Maciej Olchawa, *Gwiazdy i Tryzub: europejska integracja Ukrainy* (Krakow: Wydawnictwo Szwajpolt Fiol, 2013), 50.
6. Viktor Yanukovych, "The Future of Ukraine is With the EU," *The Wall Street Journal*, August 25, 2011.
7. Pat Cox and Aleksander Kwaśniewski, *Mission update on 18 April 2013*, Strasbourg, European Parliament Monitoring Mission to Ukraine.
8. Author's interview with Aleksander Kwaśniewski, Warsaw, December 16, 2014.
9. Małgorzata Nocuń, "Jak żyje więzień Tymoszenko," *Wprost* 20 (2012).
10. Ibid.
11. "Statement by the Spokesperson of EU High Representative Catherine Ashton on the case of Yulia Tymoshenko," *European Council*, May 26, 2011, accessed October 22, 2013, http://www.consilium.europa.eu/uedocs/cms_Data/docs/pressdata/EN/foraff/122218.pdf.
12. "Arrest of Yulia Tymoshenko in Ukraine," *European Commission*, August 8, 2011, accessed October 21, 2013, http://europa.eu/rapid/press-release_MEMO-11-551_en.htm?locale=en.
13. "Van Rompuy: 'The EU will never become the United States of Europe,'" *Euronews*, May 9, 2012, accessed November 10, 2014, http://www.euronews.com/2012/05/09/herman-van-rompuy-the-eu-will-never-become-the-united-states-of-europe/.
14. Author's interview with Aleksander Kwaśniewski, Warsaw, December 16, 2014.
15. "Cox, Kwaśniewski to monitor Tymoshenko appeal on behalf of EP," June 6, 2012, accessed October 2, 2012, http://www.europarl.europa.eu/former_ep_presidents/president-schulz-2012-2014/en/press/press_release_speeches/press_release/2012/2012-june/html/cox-kwasniewski-to-mon.
16. "Kwaśniewski w Kijowie: Nie widzę rozwiązania problemu Tymoszenko 'na już,'" *Gazeta Wyborcza.pl*, June 11, 2012, accessed April 16, 2014, http://wyborcza.pl/1,76842,11912724,Kwasniewski_w_Kijowie_Nie_widze_rozwiazania_problemu.html.
17. Małgorzata Nocuń, "Nie skreślajmy Ukrainy," *Nowa Europa Wschodnia*, October 23, 2012, accessed June 3, 2014, http://www.new.org.pl/1062,post.html.
18. Krzysztof Grzesiowski, "Rozmowa dnia: Aleksander Kwaśniewski, *Jedynka—Polskie Radio*, January 30, 2014, accessed February 2, 2014, http://www.polskieradio.pl/7/129/Artykul/1037114.
19. Paweł Wroński, "Kwaśniewski: Janukowycz nie docenił poparci ludzi dla UE," *Gazeta Wyborcza*, December 1, 2013, accessed December 2, 2013, http://m.wyborcza.pl/wyborcza/1,105226,15055961,Kwasniewski_Janukowycz_nie_docenil_poparcia_ludzi.html.
20. Ibid.
21. Piotr Kościński and Tatiana Serwetnyk, "Kwaśniewski znów na Ukrainie," *Rzeczpospolita.pl*, June 12, 2012, accessed March 19, 2013, http://www.rp.pl/artykul/11,890628-Kwasniewski-znow-na-Ukrainie.html.
22. "Unijna delegacja z Kwaśniewskim i Coxem rozpoczęła misję na Ukrainie," *EurActiv.pl*, June 12, 2012, accessed April 5, 2014, http://www.euractiv.pl/rozszerzenie/artykul/unijna-delegacja-z-kwaniewskim-i-coksem-rozpocza-misj-na-ukrainie-003697.
23. Małgorzata Nocuń, "Nie skreślajmy Ukrainy," *Nowa Europa Wschodnia*, October 23, 2012, accessed June 3, 2014, http://www.new.org.pl/1062,post.html.
24. "Kwaśniewski: Jestem przeciwnikiem bojkotu, ale Janukowycz powinien ustąpić

w sprawie Tymoszenko," *Polska The Times*, May 4, 2012, accessed September 11, 2014, http://www.polskatimes.pl/artykul/567 251,kwasniewski-jestem-przeciwnikiem-bojkotu-ale-janukowycz-powinien-usta pic-w-sprawie-tymoszenko,id,t.html.

25. "Unijna delegacja z Kwaśniewskim i Coxem rozpoczęła misję na Ukrainie," *EurActiv.pl*, June 12, 2012, accessed April 5, 2014, http://www.euractiv.pl/rozszerzenie/artykul/unijna-delegacja-z-kwaniewskim-i-coksem-rozpocza-misj-na-ukrainie-003697.

26. Marcin Wojciechowski, "Prezydent Kwaśniewski o swojej ukraińskiej misji."

27. Author's phone interview with Vadym Pozharskyi, Chicago, January 20, 2015.

28. Author's interview with Aleksander Kwaśniewski. Warsaw, December 16, 2014.

29. "Serhiy Vlasenko: I appeal to the slaves in robes: remember that you are a court," *Tymoshenko.ua*, June 24, 2011, accessed October 4, 2014, http://www.tymoshenko.ua/en/article/oe4a4z3w.

30. Author's interview with Aleksander Kwaśniewski, Warsaw, December 16, 2014.

31. *Ibid.*

32. These NGO's included the December 11 Initiative, Chesno / Civic Consortium for Election Initiatives, Opora, Committee of Voters, Amnesty International, Renaissance Foundation, and Helsinki Human Rights Union.

33. "PM Azarov meets Cox," *Ukrinform*, July 24, 2012, accessed August 5, 2014, http://www.ukrinform.ua/eng/news/pm_azarov_meets_cox_286073.

34. *Interim summary conclusions to the President of the European Parliament*, EP Monitoring Mission to Ukraine, October 4, 2012.

35. *Conference of Presidents Minutes of the Extraordinary meeting of Tuesday 2 October 2012*, European Parliament, October 2, 2012.

36. "Kwaśniewski i Cox z misją na Ukrainie do końca roku," *EurActiv.pl*, October 3, 2012, accessed March 8, 2014, http://www.euractiv.pl/rozszerzenie/artykul/misja-kwaniewskiego-i-coxa-na-ukrainie-co-najmniej-do-koca-roku-004024.

37. *Ibid.*

38. *Ibid.*

39. "Ukraine elections: how will they affect EU relations?" *European Parliament/News*, October 24, 2012, accessed April 18, 2013, http://www.europarl.europa.eu/news/en/news-room/content/20121017STO53772/html/Ukraine-elections-how-will-they-affect-EU-relations.

40. Monika Skarżyńska, "FAZ: Kwaśniewski stylizuje proces Tymoszenko na błahostkę," *Deutsche Welle*, October 27, 2012, accessed April 24, 2014, http://www.dw.de/faz-kwaśniewski-stylizuje-proces-tymoszenko-na-błahostkę/a-16337133.

41. "Kwaśniewski: Nie opóźniałem raportu ws. Tymoszenko," *Newsweek.pl*, October 29, 2012, accessed April 24, 2014, http://swiat.newsweek.pl/kwasniewski-nie-opoznialem-raportu-ws-tymoszenko,97793,1,1.html.

42. Krzysztof Grzesiowski, "Rozmowa dnia: Aleksander Kwaśniewski," *Jedynka—Polskie Radio*, January 30, 2014, accessed February 2, 2014, http://www.polskieradio.pl/7/129/Artykul/1037114. See also "Kwaśniewski: wszyscy polscy prezydenci realizowali tę samą politykę," *Wprost.pl*, October 29, 2012, accessed April 25, 2014, http://www.wprost.pl/ar/354460/Kwasniewski-wszyscy-polscy-prezydenci-realizowali-te-sama-polityke/.

43. "Kwaśniewski: Nie opóźniałem raportu ws. Tymoszenko," *Newsweek.pl*, October 29, 2012, accessed April 24, 2014, http://swiat.newsweek.pl/kwasniewski-nie-opoznialem-raportu-ws-tymoszenko,97793,1,1.html.

44. *Ibid.*

45. *Ibid.*

46. Krzysztof Grzesiowski, "Rozmowa z Aleksandrem Kwaśniewskim," *PolskieRadio.pl*, October 29, 2012, accessed April 25, 2014, http://www.polskieradio.pl/13/53/Artykul/713561,Rozmowa-z-Aleksandrem-Kwasniewskim.

47. See: "Council conclusions on Ukraine," *3209th FOREIGN AFFAIRS Council meeting*, Brussels, December 10, 2012.

48. Andrew Rettman, "EU and Ukraine trade blame over ambassador's remarks," *EUobserver*, February 29, 2012, accessed November 14, 2014, https://euobserver.com/foreign/115435.

49. "Texeira says he never had personal meeting with Yanukovych during his tenure in Ukraine," *Kyiv Post*, August 31, 2012, accessed November 14, 2014, http://www.kyivpost.com/content/politics/teixeira-

says-he-never-had-personal-meeting-with-yanukovych-during-his-tenure-in-ukraine-312360.html.
50. Author's interview with Aleksander Kwaśniewski, Warsaw, December 16, 2014.
51. *Ibid.*
52. "58. urodziny Aleksandra Kwaśniewskiego. Janukowycz: Jest pan wiernym druhem Ukrainy," *Polska The Times*, November 15, 2012, accessed July 5, 2014, http://www.polskatimes.pl/artykul/6992 47,58-urodziny-aleksandra-kwasniews kiego-janukowycz-jest-pan-wiernym-druhem-ukrainy-zdjecia,id,t.html.
53. Maciej Olchawa, *Gwiazdy i Tryzub*, 125.
54. "Kwaśniewski, Cox congratulate Azarov on his birthday and appointment as premier," *Kyiv Post*, December 19, 2012, accessed September 19, 2014, http://www.kyivpost.com/content/ukraine/kwasn iewski-cox-congratulate-azarov-on-his-birthday-and-appointment-as-premier-317844.html.
55. Тоня Туманова, "Азаров: Кокс і Кваснєвський активно підтримують процес європейської інтеграції України," *УНН – Українські Національні Новини*, December 28, 2012, accessed September 7, 2014, http://www.unn.com.ua/uk/news/ 1173681-azarov-koks-i-kvasnyevskiy-aktiv no-pidtrimuyut-protses-yevropeyskoyi-integratsiyi-ukrayini.
56. *Ibid.*
57. Krzysztof Nieczypor, "Wywiad z Jewhenią Tymoszenko," *Eastbook.eu*, December 10, 2012, accessed August 21, 2014, http://eastbook.eu/2012/12/country/ ukraine/wywiad-z-jewhenia-tymoszen ko/#.
58. "Kwaśniewski: misja PE na Ukrainie powinna być kontynuowana," *Onet.pl*, January 9, 2013, accessed June 4, 2014, http:// wiadomosci.onet.pl/swiat/kwasniewski-misja-pe-na-ukrainie-powinna-byc-kontynuowana/30t30.
59. *Ibid.*
60. "Kwaśniewski, Cox visit Ukrainian president after meeting with Tymoshenko," *Ukrinform*, February 5, 2013, accessed June 4, 2014, http://www.ukrinform.ua/eng/ne ws/kwasniewski_cox_visit_ukrainian_pre sident_after_meeting_with_tymoshenko_ 297982.
61. Maciej Olchawa, *Gwiazdy i Tryzub*, 127.

62. "Special envoy Aleksander Kwaśniewski: Ukraine's geopolitical value to Europe and the United States," *The Hill*, March 4, 2013, accessed October 3, 2014, http://thehill.com/policy/international/ 285809-special-envoy-aleksander-kwas niewski-ukraines-geopolitical-value-to-europe-and-the-united-states.
63. "Full transcript of the Atlantic Council's Third Annual Bronislaw Geremek Lecture, delivered by former President Aleksander Kwaśniewski and former National Security Advisor General Jim Jones."
64. *Ibid.*
65. *Ibid.*
66. *Ibid.*
67. *Ibid.*
68. *Ibid.*
69. "Radio Svoboda Policy Interview with Ambassador Geoffrey R. Pyatt," *Embassy of the United States—Kyiv Ukraine*, August 20, 2013, accessed October 6, 2014. http://ukraine.usembassy.gov/speeches/ amb-radio-liberty2.html.
70. "Kwaśniewski i Cox spotkali się z Julią Tymoszenko," *TVN24.pl*, February 6, 2013, accessed July 4, 2014, http://www. tvn24.pl/wiadomosci-ze-swiata,2/kwas niewski-i-cox-spotkali-sie-z-julia-tymo szenko,304593.html. See also "EP Greens leader Harms: Condition for extension of Cox-Kwaśniewski mission's mandate should be publicity of their work," *Interfax-Ukraine*, February 5, 2013, July 4, 2014, accessed http://en.interfax.com.ua/news/general/ 139140.html.
71. *Ibid.*
72. Author's interview with Aleksander Kwaśniewski, Warsaw, December 16, 2014.
73. *Ibid.*
74. Pat Cox and Aleksander Kwaśniewski, *Mission update on 18 April 2013, Strasbourg*, European Parliament Monitoring Mission to Ukraine.
75. *Ibid.*
76. "Cox–Kwaśniewski monitoring mission to Ukraine extended," *European Parliament/The President*, April 18, 2013, accessed October 1, 2014.
77. Jakub Noch, "Aleksander Kwaśniewski uwolni Julię Tymoszenko? Była premier Ukrainy wkrótce może trafić do kliniki w Niemczech," *NaTemat.pl*, accessed October 5, 2014, http://natemat.pl/63161,alek sander-kwasniewski-uwolni-julie-tymos

zenko-byla-premier-ukrainy-wkrotce-moze-trafic-do-kliniki-w-niemczech.

78. "Aleksander Kwaśniewski ma plan uwolnienia Julii Tymoszenko. Na czym on polega?" *Polska The Times*, May 30, 2013, accessed October 6, 2014, http://www.polskatimes.pl/artykul/907505,aleksander-kwasniewski-ma-plan-uwolnienia-julii-tymoszenko-na-czym-on-polega,1,id,t,sa.html.

79. *Ibid.*

80. "Tymoshenko: I will not ask for pardon under any circumstances," *Kyiv Post*, September 29, 2011, accessed October 5, 2014, http://www.kyivpost.com/content/politics/tymoshenko-i-will-not-ask-for-pardon-under-any-cir-113828.html.

81. "Tymoshenko not to ask Yanukovych for pardon, says lawyer," *Interfax-Ukraine*, October 2, 2012, accessed October 5, 2014, http://en.interfax.com.ua/news/general/120014.html.

82. "Tymoshenko family not to ask for her pardon, ex-premier's aunt says," *Interfax-Ukraine*, August 5, 2013, accessed October 5, 2014, http://en.interfax.com.ua/news/general/163173.html.

83. Author's interview with Aleksander Kwaśniewski, Warsaw, December 16, 2014.

84. Pat Cox and Aleksander Kwaśniewski, "Key observations to the Conference of Presidents of the European Parliament," *European Parliament—EP Monitoring Mission to Ukraine*, October 15, 2013.

85. "Kwaśniewski i Cox proszą o ułaskawienie Tymoszenko," *TVN24.pl*, October 4, 2013, accessed October 5, 2014, http://www.tvn24.pl/wiadomosci-ze-swiata,2/kwasniewski-i-cox-prosza-o-ulaskawienie-tymoszenko,360141.html.

86. "EU Officials In Kyiv Ask for Tymoshenko Pardon," *Radio Free Europe/Radio Liberty*, accessed October 5, 2014, http://www.rferl.org/content/ukraine-tymoshenko-eu-yanukovych/25127149.html.

87. "Kwaśniewski i Cox proszą o ułaskawienie Tymoszenko," *TVN24.pl*, October 4, 2013, accessed October 5, 2014, http://www.tvn24.pl/wiadomosci-ze-swiata,2/kwasniewski-i-cox-prosza-o-ulaskawienie-tymoszenko,360141.html.

88. Andrew Rettman, "Moment of truth for EU-Ukraine treaty," *EUobserver*, October 7, 2013, accessed October 5, 2014, https://euobserver.com/foreign/121688.

89. Pat Cox and Aleksander Kwaśniewski, "Key observations to the Conference of Presidents of the European Parliament," *European Parliament—EP Monitoring Mission to Ukraine*, October 15, 2013.

90. *Ibid.*

91. *Ibid.*

92. *Ibid.*

93. "Ukraina chwali Kwaśniewskiego: to ważny raport!" *PolskieRadio.pl*, October 15, 2013, accessed October 10, 2014, http://www.polskieradio.pl/5/3/Artykul/956436/.

94. "EU Ministers Urge Ukraine to Stop Bluffing on Tymoshenko," *Voice of America*, October 22, 2013, accessed October 7, 2014, http://www.voanews.com/content/reu-eu-ministers-urge-ukraine-to-stop-bluffing-on-tymoshenko/1774905.html.

95. "Sikorski i Bildt: koniec blefowania w rozmowach UE-Ukraine," *EurActiv.pl*, October 23, 2013, accessed October 7, 2014, http://www.euractiv.pl/rozszerzenie/artykul/sikorski-i-bildt-koniec-blefowania-w-rozmowach-ue-ukraina-005145.

96. "EU Ministers Urge Ukraine to Stop Bluffing on Tymoshenko," *Voice of America*, October 22, 2013, accessed October 7, 2014, http://www.voanews.com/content/reu-eu-ministers-urge-ukraine-to-stop-bluffing-on-tymoshenko/1774905.html.

97. Мустафа Найем, "Партія регіонів готує зрив саміту у Вільнюсі," *Українська правда*, November 8, 2013, accessed November 8, 2014, http://www.pravda.com.ua/articles/2013/11/8/7001672/.

98. *Ibid.*

99. *Ibid.*

100. Author's interview with Aleksander Kwaśniewski, Warsaw, December 16, 2014.

101. *Ibid.*

102. Pat Cox and Aleksander Kwaśniewski, "European Parliament Monitoring Mission to Ukraine—Mission Statement," *European Parliament/The President*, November 13, 2013.

103. Pat Cox and Aleksander Kwaśniewski, "European Parliament Monitoring Mission to Ukraine—Mission Statement," *European Parliament/The President*, November 13, 2013.

104. Ростислав Хотин, "Александр Кваcневський: Росія робить величезну помилку, тиснучи на горду Україну," *УНІАН*, November 14, 2013, accessed September 9, 2014, http://www.unian.ua/politics/851883-aleksandr-kvasnevskiy-rosiya-

robit-velicheznu-pomilku-tisnuchi-na-gordu-ukrajinu.html.
105. "UE czeka na decyzję Ukrainy, ale ostrzega: czas upływa; depesza," *Ministerstwo Spraw Zagranicznych RP*, November 18, 2013, accessed November 23, 2013, https://www.msz.gov.pl/pl/c/MOBILE/aktualnosci/msz_w_mediach/ue_czeka_na_decyzje_ukrainy_ale_ostrzega_czas_uplywa_.
106. "Sikorski: Polska rozczarowana decyzją Ukrainy w sprawie UE," *PolskieRadio.pl*, accessed November 23, 2013, http://www.polskieradio.pl/5/3/Artykul/984283,Sikorski-Polska-rozczarowana-decyzja-Ukrainy-w-sprawie-UE-.
107. Author's interview with Aleksander Kwaśniewski. Warsaw, December 16, 2014.
108. "У Януковича з'явилося відчуття, що йде він 'правильним шляхом,'" *Українська правда*, November 21, 2013, accessed July 17, 2014, http://www.pravda.com.ua/news/2013/11/21/7002658/.
109. Author's interview with Aleksander Kwaśniewski, Warsaw, December 16, 2014.
110. *Fakty po południu*, TVN 24, November 21, 2013.
111. *Ibid*.
112. Michał Sutowski, "Kwaśniewski: Możemy pomóc Ukraińcom raczej pod "szmatą europejską" niż flagą biało-czerwoną," *Dziennik Opinii—Krytyka Polityczna*, December 13, 2013, accessed December 16, 2013, http://www.krytykapolityczna.pl/artykuly/ukraina/20131213/kwasniewski-mozemy-pomoc-ukraincom-raczej-pod-szmata-europejska-niz-flaga.
113. "Kwaśniewski: Ukraina straciła na lata szansę zbliżenia do UE," *PolskieRadio.pl*, November 21, 2013, accessed November 23, 2013, http://www.polskieradio.pl/5/3/Artykul/983940/.
114. *Fakty po południu*, TVN 24, November 21, 2013.
115. "Kwaśniewski u Lisa: 'Rosjanie mogli mieć dokumenty, które kompromitowały Janukowycza,' 'Ratuje własną skórę,'" *TOK.FM*, February 24, 2014, accessed February 24, 2014, http://www.tokfm.pl/Tokfm/1,103085,15520926,Kwasniewski_u_Lisa_Rosjanie_mogli_miec_dokumenty_.html.
116. *Fakty po południu*, TVN 24, November 21, 2013.
117. "Yulia Tymoshenko's appeal to opposition members of parliament," *Kyiv Post*, November 22, 2013, accessed July 19, 2014, http://www.kyivpost.com/opinion/letters/yulia-tymoshenkos-appeal-to-opposition-deputies-in-the-verkhovna-rada-332300.html.
118. "ВР голосуватиме єврозакони в останній день, до цього опозиція не голосує," *Українська правда*, November 21, 2013, accessed July 19, 2014, http://www.pravda.com.ua/news/2013/11/21/7002635/.
119. Author's interview with Aleksander Kwaśniewski, Warsaw, December 16, 2014.
120. "Cox and Kwaśniewski mission: 'Deeply disappointed,'" *Kyiv Post*, November 21, 2013, accessed October 16, 2014, http://www.kyivpost.com/opinion/op-ed/cox-and-kwasniewski-mission-deeply-disappointed-332253.html.
121. *Fakty po południu*, TVN 24, November 21, 2013.
122. Jan Puhl and Christian Neef, "'Brussels Was Naïve,' Ex Polish Leader on Failed Ukraine Talks."
123. *Ibid*.
124. "Україна ніколи не була так близька до ЄС, як зараз,—Олександр Кваснєвський," Yalta European Strategy, September 21, 2013, accessed September 28, 2014, http://yes-ukraine.org/ua/news/ukrayina-nikoli-ne-bula-tak-blizka-do-yes-yak-zaraz-oleksandr-kvasnyevskiy.
125. Aleksander Kwaśniewski, *Integration of Ukraine with the EU*, European Parliament's conference, October 15, 2013.
126. *Ibid*.
127. *Ibid*.
128. Paweł Wroński, "Kwaśniewski: Janukowycz nie docenił poparci ludzi dla UE," *Gazeta Wyborcza*, December 1, 2013, accessed December 2, 2013, http://m.wyborcza.pl/wyborcza/1,105226,15055961,Kwasniewski_Janukowycz_nie_docenil_poparcia_ludzi.html.
129. Monika Olejnik, "Gość Radia ZET: Aleksander Kwaśniewski," *Radio ZET*, November 26, 2013, accessed November 27, 2013, http://www.radiozet.pl/Programy/Gosc-Radia-ZET/Blog/Gosc-Radia-ZET-Aleksander-Kwasniewski.
130. Paweł Wroński, "Kwaśniewski: Janukowycz nie docenił poparci ludzi dla UE," *Gazeta Wyborcza*, December 1, 2013, accessed December 2, 2013, http://m.wyborcza.pl/wyborcza/1,105226,15055961,Kwasniewski_Janukowycz_nie_docenil_poparcia_ludzi.html.

131. *Ibid.*
132. Michał Sutowski, "Kwaśniewski: Możemy pomóc Ukraińcom raczej pod "szmatą europejską" niż flagą biało-czerwoną," *Dziennik Opinii—Krytyka Polityczna*, December 13, 2013, accessed December 16, 2013, http://www.krytykapolityczna.pl/artykuly/ukraina/20131213/kwasniewski-mozemy-pomoc-ukraincom-raczej-pod-szmata-europejska-niz-flaga.
133. "Kwaśniewski u Lisa: 'Rosjanie mogli mieć dokumenty, które kompromitowały Janukowycza,' 'Ratuje własną skórę,'" *TOK.FM*, February 24, 2014, accessed February 24, 2014, http://www.tokfm.pl/Tokfm/1,103085,15520926,Kwasniewski_u_Lisa_Rosjanie_mogli_miec_dokumenty_.html.
134. Jan Puhl and Christian Neef, "'Brussels Was Naïve,' Ex Polish Leader on Failed Ukraine Talks."
135. Zbigniew Parafianowicz and Michał Potocki, *Wilki żyją poza prawem. Jak Janukowycz przegrał Ukrainę* (Wołowiec: Wydawnictwo Czarne, 2015), 158–159.
136. Monika Olejnik, "Opozycja nie powinna odrzucić zaproszenia do dialogu," *Kropka nad i*," TVN24.pl, December 11, 2013, accessed December 11, 2013, http://www.tvn24.pl/kropka-nad-i,3,m/opozycja-nie-powinna-odrzucic-zaproszenia-do-dialogu,378913.html.
137. Jan Puhl and Christian Neef, "'Brussels Was Naïve,' Ex Polish Leader on Failed Ukraine Talks."
138. *Ibid.*
139. "Kwaśniewski u Tomasza Lisa: Majdan to 'Solidarność' pionierskiego okresu," *Newsweek.pl*, February 24, 2014, accessed February 27, 2014, http://polska.newsweek.pl/aleksander-kwasniewski-o-ukrainie-u-tomasza-lisa-newsweek-pl,artykuly,281203,1.html.
140. "Kwaśniewski o Ukrainie: cud się nie wydarzy, szukamy planu 'B,'" *TVN24 Fakty po faktach*, November 26, 2013, accessed November 27, 2013, http://faktypofaktach.tvn24.pl/kwasniewski-o-ukrainie-cud-sie-nie-wydarzy-szukamy-planu-b,374867.html.
141. Jan Puhl and Christian Neef, "'Brussels Was Naïve,' Ex Polish Leader on Failed Ukraine Talks."
142. "Kwaśniewski: Ukraina straciła na lata szansę zbliżenia do UE," *PolskieRadio.pl*, November 21, 2013, accessed November 23, 2013, http://www.polskieradio.pl/5/3/Artykul/983940/.
143. *Fakty po południu*, TVN 24, November 21, 2013.
144. Renata Grochal, "Kwaśniewski: Eurowybory wygra PiS. Niska frekwencja sprzyja Kaczyńskiemu i radykałom," *Gazeta Wyborcza*, February 17, 2014, accessed February 20, 2014, http://wyborcza.pl/1,75478,15470060,Kwasniewski_PO_juz_nie_chroni_przed_PiS_Zaluje_.html#ixzz2tiMvkdTx.
145. Monika Olejnik, "Gość Radia ZET: Aleksander Kwaśniewski," *Radio ZET*, November 26, 2013, accessed November 27, 2013, http://www.radiozet.pl/Programy/Gosc-Radia-ZET/Blog/Gosc-Radia-ZET-Aleksander-Kwasniewski.
146. *Ibid.*
147. "Kwaśniewski o Ukrainie: cud się nie wydarzy, szukamy planu 'B,'" *TVN24 Fakty po faktach*, November 26, 2013, accessed November 27, 2013, http://faktypofaktach.tvn24.pl/kwasniewski-o-ukrainie-cud-sie-nie-wydarzy-szukamy-planu-b,374867.html.
148. *Ibid.*
149. Jędrzej Bielecki, "Tymoszenko to największy problem," *Rzeczpospolita*, September 20, 2013, accessed September 21, 2013, http://www.rp.pl/artykul/1049896-Tymoszenko-to-najwiekszy-problem.html.
150. Aleksander Kwaśniewski, *Integration of Ukraine with the EU*, European Parliament's conference, October 15, 2013.
151. Krzysztof Grzesiowski, "Rozmowa dnia: Aleksander Kwaśniewski," *Jedynka—Polskie Radio*, January 30, 2014, accessed February 2, 2014, http://www.polskieradio.pl/7/129/Artykul/1037114.
152. *Fakty po faktach*, TVN 24, February 19, 2014.
153. *Ibid.*
154. *Ibid.*
155. "Kwaśniewski u Lisa: 'Rosjanie mogli mieć dokumenty, które kompromitowały Janukowycza,' 'Ratuje własną skórę,'" *TOK.FM*, February 24, 2014, accessed February 24, 2014, http://www.tokfm.pl/Tokfm/1,103085,15520926,Kwasniewski_u_Lisa_Rosjanie_mogli_miec_dokumenty_.html.
156. Author's interview with Aleksander Kwaśniewski. Warsaw, December 16, 2014.
157. *Ibid.*
158. "Kwaśniewski o Ukrainie: cud się nie wydarzy, szukamy planu 'B,'" *TVN24*

Notes—Chapter II

Fakty po faktach, November 26, 2013, accessed November 27, 2013, http://faktypofaktach.tvn24.pl/kwasniewski-o-ukrainie-cud-sie-nie-wydarzy-szukamy-planu-b,374867.html.

159. Agnieszka Kublik, "Zaufać krwawemu Janukowyczowi? Aleksander Kwaśniewski analizuje porozumienie na Ukrainie," *Gazeta Wyborcza.pl*, February 21, 2014, accessed February 24, 2014, http://wyborcza.pl/1,75478,15507005,Zaufac_krwawemu_Janukowyczowi_Aleksander_Kwasniewski.html.

160. *Poranek Polsat News*, Polsat News, February 19, 2014.

161. "Kwaśniewski o Ukrainie: cud się nie wydarzy, szukamy planu 'B,'" *TVN24 Fakty po faktach*, November 26, 2013, accessed November 27, 2013, http://faktypofaktach.tvn24.pl/kwasniewski-o-ukrainie-cud-sie-nie-wydarzy-szukamy-planu-b,374867.html.

162. Monika Olejnik, "Gość Radia ZET: Aleksander Kwaśniewski," *Radio ZET*, November 26, 2013, accessed November 27, 2013, http://www.radiozet.pl/Programy/Gosc-Radia-ZET/Blog/Gosc-Radia-ZET-Aleksander-Kwasniewski.

163. *Kwaśniewski o Ukrainie: Możemy znaleźć się w spirali wydarzeń, która będzie nie do zahamowania*, *TVN24.pl*, January 22, 2014, accessed January 23, 2014, http://www.tvn24.pl/wiadomosci-ze-swiata,2/kwasniewski-o-ukrainie-mozemy-znalezc-sie-w-spirali-wydarzen-ktora-bedzie-nie-do-zahamowania,390248.html.

164. Jan Puhl and Christian Neef, "'Brussels Was Naïve,' Ex Polish Leader on Failed Ukraine Talks."

165. Michał Sutowski, "Kwaśniewski: Możemy pomóc Ukraińcom raczej pod 'szmatą europejską' niż flagą biało-czerwoną," *Dziennik Opinii—Krytyka Polityczna*, December 13, 2013, accessed December 16, 2013, http://www.krytykapolityczna.pl/artykuly/ukraina/20131213/kwasniewski-mozemy-pomoc-ukraincom-raczej-pod-szmata-europejska-niz-flaga.

166. "Aleksander Kwaśniewski: W Wilnie nie dojdzie do podpisania umowy z Ukrainą," *Jedynka–Polskie Radio*, November 27, 2013, accessed December 16, 2013, http://www.polskieradio.pl/7/15/Artykul/987899,Aleksander-Kwasniewski-w-Wilnie-nie-dojdzie-do-podpisania-umowy-z-Ukraina.

167. Monika Olejnik, "Gość Radia ZET: Aleksander Kwaśniewski," *Radio ZET*, November 26, 2013, accessed November 27, 2013, http://www.radiozet.pl/Programy/Gosc-Radia-ZET/Blog/Gosc-Radia-ZET-Aleksander-Kwasniewski.

168. *Ibid*.

169. Agaton Koziński, "Aleksander Kwaśniewski: Unia zrobiła za mało dla Ukrainy," *Polska The Times*, November 29, 2013, accessed November 29, 2013, http://www.polskatimes.pl/artykul/1053850,aleksander-kwasniewski-unia-zrobila-za-malo-dla-ukrainy,id,t.html?cookie=1#drukuj_dol.

170. *Ibid*.

171. Monika Olejnik, "Gość Radia ZET: Aleksander Kwaśniewski," *Radio ZET*, November 26, 2013, accessed November 27, 2013, http://www.radiozet.pl/Programy/Gosc-Radia-ZET/Blog/Gosc-Radia-ZET-Aleksander-Kwasniewski.

172. *Poranek Polsat News*, Polsat News, February 19, 2014.

173. *Ibid*.

174. Jan Puhl and Christian Neef, "'Brussels Was Naïve,' Ex Polish Leader on Failed Ukraine Talks."

175. "Wspólna deklaracja szefów MSZ Polski i Niemiec ws. Ukrainy," *Ministerstwo Spraw Zagranicznych RP*, November 26, 2013, accessed November 27, 2013, http://www.msz.gov.pl/pl/p/msz/aktualnosci/wiadomosci/wspolna_deklaracja_szefow_msz_polski_i_niemiec_ws_ukrainy.

176. "Ashton: Yanukovych Promised Solution Within 24 Hours," *Radio Free Europe/Radio Liberty*, December 11, 2013, accessed December 15, 2014, http://www.rferl.org/content/ukraine-protests-nuland-yanukovych/25197108.html.

177. Monika Olejnik, "Opozycja nie powinna odrzucić zaproszenia do dialogu," *Kropka nad i*, TVN24.pl, December 11, 2013, accessed December 11, 2013, http://www.tvn24.pl/kropka-nad-i,3,m/opozycja-nie-powinna-odrzucic-zaproszenia-do-dialogu,378913.html.

178. *Ibid*.

179. Jan Puhl and Christian Neef, "'Brussels Was Naïve,' Ex Polish Leader on Failed Ukraine Talks."

180. Monika Olejnik, "Opozycja nie powinna odrzucić zaproszenia do dialogu," *Kropka nad i*, TVN24.pl, December 11, 2013, accessed December 11, 2013, http://

Notes—Chapter II

www.tvn24.pl/kropka-nad-i,3,m/opozycja-nie-powinna-odrzucic-zaproszenia-do-dialogu,378913.html.
181. Michał Sutowski, "Kwaśniewski: Możemy pomóc Ukraińcom raczej pod "szmatą europejską" niż flagą biało-czerwoną," *Dziennik Opinii—Krytyka Polityczna*, December 13, 2013, accessed December 16, 2013, http://www.krytykapolityczna.pl/artykuly/ukraina/20131213/kwasniewski-mozemy-pomoc-ukraincom-raczej-pod-szmata-europejska-niz-flaga.
182. *Ibid.*
183. *Ibid.*
184. *Ibid.*
185. Monika Olejnik, "Opozycja nie powinna odrzucić zaproszenia do dialogu," *Kropka nad i*, TVN24.pl, December 11, 2013, accessed December 11, 2013, http://www.tvn24.pl/kropka-nad-i,3,m/opozycja-nie-powinna-odrzucic-zaproszenia-do-dialogu,378913.html.
186. Monika Olejnik, "Kwaśniewski: USA miały w Polsce bazę. O torturach nie rozmawialiśmy," *Kropka nad i*, TVN24.pl, January 30, 2014, accessed February 2, 2014, http://www.tvn24.pl/kropka-nad-i,3,m/kwasniewski-usa-mialy-w-polsce-baze-o-torturach-nie-rozmawialismy,393027.html.
187. Monika Olejnik, "Opozycja nie powinna odrzucić zaproszenia do dialogu," *Kropka nad i*, TVN24.pl, December 11, 2013, accessed December 11, 2013, http://www.tvn24.pl/kropka-nad-i,3,m/opozycja-nie-powinna-odrzucic-zaproszenia-do-dialogu,378913.html.
188. *Kwaśniewski o Ukrainie: Możemy znaleźć się w spirali wydarzeń, która będzie nie do zahamowania*, TVN24.pl, January 22, 2014, accessed January 23, 2014, http://www.tvn24.pl/wiadomosci-ze-swiata,2/kwasniewski-o-ukrainie-mozemy-znalezc-sie-w-spirali-wydarzen-ktora-bedzie-nie-do-zahamowania,390248.html.
189. *Ibid.*
190. "'Boję się odpowiadać matkom, dlaczego zginęły ich dzieci,'" *TVP Info*, January 24, 2014, accessed January 24, 2014, http://tvp.info/informacje/swiat/boje-sie-odpowiadac-matkom-dlaczego-zginely-ich-dzieci/13750343.
191. Monika Olejnik, "Kwaśniewski: USA miały w Polsce bazę. O torturach nie rozmawialiśmy," *Kropka nad i*, TVN24.pl, January 30, 2014, accessed February 2, 2014, http://www.tvn24.pl/kropka-nad-i,3,m/kwasniewski-usa-mialy-w-polsce-baze-o-torturach-nie-rozmawialismy,393027.html.
192. "To nie pułapka, tylko krok naprzód," *TVP Info*, January 28, 2014, accessed January 29, 2014, http://tvp.info/informacje/polska/to-nie-pulapka-tylko-krok-naprzod/13798335.
193. *Ibid.*
194. Jacek Pawlicki, "Trzy Ukrainy," *Newsweek Polska* 6 (2014).
195. Konrad Piasecki, "Sikorski: Władza w Kijowie mobilizuje siły. Stan wyjątkowy wciąż możliwy," *Kontrwywiad*, RMF FM, January 29, 2014, accessed February 6, 2014, http://www.rmf.pl/tylko-w-rmf24/wywiady/kontrwywiad/news-sikorski-wladza-w-kijowie-mobilizuje-sily-stan-wyjatkowy-wci,nId,1097065.
196. "Kwaśniewski u Tomasza Lisa: Majdan to 'Solidarność' pionierskiego okresu," *Newsweek.pl*, February 24, 2014, accessed February 27, 2014, http://polska.newsweek.pl/aleksander-kwasniewski-o-ukrainie-u-tomasza-lisa-newsweek-pl,artykuly,281203,1.html.
197. Monika Olejnik, "Kwaśniewski: USA miały w Polsce bazę. O torturach nie rozmawialiśmy," *Kropka nad i*, TVN24.pl, January 30, 2014, accessed February 2, 2014, http://www.tvn24.pl/kropka-nad-i,3,m/kwasniewski-usa-mialy-w-polsce-baze-o-torturach-nie-rozmawialismy,393027.html.
198. *Kwaśniewski o Ukrainie: Możemy znaleźć się w spirali wydarzeń, która będzie nie do zahamowania*, TVN24.pl, January 22, 2014, accessed January 23, 2014, http://www.tvn24.pl/wiadomosci-ze-swiata,2/kwasniewski-o-ukrainie-mozemy-znalezc-sie-w-spirali-wydarzen-ktora-bedzie-nie-do-zahamowania,390248.html.
199. Krzysztof Grzesiowski, "Rozmowa dnia: Aleksander Kwaśniewski," *Jedynka—Polskie Radio*, January 30, 2014, accessed February 2, 2014, http://www.polskieradio.pl/7/129/Artykul/1037114.
200. *Ibid.*
201. *Ibid.*
202. "Władza nie ma wyjścia. Ma krew na rękach," *TVP Info*, February 19, 2014, accessed February 19, 2014, http://tvp.info/informacje/polska/wladza-nie-ma-wyjscia-ma-krew-na-rekach/14077881.
203. Jacek Lepiarz, "Kwaśniewski: Janu-

Notes—Chapter II

kowycz nie jest gotowy do kompromisu," *Polska Agencja Prasowa*, February 18, 2014, accessed February 25, 2014, http://www.pap.pl/palio/html.run?_Instance=cms_www.pap.pl&_PageID=1&s=infopakiet&dz=swiat&idNewsComp=145255&filename=&idnews=148566&data=&status=biezace&_CheckSum=-1443104530.

204. "Ukraina na trudnej drodze do Europy. Aleksander Kwaśniewski gościem Salonu InMitte."

205. *Poranek Polsat News*, Polsat News, February 19, 2014.

206. "Władza nie ma wyjścia. Ma krew na rękach," *TVP Info*, February 19, 2014, accessed February 19, 2014, http://tvp.info/informacje/polska/wladza-nie-ma-wyjscia-ma-krew-na-rekach/14077881.

207. *Ibid*.
208. *Ibid*.
209. *Ibid*.

210. "To nie pułapka, tylko krok naprzód," *TVP Info*, January 28, 2014, accessed January 29, 2014, http://tvp.info/informacje/polska/to-nie-pulapka-tylko-krok-naprzod/13798335.

211. "Ukraina na trudnej drodze do Europy. Aleksander Kwaśniewski gościem Salonu InMitte."

212. Bartosz T. Wieliński, "Jak Rosja straciła Ukrainę," *Gazeta Wyborcza*, February 12, 2015, accessed February 12, 2015, http://wyborcza.pl/1,75248,17393699,Jak_Rosja_stracila_Ukraine.html.

213. *Fakty po faktach*, TVN 24, February 19, 2014.

214. *Ibid*.

215. *Poranek Polsat News*, Polsat News, February 19, 2014.

216. Roman Olearchyk and Neil Buckley, "Papers reveal Yanukovich plans to turn army against protesters," *Financial Times*, February 24, 2014.

217. Renata Grochal, "Janukowycz zbladł—Sikorski dla 'Gazety Wyborczej' o negocjacjach w Kijowie," *Gazeta Wyborcza*, February 21, 2014, accessed February 28, 2014, http://wyborcza.pl/1,75478,155 05910,Janukowycz_zbladl.html

218. Bartosz T. Wieliński, "Jak Rosja straciła Ukrainę," *Gazeta Wyborcza*, February 12, 2015, accessed February 12, 2015, http://wyborcza.pl/1,75248,17393699,Jak_Rosja_stracila_Ukraine.html.

219. Renata Grochal, "Janukowycz zbladł—Sikorski dla 'Gazety Wyborczej' o negocjacjach w Kijowie," *Gazeta Wyborcza*, February 21, 2014, accessed February 28, 2014, http://wyborcza.pl/1,75478,1550 5910,Janukowycz_zbladl.html

220. Agnieszka Kublik, "Zaufać krwawemu Janukowyczowi? Aleksander Kwaśniewski analizuje porozumienie na Ukrainie," *GazetaWyborcza.pl*, February 21, 2014, accessed February 24, 2014, http://wyborcza.pl/1,75478,15507005,Zaufac_krwawemu_Janukowyczowi_Aleksander_Kwasniewski.html.

221. "Kwaśniewski u Tomasza Lisa: Majdan to 'Solidarność' pionierskiego okresu," *Newsweek.pl*, February 24, 2014, accessed February 27, 2014, http://polska.newsweek.pl/aleksander-kwasniewski-o-ukrainie-u-tomasza-lisa-newsweek-pl,artykuly,28120 3,1.html.

222. "Kwaśniewski u Lisa: 'Rosjanie mogli mieć dokumenty, które kompromitowały Janukowycza,' 'Ratuje własną skórę,'" *TOK FM*, February 24, 2014, http://www.tokfm.pl/Tokfm/1,103085,15520926,Kwasniewski_u_Lisa_Rosjanie_mogli_miec_dokumenty_.html.

223. "Kwaśniewski: nowy ukraiński rząd będzie potrzebował wsparcia UE," *Polska Agencja Prasowa*, February 12, 2014, accessed February 26, 2014, http://www.pap.pl/palio/html.run?_Instance=cms_www.pap.pl&_PageID=1&s=infopakiet&dz=kraj&idNewsComp=&filename=&idnews=149931&data=&status=biezace&_CheckSum=1382051473.

224. Agnieszka Kublik, "Zaufać krwawemu Janukowyczowi? Aleksander Kwaśniewski analizuje porozumienie na Ukrainie," *GazetaWyborcza.pl*, February 21, 2014, accessed February 24, 2014, http://wyborcza.pl/1,75478,15507005,Zaufac_krwawemu_Janukowyczowi_Aleksander_Kwasniewski.html.

225. *Ibid*.
226. *Ibid*.
227. *Ibid*.

228. Jacek Lepiarz, "Kwaśniewski: Janukowycz nie jest gotowy do kompromisu," *Polska Agencja Prasowa*, February 18, 2014, accessed February 25, 2014, http://www.pap.pl/palio/html.run?_Instance=cms_www.pap.pl&_PageID=1&s=infopakiet&dz=swiat&idNewsComp=145255&filename=&idnews=148566&data=&status=biezace&_CheckSum=-1443104530.

229. Agnieszka Kublik, "Zaufać krwawe-

Notes—Chapter II

mu Janukowyczowi? Aleksander Kwaśniewski analizuje porozumienie na Ukrainie," *Gazeta Wyborcza.pl*, February 21, 2014, accessed February 24, 2014, http://wyborcza.pl/1,75478,15507005,Zaufac_krwawemu_Janukowyczowi_Aleksander_Kwasniewski.html.

230. Daisy Sindelar, "Was Yanukovych's Ouster Constitutional?" *Radio Free Europe/Radio Liberty*, February 23, 2014, accessed June 9, 2014, http://www.rferl.org/content/was-yanukovychs-ouster-constitutional/25274346.html.

231. Sergii Leshchenko and Mustafa Nayyem, "A Day and a Night of Viktor Yanukovych," *Ukrainska Pravda*, December 8, 2013, accessed November 7, 2014, http://www.pravda.com.ua/articles/2013/12/8/7005339/.

232. Sergii Leshchenko, "Yanukovych, the luxury residence and the money trail that leads to London," *Open Democracy*, June 8, 2012, accessed October 7, 2014, https://www.opendemocracy.net/od-russia/serhij-leschenko/yanukovych-luxury-residence-and-money-trail-that-leads-to-london.

233. "In pictures: Inside the palace Yanukovych didn't want Ukraine to see," *The Telegraph*, accessed October 7, 2014, http://www.telegraph.co.uk/news/worldnews/europe/ukraine/10656023/In-pictures-Inside-the-palace-Yanukovych-didnt-want-Ukraine-to-see.html?frame=2834846.

234. "Kwaśniewski u Lisa: 'Rosjanie mogli mieć dokumenty, które kompromitowały Janukowycza,' 'Ratuje własną skórę,'" *TOK. FM*, February 24, 2014, accessed February 24, 2014, http://www.tokfm.pl/Tokfm/1,103085,15520926,Kwasniewski_u_Lisa_Rosjanie_mogli_miec_dokumenty_.html.

235. Piotr Najsztub, "Za Ukrainę!" *Wprost* 16 (2013).

236. Piotr Kraśko, *Dziś Wieczorem*, TVP Info, February 27, 2014. See also Renata Grochal, "Janukowycz zbladł—Sikorski dla 'Gazety Wyborczej' o negocjacjach w Kijowie," *Gazeta Wyborcza*, February 21, 2014, accessed February 28, 2014, http://wyborcza.pl/1,75478,15505910,Janukowycz_zbladl.html and oraz Jacek Pawlicki's interview with Sikorski: "O porażkach poinformuje opozycja," *Newsweek Polska* 14 (2014).

237. Author's interview with Aleksander Kwaśniewski, Warsaw, December 16, 2014.

238. "Sikorski: Putin chciał stłumienia Majdanu," *Deutsche Welle*, January 25, 2015, accessed January 25, 2015, http://www.dw.de/sikorski-putin-chciał-stłumienia-majdanu/a-18213766.

239. "Radosław Sikorski ujawnia: Władimir Putin chciał krwawego stłumienia protestów na Majdanie," *Wirtualna Polska*, January 25, 2015, accessed January 25, 2015, http://wiadomosci.wp.pl/kat,1374,title,Radoslaw-Sikorski-ujawnia-Wladimir-Putin-chcial-krwawego-stlumienia-protestow-na-Majdanie,wid,17205231,wiadomosc.html.

240. Author's interview with Aleksander Kwaśniewski, Warsaw, December 16, 2014.

241. Ibid.

242. Ibid.

243. "Statement by Pat Cox, former president of the European Parliament and Aleksander Kwaśniewski, former president of Poland, co-chairmen of European Parliament Monitoring Mission to Ukraine," *EU Reporter*, February 24, 2014, accessed February 24, 2014, http://www.eureporter.co/frontpage/2014/02/24/statement-by-pat-cox-former-president-of-the-european-parliament-and-aleksander-kwasniewski-former-president-of-poland-co-chairmen-of-european-parliament-monitoring-mission-to-ukraine/. See also "ЄС повинен негайно підтримати Україну—Кокс і Кваснєвський," *Радіо Свобода*, February 24, 2014, accessed February 25, 2014, http://www.radiosvoboda.org/content/article/25275181.html.

244. "Kwaśniewski: nowy ukraiński rząd będzie potrzebował wsparcia UE," *Polska Agencja Prasowa*, February 12, 2014, accessed February 26, 2014, http://www.pap.pl/palio/html.run?_Instance=cms_www.pap.pl&_PageID=1&s=infopakiet&dz=kraj&idNewsComp=&filename=&idnews=149931&data=&status=biezace&_CheckSum=1382051473.

245. "Kwaśniewski: Rosja nie zgodzi się na utratę wpływów na Ukrainie," *PolskieRadio.pl*, February 25, 2014, accessed February 28, 2014, http://www.polskieradio.pl/5/3/Artykul/1061399,Kwasniewski-Rosja-nie-zgodzi-sie-na-utrate-wplywow-na-Ukrainie.

246. Ibid.

247. "Kwaśniewski u Tomasza Lisa: Majdan to 'Solidarność' pionierskiego okresu," *Newsweek.pl*, February 24, 2014, accessed

Notes—Chapter II

February 27, 2014, http://polska.newsweek.pl/aleksander-kwasniewski-o-ukrainie-u-tomasza-lisa-newsweek-pl,artykuly,281203,1.html.

248. Krzysztof Grzesiowski, "Rozmowa dnia: Aleksander Kwaśniewski," *Jedynka—Polskie Radio*, January 30, 2014, accessed February 2, 2014, http://www.polskieradio.pl/7/129/Artykul/1037114.

249. Piotr Najsztub, "Za Ukrainę!" *Wprost* 16 (2013).

250. *Ibid*.

251. "Ukraina na trudnej drodze do Europy. Aleksander Kwaśniewski gościem Salonu InMitte."

252. See Petro Poroszenko's profile in *Forbes*: http://www.forbes.com/profile/petro-poroshenko/.

253. Sarah A. Topol, "The Chocolate King Who Would Be President," *Politico*, May 22, 2014, accessed July 11, 2014, http://www.politico.com/magazine/story/2014/05/the-chocolate-king-who-would-be-president-106998.html#.VNy_jlpN3zI.

254. Daisy Sindelar, *"Moscow's Latest War On Good Taste: No To Ukrainian Chocolate,"* Radio Free Europe/Radio Liberty, July 30, 2013, accessed July 11, 2014, http://www.rferl.org/content/russia-ukrainian-chocolate-ban/25060451.html.

255. "Kwaśniewski: nowy ukraiński rząd będzie potrzebował wsparcia UE," *Polska Agencja Prasowa*, February 12, 2014, accessed February 26, 2014, http://www.pap.pl/palio/html.run?_Instance=cms_www.pap.pl&_PageID=1&s=infopakiet&dz=kraj&idNewsComp=&filename=&idnews=149931&data=&status=biezace&_CheckSum=1382051473.

256. *Ibid*.

257. "Kwaśniewski: nowy ukraiński rząd będzie potrzebował wsparcia UE," *Polska Agencja Prasowa*, February 12, 2014, accessed February 26, 2014, http://www.pap.pl/palio/html.run?_Instance=cms_www.pap.pl&_PageID=1&s=infopakiet&dz=kraj&idNewsComp=&filename=&idnews=149931&data=&status=biezace&_CheckSum=1382051473.

258. Krzysztof Grzesiowski, "Rozmowa dnia: Aleksander Kwaśniewski," *Jedynka—Polskie Radio*, January 30, 2014, accessed February 2, 2014, http://www.polskieradio.pl/7/129/Artykul/1037114.

259. Renata Grochal, "Kwaśniewski: Nie pojechałbym dziś do Moskwy," *Wyborcza.pl*,

May 13, 2014, accessed July 7, 2014, http://wyborcza.pl/politykaekstra/1,137934,15955837,Kwasniewski_Nie_pojechalbym_dzis_do_Moskwy.html.

260. Monika Olejnik, "Gość Radia ZET: Aleksander Kwaśniewski," *Radio ZET*, November 26, 2013, accessed November 27, 2913, http://www.radiozet.pl/Programy/Gosc-Radia-ZET/Blog/Gosc-Radia-ZET-Aleksander-Kwasniewski.

261. Author's interview with Aleksander Kwaśniewski, Warsaw, December 16, 2014.

262. *Ibid*.

263. Jan Puhl and Christian Neef, "'Brussels Was Naïve,' Ex Polish Leader on Failed Ukraine Talks."

264. Renata Grochal, "Kwaśniewski: Eurowybory wygra PiS. Niska frekwencja sprzyja Kaczyńskiemu i radykałom," *Gazeta Wyborcza*, February 17, 2014, accessed February 20, 2014, http://wyborcza.pl/1,75478,15470060,Kwasniewski_PO_juz_nie_chroni_przed_PiS_Zaluje_.html#ixzz2tiMvkdTx.

265. "Aleksander Kwaśniewski: W Wilnie nie dojdzie do podpisania umowy z Ukrainą," *Jedynka–Polskie Radio*, November 27, 2013, accessed December 16, 2013, http://www.polskieradio.pl/7/15/Artykul/987899,Aleksander-Kwasniewski-w-Wilnie-nie-dojdzie-do-podpisania-umowy-z-Ukraina.

266. Aleksander Kwaśniewski, *Integration of Ukraine with the EU*, European Parliament's conference, October 15, 2013.

267. Jan Puhl and Christian Neef, "'Brussels Was Naïve,' Ex Polish Leader on Failed Ukraine Talks."

268. Author's interview with Aleksander Kwaśniewski, Warsaw, December 16, 2014.

269. "Kwaśniewski o Ukrainie: cud się nie wydarzy, szukamy planu 'B,'" *TVN24 Fakty po faktach*, November 26, 2013, accessed November 27, 2013, http://faktypofaktach.tvn24.pl/kwasniewski-o-ukrainie-cud-sie-nie-wydarzy-szukamy-planu-b,374867.html.

270. Jan Puhl and Christian Neef, "'Brussels Was Naïve,' Ex Polish Leader on Failed Ukraine Talks."

271. Author's interview with Aleksander Kwaśniewski, Warsaw, December 16, 2014.

272. *Ibid*.

273. *Ibid*.

274. "Ukraine: EPP Group wants Cox/Kwaśniewski mission to now focus on free-

ing Tymoshenko," *EPP Group in the European Parliament*, October 15, 2013, accessed September 3, 2014, http://www.epp group.eu/press-release/Cox/Kwasniewski-mission-must-focus-on-freeing-Tymo shenko.

275. Author's interview with Aleksander Kwaśniewski. Warsaw, December 16, 2014.

276. Monika Olejnik, "Gość Radia ZET: Aleksander Kwaśniewski," *Radio ZET*, November 26, 2013, accessed November 27, 2013, http://www.radiozet.pl/Programy/Gosc-Radia-ZET/Blog/Gosc-Radia-ZET-Aleksander-Kwasniewski.

277. Krzysztof Grzesiowski, "Rozmowa dnia: Aleksander Kwaśniewski," *Jedynka—Polskie Radio*, January 30, 2014, accessed February 2, 2014, http://www.polskieradio.pl/7/129/Artykul/1037114.

278. Małgorzata Nocuń, "Jak żyje więzień Tymoszenko," *Wprost* 20 (2012).

279. "Yulia Tymoshenko: Darwinism can't transform a jackal into a lion," Tymoshenko.com, October 19, 2012, accessed October 10, 2013, http://www.tymoshenko.ua/en/article/yulia_tymoshenko_19_10_2012_03.

280. Author's interview with Aleksander Kwaśniewski. Warsaw, December 16, 2014.

281. *Ibid.*

282. *Ibid.*

283. *Ibid.*

284. "Condoleeza Rice sends letter of support to Tymoshenko," *Kyiv Post*, October 4, 2012, accessed January 10, 2015, http://www.kyivpost.com/content/politics/condoleezza-rice-sends-letter-of-support-to-tymoshenko-313876.html.

285. Author's interview with Aleksander Kwaśniewski. Warsaw, December 16, 2014.

286. *Ibid.*

287. *Ibid.*

288. "Tymoszenko zleciła morderstwo? 'Mam dowody,'" *Polskie Radio*, April 4, 2012, accessed December 20, 2014, http://www.polskieradio.pl/5/3/Artykul/579899,Tymoszenko-zlecila-morderstwo-Mam-dowody/?utm_source=box&utm_medium=link&utm_campaign=related.

289. Author's interview with Aleksander Kwaśniewski, Warsaw, December 16, 2014.

290. *Ibid.*

291. "Kwaśniewski: nowy ukraiński rząd będzie potrzebował wsparcia UE," *Polska Agencja Prasowa*, February 12, 2014, accessed February 26, 2014, http://www.pap. pl/palio/html.run?_Instance=cms_www. pap.pl&_PageID=1&s=infopakiet&dz= kraj&idNewsComp=&filename=&idnews= 149931&data=&status=biezace&_Check Sum=1382051473.

292. "Kwaśniewski u Lisa: 'Rosjanie mogli mieć dokumenty, które kompromitowały Janukowycza,' 'Ratuje własną skórę,'" *TOK. FM*, February 24, 2014, accessed February 24, 2014, http://www.tokfm.pl/Tokfm/1,10 3085,15520926,Kwasniewski_u_Lisa_Rosjanie_mogli_miec_dokumenty_.html.

293. Author's interview with Aleksander Kwaśniewski. Warsaw, December 16, 2014.

294. Krzysztof Grzesiowski, "Rozmowa dnia: Aleksander Kwaśniewski," *Jedynka—Polskie Radio*, January 30, 2014, accessed February 2, 2014, http://www.polskieradio.pl/7/129/Artykul/1037114.

295. *Ibid.*

296. "Місія Кокса-Квасневського нарешті завершилась успіхом," *5 канал*, June 7, 2014, accessed September 8, 2014, http://www.5.ua/ukrajina/suspilstvo/item/385842-misiia-koksa-kvasnevskoho-nareshti-zavershylas-uspikhom.

297. Martin Schulz, "Speech at the Yalta European Strategy—YES conference," *European Parliament/The President*, September 12, 2014, September 20, 2014, http://www.europarl.europa.eu/the-president/en/press/press_release_speeches/speeches/speeches-2014/speeches-2014-september/html/speech-at-the-yalta-european-strategy-yes-conference.

Chapter III

1. Monika Olejnik, "Kwaśniewski: USA miały w Polsce bazę. O torturach nie rozmawialiśmy," *Kropka nad i*, TVN24.pl, January 30, 2014, accessed February 2, 2014, http://www.tvn24.pl/kropka-nad-i,3,m/kwasniewski-usa-mialy-w-polsce-baze-o-torturach-nie-rozmawialismy,39 3027.html.

2. *Ibid.*

3. Monika Olejnik, "Gość Radia ZET: Aleksander Kwaśniewski," *Radio ZET*, November 26, 2013, accessed November 27, 2013, http://www.radiozet.pl/Programy/Gosc-Radia-ZET/Blog/Gosc-Radia-ZET-Aleksander-Kwasniewski.

4. "Kwaśniewski u Tomasza Lisa: Majdan to 'Solidarność' pionierskiego okresu,"

Notes—Chapter III

Newsweek.pl, February 24, 2014, accessed February 27, 2014, http://polska.newsweek.pl/aleksander-kwasniewski-o-ukrainie-u-tomasza-lisa-newsweek-pl,artykuly,281203,1.html.

5. Renata Grochal, "Kwaśniewski: Tusk jako prezydent Unii nie ucieknie od problemu Ukrainy," *Wyborcza.pl*, October 30, 2014, accessed November 10, 2014, http://wyborcza.pl/1,76842,16886925,Kwasniewski_Tusk_jako_prezydent_Unii_nie_ucieknie.html.

6. Michał Sutowski, "Kwaśniewski: Możemy pomóc Ukraińcom raczej pod "szmatą europejską" niż flagą biało-czerwoną," *Dziennik Opinii—Krytyka Polityczna*, December 13, 2013, accessed December 16, 2013, http://www.krytykapolitycz na.pl/artykuly/ukraina/20131213/kwasniewski-mozemy-pomoc-ukraincom-raczej-pod-szmata-europejska-niz-flaga.

7. *Ibid.*

8. Monika Olejnik, "Gość Radia ZET: Aleksander Kwaśniewski," *Radio ZET*, November 26, 2013, accessed November 27, 2013, http://www.radiozet.pl/Programy/Gosc-Radia-ZET/Blog/Gosc-Radia-ZET-Aleksander-Kwasniewski.

9. *Ibid.*

10. Michał Sutowski, "Kwaśniewski: Mozemy pomóc Ukraincom raczej pod "szmatą europejską" niż flagą biało-czerwoną," *Dziennik Opinii—Krytyka Polityczna*, December 13, 2013, accessed December 16, 2013, http://www.krytykapolitycz na.pl/artykuly/ukraina/20131213/kwasniewski-mozemy-pomoc-ukraincom-raczej-pod-szmata-europejska-niz-flaga.

11. *Ibid.*

12. Monika Olejnik, "Gość Radia ZET: Aleksander Kwaśniewski," *Radio ZET*, November 26, 2013, accessed November 27, 2013, http://www.radiozet.pl/Programy/Gosc-Radia-ZET/Blog/Gosc-Radia-ZET-Aleksander-Kwasniewski.

13. Monika Olejnik, "Kwaśniewski: USA miały w Polsce bazę. O torturach nie rozmawialiśmy," *Kropka nad i*, TVN24.pl, January 30, 2014, accessed February 2, 2014, http://www.tvn24.pl/kropka-nad-i,3,m/kwasniewski-usa-mialy-w-polsce-baze-o-torturach-nie-rozmawialismy,393027.html.

14. Michał Sutowski, "Kwaśniewski: Możemy pomóc Ukraińcom raczej pod "szmatą europejską" niż flagą biało-czerwoną," *Dziennik Opinii—Krytyka Polity-czna*, December 13, 2013, accessed December 16, 2013, http://www.krytykapolitycz na.pl/artykuly/ukraina/20131213/kwasniewski-mozemy-pomoc-ukraincom-raczej-pod-szmata-europejska-niz-flaga.

15. "Kwaśniewski: Rosja nie zgodzi się na utratę wpływów na Ukrainie," *Polskie Radio.pl*, February 25, 2014, accessed February 28, 2014, http://www.polskieradio.pl/5/3/Artykul/1061399,Kwasniewski-Rosja-nie-zgodzi-sie-na-utrate-wplywow-na-Ukrainie.

16. The treaty was signed by Algirdas Brazauskas and Lech Wałęsa on April 26, 1994.

17. Aleksandra Akińczo, "Kwaśniewski: przełom w stosunkach polsko-litewskich możliwy po wyborach," *GazetaWyborcza.pl*, February 27, 2014, accessed February 28, 2014, http://wyborcza.pl/1,91446,15537190,Kwasniewski_przelom_w_stosun kach_polsko_litewskich.html.

18. Kathy Lally, Will Englund and William Booth, "Russian parliament approves use of troops in Ukraine," *Washington Post*, March 1, 2014, accessed March 2, 2014, http://www.washingtonpost.com/world/europe/russian-parliament-approves-use-of-troops-in-crimea/2014/03/01/d1775f70-a151-11e3-a050-dc3322a94fa7_story.html.

19. Renata Grochal, "Kwaśniewski: To powrót do Związku Radzieckiego," *Gazeta Wyborcza*, March 1, 2014, accessed March 2, 2014, http://wyborcza.pl/1,134642,15549604,Kwasniewski_To_powrot_do_Zwia zku_Radzieckiego.html?google_editors_picks=true#ixzz2wswiHBLX.

20. *Ibid.*

21. *Ibid.*

22. Agaton Koziński, "Kwaśniewski: NATO dobrze reaguje na ukraiński kryzys. Ale musi być gotowe na czarne scenariusze," *Polska The Times*, March 10, 2014, accessed March 18, 2014, http://www.polskatimes.pl/artykul/3360081,kwasniewski-nato-dobrze-reaguje-na-ukrainski-kryzys-ale-musi-byc-gotowe-na-czarne-scena riusze,2,id,t,sa.html.

23. Renata Grochal, "Kwaśniewski: To powrót do Związku Radzieckiego," *Gazeta Wyborcza*, March 1, 2014, accessed March 2, 2014, http://wyborcza.pl/1,134642,15549604,Kwasniewski_To_powrot_do_Zwia zku_Radzieckiego.html?google_editors_picks=true#ixzz2wswiHBLX.

24. *Ibid.*

Notes—Chapter III

25. Adam Taylor, "A brief rundown of Vladimir Putin's strange, rambling press conference," *Washington Post*, March 4, 2014, accessed March 5, 2014, http://www.washingtonpost.com/blogs/worldviews/wp/2014/03/04/a-brief-rundown-of-vladimir-putins-strange-rambling-press-conference/.

26. Monika Olejnik, "Kwaśniewski: Trzecia wojna światowa nam nie grozi. Ciężkie czasy—tak," *Kropka nad i*, TVN 24, March 4, 2014, accessed March 6, 2014, http://www.tvn24.pl/kropka-nad-i,3,m/kwasniewski-trzecia-wojna-swiatowa-nam-nie-grozi-ciezkie-czasy-tak,404463.html.

27. "Putin: Rosja była słaba i ją ograbiono," *Gazeta Wyborcza*, March 21, 2014, accessed April 4, 2014, http://wyborcza.pl/magazyn/1,136823,15666360,Putin_Rosja_byla_slaba_i_ja_ograbiono.html.

28. Putin failed to add that 54% of voters in that referendum chose to be part of Ukraine. See Glenn Kessler, "Fact Checking Vladimir Putin's speech on Crimea (video)," *Washington Post*, March 19, 2014, accessed October 10, 2014, http://www.washingtonpost.com/blogs/fact-checker/wp/2014/03/19/fact-checking-vladimir-putins-speech-on-crimea/.

29. "Putin: Rosja była słaba i ją ograbiono," *Gazeta Wyborcza*, March 21, 2014, accessed April 4, 2014, http://wyborcza.pl/magazyn/1,136823,15666360,Putin_Rosja_byla_slaba_i_ja_ograbiono.html.

30. "Kwaśniewski: Krym nie spełni wszystkich marzeń Putina. On chce odbudować supermocarstow i potrzebuje całej Ukrainy," *Gazeta Wyborcza*, March 18, 2014, accessed February 21, 2014, http://wyborcza.pl/1,75478,15645547,Kwasniewski_Krym_nie_spelni_wszystkich_marzen_Putina_.html.

31. *Ibid.*
32. *Ibid.*
33. *Ibid.*

34. Sherman Garnett, "U.S.–Ukraine Relations," *Harvard Ukrainian Studies* 20 (1998): 113. See Maciej Olchawa, *Imperialna Rozgrywka*, 77.

35. See Maciej Olchawa, *Imperialna Rozgrywka*, 78.

36. Agaton Koziński, "Kwaśniewski: NATO dobrze reaguje na ukraiński kryzys. Ale musi być gotowe na czarne scenariusze," *Polska The Times*, March 10, 2014, accessed March 18, 2014, http://www.polskatimes.pl/artykul/3360081,kwasniewski-nato-dobrze-reaguje-na-ukrainski-kryzys-ale-musi-byc-gotowe-na-czarne-scenariusze,2,id,t,sa.html.

37. Sherman W. Garnett, "Ukraine's Decision to Join the NPT," *Arms Control NOW: The blog of the Arms Control Association*, accessed April 4, 2016, https://armscontrolnow.org/2014/03/08/ukraine-russia-and-the-npt/.

38. "Putin: Rosja była słaba i ją ograbiono," *Gazeta Wyborcza*, March 21, 2014, accessed April 4, 2014, http://wyborcza.pl/magazyn/1,136823,15666360,Putin_Rosja_byla_slaba_i_ja_ograbiono.html.

39. "Kwaśniewski: Krym nie spełni wszystkich marzeń Putina. On chce odbudować supermocarstow i potrzebuje całej Ukrainy," *Gazeta Wyborcza*, March 18, 2014, accessed February 21, 2014, http://wyborcza.pl/1,75478,15645547,Kwasniewski_Krym_nie_spelni_wszystkich_marzen_Putina_.html.

40. *Poranek Polsat News*, Polsat News, February 19, 2014.

41. Monika Olejnik, "Kwaśniewski: Trzecia wojna światowa nam nie grozi. Ciężkie czasy—tak," *Kropka nad i*, TVN 24, March 4, 2014, accessed March 6, 2014, http://www.tvn24.pl/kropka-nad-i,3,m/kwasniewski-trzecia-wojna-swiatowa-nam-nie-grozi-ciezkie-czasy-tak,404463.html.

42. Josh Rogin and Eli Lake, "Kerry: U.S. Taped Moscow's Calls to Its Ukraine Spies," *The Daily Beast*, April 29, 2014, accessed September 7, 2014, http://www.thedailybeast.com/articles/2014/04/29/kerry-u-s-taped-moscow-s-calls-to-its-ukraine-spies.html.

43. "Ukraina na trudnej drodze do Europy. Aleksander Kwaśniewski gościem Salonu InMitte."

44. Małgorzata Nocuń, "Nie skreślajmy Ukrainy," *Nowa Europa Wschodnia*, October 23, 2012, accessed June 3, 2014, http://www.new.org.pl/1062,post.html.

45. Renata Grochal, "Kwaśniewski: Tusk jako prezydent Unii nie ucieknie od problemu Ukrainy," *Wyborcza.pl*, October 30, 2014, accessed November 10, 2014, http://wyborcza.pl/1,76842,16886925,Kwasniewski_Tusk_jako_prezydent_Unii_nie_ucieknie.html.

46. Agaton Koziński, "Kwaśniewski: NATO dobrze reaguje na ukraiński kryzys. Ale musi być gotowe na czarne scenar-

Notes—Chapter IV

iusze," *Polska The Times*, March 10, 2014, accessed March 18, 2014, http://www.polskatimes.pl/artykul/3360081,kwasniewski-nato-dobrze-reaguje-na-ukrainski-kryzys-ale-musi-byc-gotowe-na-czarne-scenariusze,2,id,t,sa.html.

47. Author's interview with Aleksander Kwaśniewski. Warsaw, December 16, 2014.

Chapter IV

1. "Putin: Crimea similar to Kosovo, West is rewriting its own rule book," Russia Today, March 18, 2014, accessed November 20, 2014, https://www.rt.com/news/putin-address-parliament-crimea-562/.

2. John Lewis Gaddis, *The Cold War: A New History* (New York: Penguin Press, 2005), 247–248.

3. "Kuchma News Conference Discusses Current Issues: Kiev Radio Ukraine World Service, 29 May 1995 [FBIS Translation], Excerpts," in *Russia and the Commonwealth of Independent States: Documents, Data, and Analysis*, ed. Zbigniew Brzeziński and Paige Sullivan (New York: M.E. Sharpe, 1997), 281.

4. "Brzezinski Suggests Finland as Model for Ukraine (Transcript)," *Bloomberg*, April 11, 2014, accessed November 20, 2014, http://www.bloomberg.com/news/2014-04-11/brzezinski-suggests-finland-as-model-for-ukraine-transcript-.html.

5. Zbigniew Brzeziński, "What Obama Should Tell Americans About Ukraine," *Politico Magazine*, May 2, 2014. See also Zbigniew Brzeziński, "Russia needs to be offered a 'Finland option' for Ukraine," *Financial Times*, February 22, 2014.

6. Zbigniew Brzeziński, "Putin's three choices on Ukraine," *Washington Post*, July 8, 2014.

7. Богдана Костюк, "Фінляндизація» системи європейської безпеки: чи знайдеться місце Україні?" *Радіо Свобода*, May 15, 2010, accessed April 22, 2014, http://www.radiosvoboda.org/content/article/2072734.html.

8. James Kirchick, "Finlandization Is Not a Solution for Ukraine," *The American Interest*, July 27, 2014, accessed July 28, 2014, http://www.the-american-interest.com/2014/07/27/finlandization-is-not-a-solution-for-ukraine/.

9. Ibid.

10. Mark P. Lagon and Will Moreland, "'Finlandization' Abandons Ukraine," *Foreign Policy*, November 3, 2014, accessed November 10, 2014, http://shadow.foreignpolicy.com/posts/2014/11/03/finlandization_abandons_ukraine.

11. Francisco de Borja Lasheras, "Sobre la finlandización de Ucrania," *El Mundo*, November 2, 2014, accessed November 7, 2014, http://www.elmundo.es/internacional/2014/11/02/5455227be2704e81368b457b.html.

12. Kathleen Miles, "Former NATO Commander Wesley Clark Urges U.S. Backing for Ukrainians," *The Huffington Post*, April 28, 2014, accessed November 20, 2014, http://www.huffingtonpost.com/2014/04/28/wesley-clark-ukraine_n_5228187.html.

13. "Brzezinski Suggests Finland as Model for Ukraine (Transcript)," *Bloomberg*, April 11, 2014, accessed November 20, 2014, http://www.bloomberg.com/news/2014-04-11/brzezinski-suggests-finland-as-model-for-ukraine-transcript-.html.

14. Nathan Gardels, "NATO Should Stop Putin From Restoring Czarist Empire, Zbigniew Brzezinski Says," *The WorldPost*, March 9, 2014, http://www.huffingtonpost.com/2014/09/03/zbigniew-brzezinski-nato-putin-ukraine_n_5760068.html.

15. Renata Grochal, "Kwaśniewski: Zazdroszczę Tuskowi," *Wyborcza.pl*, September 9, 2014, accessed September 9, 2014, http://wyborcza.pl/politykaekstra/1,140681,16614668,Kwasniewski_Zazdroszcze_Tuskowi.html#TRrelSST.

16. Author's interview with Aleksander Kwaśniewski, Warsaw, December 16, 2014.

17. Ibid.

18. Agaton Koziński, "Kwaśniewski: NATO dobrze reaguje na ukraiński kryzys. Ale musi być gotowe na czarne scenariusze," *Polska The Times*, March 10, 2014, accessed March 18, 2014, http://www.polskatimes.pl/artykul/3360081,kwasniewski-nato-dobrze-reaguje-na-ukrainski-kryzys-ale-musi-byc-gotowe-na-czarne-scenariusze,2,id,t,sa.html.

19. "Kwaśniewski u Tomasza Lisa: Majdan to 'Solidarność' pionierskiego okresu," *Newsweek.pl*, February 24, 2014, accessed February 27, 2014, http://polska.newsweek.pl/aleksander-kwasniewski-o-ukrainie-u-tomasza-lisa-newsweek-pl,artykuly,281203,1.html.

Notes—Chapter IV

20. Paulina Nowosielska, "Kwaśniewski: Ukraina w NATO to gwarancja naszego bezpieczeństwa," *Polska The Times*, August 20, 2008, accessed October 15, 2014, http://www.polskatimes.pl/artykul/37201,kwasniewski-ukraina-w-nato-to-gwarancja-naszego-bezpieczenstwa,1,id,t,sa.html.

21. *Wygraliśmy przyszłość: przemówienia, wywiady, dokumenty (wybór)*, *10 lat prezydentury Aleksandra Kwaśniewskiego* (Warsaw: Amicus Europea, 2008), 410.

22. *Ibid.*, 413.

23. "Putin: Rosja była słaba i ją ograbiono," *Gazeta Wyborcza*, March 21, 2014, accessed April 4, 2014, http://wyborcza.pl/magazyn/1,136823,15666360,Putin_Rosja_byla_slaba_i_ja_ograbiono.html.

24. *Ibid.*

25. "Putin's Prepared Remarks at 43rd Munich Conference on Security Policy," *Washington Post*, February 12, 2007, accessed June 6, 2014, http://www.washingtonpost.com/wp-dyn/content/article/2007/02/12/AR2007021200555.html.

26. "Putin: Rosja była słaba i ją ograbiono," *Gazeta Wyborcza*, March 21, 2014, accessed April 4, 2014, http://wyborcza.pl/magazyn/1,136823,15666360,Putin_Rosja_byla_slaba_i_ja_ograbiono.html.

27. Catherine A. Fitzpatrick, "Gorbachev Confirms There Was No NATO 'Non-Expansion' Pledge," *The Interpreter*, October 18, 2014, accessed October 20, 2014, http://www.interpretermag.com/russia-this-week-hundreds-of-russians-poisoned-25-dead-in-spice-drug-epidemic/.

28. *Ibid.*

29. Steven Pifer, "Did NATO Promise Not to Enlarge? Gorbachev Says 'No,'" *The Brookings Institution*, November 6, 2014, accessed November 7, 2014, http://www.brookings.edu/blogs/up-front/posts/2014/11/06-nato-no-promise-enlarge-gorbachev-pifer.

30. Juliane von Mittelstaedt and Erich Follath, "Interview with Henry Kissinger: 'Do We Achieve World Order Through Chaos or Insight?'" *SPIEGEL ONLINE*, November 13, 2014, accessed November 18, 2014, http://www.spiegel.de/international/world/interview-with-henry-kissinger-on-state-of-global-politics-a-1002073-2.html.

31. *Wygraliśmy przyszłość: przemówienia, wywiady, dokumenty (wybór)*, *10 lat prezydentury Aleksandra Kwaśniewskiego* (Warsaw: Amicus Europea, 2008), 389–390.

32. Ronald D. Asmus, *A Little War That Shook the World* (New York: Palgrave Macmillan, 2010), 112.

33. *Ibid.*, 139.

34. "Special envoy Aleksander Kwaśniewski: Ukraine's geopolitical value to Europe and the United States," *The Hill*, March 4, 2013, accessed October 3, 2014, http://thehill.com/policy/international/285809-special-envoy-aleksander-kwasniewski-ukraines-geopolitical-value-to-europe-and-the-united-states.

35. *Ibid.*

36. Agaton Koziński, "Kwaśniewski: NATO dobrze reaguje na ukraiński kryzys. Ale musi być gotowe na czarne scenariusze," *Polska The Times*, March 10, 2014, accessed March 18, 2014, http://www.polskatimes.pl/artykul/3360081,kwasniewski-nato-dobrze-reaguje-na-ukrainski-kryzys-ale-musi-byc-gotowe-na-czarne-scenariusze,2,id,t,sa.html.

37. *Ibid.*

38. *Ibid.*

39. Author's interview with Aleksander Kwaśniewski, Warsaw, December 16, 2014.

40. *Ibid.*

41. *Ibid.*

42. Renata Grochal, "Kwaśniewski: To powrót do Związku Radzieckiego," *Gazeta Wyborcza*, March 1, 2014, accessed March 2, 2014, http://wyborcza.pl/1,134642,15549604,Kwasniewski_To_powrot_do_Zwiazku_Radzieckiego.html?google_editors_picks=true#ixzz2wswiHBLX.

43. "Obama warns Russia not to invade Ukraine," *Washington Post—post tv*, February 28, 2014, accessed February 29, 2014, http://www.washingtonpost.com/posttv/politics/obama-there-will-be-costs-if-russia-invades-ukraine/2014/02/28/3ea663c6-a0c5-11e3-878c-65222df220eb_video.html. See also: William Booth and Karen DeYoung, "Reports of Russian military activity in Crimea prompts stern warning from Obama," *Washington Post*, February 28, 2014, accessed February 29, 2014, http://www.washingtonpost.com/world/ukraine-calls-russian-troops-invasion/2014/02/28/e066bfc8-a0be-11e3-878c-65222df220eb_story.html.

44. Peter Baker and Rick Lymanjune, "With Ukraine Still Unsettled, Obama Sets Off to Soothe European Friends," *New York Times*, June 1, 2014, accessed June 1, 2014, http://www.nytimes.com/2014/06/02/

world/europe/with-ukraine-crisis-cooling-obama-sets-off-to-soothe-european-friends.html?_r=0.

45. Agnieszka Kublik, "Zaufać krwawemu Janukowyczowi? Aleksander Kwaśniewski analizuje porozumienie na Ukrainie," *Gazeta Wyborcza.pl*, February 21, 2014, accessed February 24, 2014, http://wyborcza.pl/1,75478,15507005,Zaufac_krwawemu_Janukowyczowi_Aleksander_Kwasniewski.html.

Epilogue

1. Aleksander Kwaśniewski, *Integration of Ukraine with the EU*, European Parliament's conference, October 15, 2013.
2. "Ukraina na trudnej drodze do Europy. Aleksander Kwaśniewski gościem Salonu InMitte."
3. Aleksander Kwaśniewski, *Integration of Ukraine with the EU*, European Parliament's conference, October 15, 2013.
4. Małgorzata Nocuń, "Nie skreślajmy Ukrainy," *Nowa Europa Wschodnia*, October 23, 2012, accessed June 3, 2014, http://www.new.org.pl/1062,post.html.
5. Author's interview with Aleksander Kwaśniewski. Warsaw, December 16, 2014.
6. Ibid.
7. Ibid.
8. Ibid.
9. Michał Kacewicz and Michał Krzymowski, "Aleksander Kwaśniewski: Inna liga."
10. Max Seddon, "Biden's Son, Polish Ex-President Quietly Sign On To Ukrainian Gas Company," *Buzzfeed*, May 14, 2014, accessed October 10, 2014, http://www.buzzfeed.com/maxseddon/bidens-son-polish-ex-president-quietly-sign-on-to-ukrainian#.mjrm8RYYM.
11. Michael Scherer, "Ukrainian Employer of Joe Biden's Son Hires a D.C. Lobbyist," *Time*, July 7, 2014, accessed October 10, 2014, http://time.com/2964493/ukraine-joe-biden-son-hunter-burisma/.
12. Max Seddon, "Biden's Son, Polish Ex-President Quietly Sign On To Ukrainian Gas Company."

13. "Statement of the Office of Aleksander Kwaśniewski," May 14, 2014.
14. Bogdan Rymanowski, *Jeden na jeden*, TVN24.pl, May 16, 2014, accessed October 10, 2014, http://www.tvn24.pl/jeden-na-jeden,44,m/kwasniewski-nie-zamierzam-wycofac-sie-z-zarzadu-ukrainskiej-spolki,428900.html.
15. "Statement of the Office of Aleksander Kwaśniewski," May 14, 2014.
16. Joanna Miziołek, "Aleksander Kwaśniewski: Robię coś niewłaściwego, A Poroszenko był w rządzie Azarowa..." *Polska The Times*, May 16, 2014, accessed June 6, 2014, http://www.polskatimes.pl/artykul/3437651,aleksander-kwasniewski-robie-cos-niewlasciwego-a-poroszenko-byl-w-rzadzie-azarowa,1,id,t,sa.html.
17. Bogdan Rymanowski, *Jeden na jeden*, TVN24.pl, May 16, 2014, accessed October 10, 2014, http://www.tvn24.pl/jeden-na-jeden,44,m/kwasniewski-nie-zamierzam-wycofac-sie-z-zarzadu-ukrainskiej-spolki,428900.html.
18. Author's interview with Aleksander Kwaśniewski, Warsaw, December 16, 2014.
19. Ibid.
20. Agaton Koziński, "Kwaśniewski: NATO dobrze reaguje na ukraiński kryzys. Ale musi być gotowe na czarne scenariusze," *Polska The Times*, March 10, 2014, accessed March 18, 2014, http://www.polskatimes.pl/artykul/3360081,kwasniewski-nato-dobrze-reaguje-na-ukrainski-kryzys-ale-musi-byc-gotowe-na-czarne-scenariusze,2,id,t,sa.html.
21. Author's interview with Aleksander Kwaśniewski, Warsaw, December 16, 2014.
22. Ibid.
23. Ростислав Хотин, "Александр Квасневський: Росія робить величезну помилку, тиснучи на горду Україну," *УНІАН*, November 14, 2013, accessed September 9, 2014, http://www.unian.ua/politics/851883-aleksandr-kvasnevskiy-rosiya-robit-velicheznu-pomilku-tisnuchi-na-gordu-ukrajinu.html.
24. Author's interview with Aleksander Kwaśniewski, Warsaw, December 16, 2014.
25. Ibid.

Bibliography

Books

Asmus, Ronald D. *A Little War That Shook the World*. New York: Palgrave Macmillan, 2010.
Brzezinski, Zbigniew. *Strategic Vision: America and the Crisis for Global Power*. New York: Basic Books, 2012.
Brzezinski, Zbigniew, and Paige Sullivan. *Russia and the Commonwealth of Independent States: Documents, Data, and Analysis*. New York: M.E. Sharpe, 1997.
Gaddis, John Lewis. *The Cold War: A New History*. New York: Penguin Press, 2005.
Grünberg, Karol, and Bolesław Sprengel. *Trudne sąsiedztwo: stosunki polsko-ukraińskie w X-XX wieku*. Warsaw: Książka i Wiedza, 2005.
Hoffmann, Lutz, and Felicitas Möllers. *Ukraine on the Road to Europe*. Heidelberg: Physica-Verlag HD, 2001.
Olchawa, Maciej. *Gwiazdy i Tryzub: europejska integracja Ukrainy*. Kraków: Wydawnictwo Szwajpolt Fiol, 2013.
Olchawa, Maciej. *Imperialna rozgrywka: Ukraina w geopolitycznej strategii Stanów Zjednoczonych*. Kraków: Arcana, 2009.
Parafianowicz, Zbigniew, and Michał Potocki. *Wilki żyją poza prawem. Jak Janukowycz przegrał Ukrainę*. Wołowiec: Wydawnictwo Czarne, 2015.
Wilson, Andrew. *Ukraine's Orange Revolution*. New Haven: Yale University Press, 2005.
Wygraliśmy przyszłość: przemówienia, wywiady, dokumenty (wybór), 10 lat prezydentury Aleksandra Kwaśniewskiego. Warsaw: Amicus Europea, 2008.

Journal Articles

Garnett, Sherman. "U.S.–Ukraine Relations," *Harvard Ukrainian Studies* 20 (1998).
Pifer, Steven. "European Mediators and Ukraine's Orange Revolution." *Problems of Post-Communism* 6 (2007).
Schneider, William. "Ukraine's 'Orange Revolution.'" *National Journal* 50 (2004).
Streetly, Martin. "Jane's Radar and Electronic Warfare Systems 2008–2009." *Jane's Information Group*, Surrey 2006.

Newspapers and Weeklies

Bloomberg
Financial Times
Gazeta Wyborcza
Krytyka Polityczna
New York Times
PAP-Polska Agencja Prasowa
Politico Magazine
Polityka
Polska The Times
Rzeczpospolita
SPIEGEL
Time
The Telegraph
The Wall Street Journal

Bibliography

Tygodnik Powszechny
UNIA News Agency
Washington Post
Wprost

Websites

Arms Control Today
BBC News
Buzzfeed
CNN
Deutsche Welle
Eastbook.eu
El Mundo
EUobserver
EurActiv.pl
Euronews
5 Kanal
ForeignPolicy.com
Interfax Ukraine
KyivPost.com
NaTemat.pl
Newsweek.pl
Onet
Radio Free Europe/Radio Liberty
Radio Svoboda
Radio ZET
Politico
Polsat News
PolskieRadio.pl
RMF FM
Russia Today
Rzeczpospolita.pl
Spiegel Online
The American Interest
The Daily Beast
The Hill
The Huffington Post
The Interpreter
The WorldPost
TOK FM
TVN24
TVP Info
Tymoshenko.ua
Ukrainska Pravda
Ukrinform.ua
UNN.com
Wirtualna Polska
Voice of America
Wyborcza.pl

Organizations

Amicus Europea
Atlantic Council
The Brookings Institution
Embassy of the United States—Kyiv Ukraine
EPP Group in the European Parliament
European Commission
European Council
European Parliament
Ministry of Foreign Affairs of the Republic of Poland
Yalta European Strategy

Index

Numbers in ***bold italics*** indicate pages with photographs.

AA *see* Association Agreement
Adamkus, Valdas 3, 26–28, 34
Amsterdam 5
Archer, Devon 140
Armenia 36, 114
Arms Control Today 120
Ashton, Catherine 38, 40, 51–52, 84, 86, 88
Asmus, Ronald D. 133
Association Agreement (AA) 1, 2, 8–10, 13, 22, 36, 39, 41, 43, 51, **53**–57, 62–63, 66, 68–75, 78–82, 84–86, 98–99, 102–106, 112–114, 130, 137–138, 142
Astana 15
Atlantic Council 16, 55–56
Austria 26, 70
authoritarianism 81, 96, 128
Azarov, Mykola 8, 9, 30, 38–39, 44, 46–47, 53–54, 65, 69–71, 83, 88, 101, 139–140
Azerbaijan 36, 113–114

Baker, James 131
Balkenende, Jan Peter 26
Baltic republics 113, 130
Baltic states *see* Baltic republics
Barroso, José Manuel 40, 55, 86
Batkivshchyna 37, 50, 58, 105–106
Belarus 14, 20, 22, 37, 50
Belgium 1
Berkut 75, 90, 91, 95, 97
Berlin 9, 12, 27, 61, 63, 90, 91
Berlusconi, Silvio 39
Biden, Hunter 140
Bildt, Carl 10, 35, 63
Black Sea 77
Black Sea Fleet 118, 120
BMW 76
Bolsheviks 118
Boyko, Yuriy 69
Brexit 17–19
Brezhnev Doctrine 125
Brussels 32, 35, 38, 40–**42**, 44, **47**, 52, 54–55, 58, 61–62, 66–**67**, 69, 74, 79, 82–84, 86, 98, 104, 106, 126, 132, 141
Brzezinski, Zbigniew 1, 21, 127, 129
Budapest Memorandum 119–120
Bulgaria 130
Burisma 140–141
Bush, George W. 32
Buzek, Jerzy 40
BuzzFeed 140

casualties 75, 90–91, 94–95, 99
Catherine the Great 113, 115
Catholic Church 12–13
Central and Eastern Europe 12, 18
Central Intelligence Agency (CIA) 98
Charité Clinique 61
Chechnya 117
Cherkasy 84
Chersonesus 118
Chevron 133
China 14, 16, 19, 44
Chirac, Jacques 26
Churchill, Winston 130
CIA *see* Central Intelligence Agency
Ciosek, Stanisław 25
civil society 23, 59, 87, 90
Clinton, Bill 119, 130
Clinton, Hillary 109
Cold War 23, 128, 130, 132, 136
Commonwealth of Independent States 137
Conference of Presidents (European Parliament) 48, **53**, 61, 66
corruption 6, 9, 11, 35, 37, 95, 100, 119, 139
Council of Europe 52, 117
Council of the European Union 50, 52–53, 62
Cox, Pat 2, 5–10, 35, 40–51, 53–54, 57–68, 71, 73, 77, 99, 102, 104, 106–107, 111–112, 138–139, 143
Cox-Kwaśniewski Special Envoy Mission 2, 5, 35, 41, 48, 57, 59, 106–107;

INDEX

achievements 2, 54, 58–59, 107–108, 112, 139; creation 7–8; criticism 49, 58; extension of mandate 48, 62, 66, 111; objectives 7–8, 43, 102–104
Crimea 2–3, 10, 23, 77, 99, 115–124, 127
Crimea: The Return to the Homeland 99
Crimean Tatars 117
Cuba 50
Czech Republic 26, 130

Davos 86
DCFTA *see* Deep and Comprehensive Free Trade Area
Deep and Comprehensive Free Trade Area (DCFTA) 36, 41, 69, 75, 79
democracy 13, 30, 33, 62, 81, 83, 96, 100, 109, 128, 132
Dnipropetrovsk 87
Donbas 121–122
Donetsk 24, 109–110, 122, 124, 129
Donetsk Republic 122, 124
Dublin 5

Eastern Partnership 36; summit 1, 53, 61–64, 67, 69, 82, 102, 137–138
EEAS *see* European External Action Service
embargo 9, 71, 74, 77–83, 101, 103, 114, 135, 142
energy security 21, 45, 133, 140–141
EPP *see* European People's Party
Estonia 125
Eurasia 8, 35, 124, 128
Eurasian Customs Union 14, 57, 82, 98, 113–114
Euro-Atlantic Partnership Council 32, 125
Euromaidan 2, 9–10, 22–23, 73, 75, 79, 84, 94, 98, 100–101, 107, 118, 124, 142
European Commission 6, 36, 38–40, 55, 72
European Court of Human Rights 49, 52
European External Action Service (EEAS) 51–52
European Parliament 1–2, **6**, 7–8, 10, 20, 22, 34, 38–**42**, 48–49, 53–54, 57–58, 61, 63, 66, 68, 81, 106–107, 111, 139, 141
European People's Party (EPP) 39, 40–41, 105–106
European Union (EU) 1, 2, 5–11, 13–24, 26, 30, 33, 35–42, **47**, 50–57, 59–64, 66–75, 78–88, 90–91, 94, 98–107, 111, 122–125, 127–128, 130, 133–135, 137–139, 141, 143; assistance for Ukraine 21, 81, 90–91, 100, 135; enlargement 13, 20–21; global player 14, 16–17, 19–21; position on Tymoshenko 2, 7, 36–39, 61–62, 102–106, 138; special envoy initiative 7–8
Eurozone 19

Fabius, Laurent 94
Finland 127–128
Finlandization 125, 127–128, 130
Fischer, Heinz 70
Forbes 59
France 18–19, 26, 52, 92
Frankfurter Allgemeine Zeitung 49–50
Füle, Štefan 10, 38, **47**, 69

gas 36–37, 44–46, 56, 71, 74, 78, 80, 82–83, 104, 133, 140–142
Gauck, Joachim 90
Gazeta Wyborcza 116
Gazprom 45
Geneva 123
Georgia 36, 114, 130, 133–134
Gerasimov, Gennadi 125
Germany 9, 19, 59–61, 63, 73, 84, 92–93, 105, 111, 130
Gongadze, Georgiy 32, 126
Gorbachev, Mikhail 124, 131–132, 137–138
Great Britain *see* United Kingdom
Greece 35
Gryzlov, Boris 28

Harms, Rebecca 58
Heavenly Hundred 10, 142
The Hill 133
Hryshchenko, Konstantin 62
Hungary 125, 130
Hussein, Saddam 32
hybrid warfare 121–122, 124

IMF *see* International Monetary Fund
imperialism 113–115, 121, 123–124
Institute of World Politics 10
International Monetary Fund (IMF) 56, 81–83
Iron Curtain 13
Italy 19, 22
Ivano-Frankivsk 84
Ivashchenko, Valeriy 47–48
Iwaniak, Olga 25

Jordan 52
Juncker, Jean-Claude 40

Kaczyński, Lech 5
Kamyshev, Serhiy 44
Kazakhstan 14, 32, 114

Index

Kekkonen, Urho 128
Kerry, John 140
Kharkiv 6, 45–48, 54, 59–61, 95, 97, 107, 122
Khreshchatyk Street 98
Khrushchev, Nikita 115, 118
Kiev *see* Kyiv
Kievan Rus 115
Kissinger, Henry 132
Klaus, Václav 26
Klitschko, Vitali 10, *17*, 87, 90, 93–94
Kluczkowski, Jacek 25, 27
Klyuyev, Andriy 66, 80
Kolchuga 32, 126
Komorowski, Bronisław 10
Korolevska, Natalia 17
Kowal, Paweł 3, 10
Kozhara, Leonid 97
Kraków 1
Kramatorsk 123
Kravchuk, Leonid 28, 88, 137
Kremlin 2, 26, 44, 74, 78–79, 98, 114, 116–118, 122–124, 128, 130–131, 133, 135, 140, 142
Kubiš, Ján 28
Kuchma, Leonid 17, 24–33, 42, 88, 120, 125–126, 138
Kuzmin, Renat 46, 60
Kwaśniewski, Aleksander: on energy 45, 113, 133, 141; on EU enlargement 13, 20–21; on Eurasian Customs Union 56–57, 82, 114; meetings with Yanukovych 9, 44, 48–50, 54, 63, 72, 77, 89, 109–110; Orange Revolution 2, 23–34, 42; president of Poland 11, 23, 130, 132; Putin's blackmail of Yanukovych 79–80, 98, 103; on sanctions 86–87; Soviet Union 12, 14, 22–23, 55, 57, 115–116; on U.S. policy toward Ukraine 55–57, 91, 122, 135–136
Kyiv 1, 5–7, 9–12, 15, 22, 24–26, 29, 32, 35–36, 38–41, 43–48, 51, 53, 55–56, 61–62, 66, 68–70, 78, 82–84, 86–87, 90–92, 95, 97–100, 102, 107, 112, 115, 119, 124, 126, 128, 133–134, 138, 140–142

Lady Yu *see* Tymoshenko, Yulia
Latin America 16
Latvia 125
Leiter, David 140
Lithuania 3, 8, 26, 116, 125, 129
The Little War That Shook the World 133
London 16, 120
Luhansk 27, 122, 124

Lutkovska, Valeriya 47
Lutsenko, Yuriy 43, 46–48, 54–55, 58, 61, 89, 103
Lviv 84
Lytvyn, Volodymyr 28–29, 48

Maidan Nezalezhnosti *see* Maidan Square
Maidan of Independence *see* Maidan Square
Maidan Square 9, 12, 23–25, 29, 33, 70, 73, 75, 77, 79, 84, 87–88, 90–102, 107–108, 110–111, 113, 119, 124, 138
Mandela, Nelson 110
Mariyinsky Palace 26
Medvedev, Dmitry 71
Melnychenko, Mykola 31–32
Merkel, Angela 90, 105–106, 109
Mezhyhirya 95–96
Mokry, Włodzimierz 1, 3
Moldova 36, 114
Molotov-Ribbentrop pact 80
Moroz, Oleksandr 32–33, 48
Moscow 11–12, 15, 25–26, 34, 44, 69, 78–79, 83, 98, 102, 114–115, 117, 121, 123, 126–127, 133–135, 140, 142

NATO *see* North Atlantic Treaty Organization
Nazarbayev, Nursultan 32
NEA *see* New Enhanced Agreement
Nemyria, Hryhoriy 43, 59
Netherlands 18, 26
New Enhanced Agreement (NEA) 36
The New York Times 135
Nocuń, Małgorzata 37
North Atlantic Alliance *see* North Atlantic Treaty Organization
North Atlantic Treaty Organization (NATO) 11, 13, 32–33, 121, 125–134
Northern Ireland 18
Novo Ogaryovo residence 117

Obama, Barack 127, 135
Odessa 84, 122, 126
oligarchs 6, 11, 22, 37, 45, 89, 96, 100–101
Oliynyk, Volodymyr 65
Orange Revolution 1–2, 11–12, 15, 23–25, 29–30, 33–34, 42, 48, 85, 101, 105, 110–111, 115, 125
Organization for Security and Co-operation in Europe (OSCE) 122–123
Orthodoxy 13, 118
OSCE *see* Organization for Security and Co-operation in Europe

171

Index

Parafianowicz, Zbigniew 76
Partnership and Cooperation Agreement (PCA) 36
Party of Regions 6, 38–41, 50–51, 61, 63–66, 68, 71–73, 77, 88–89, 97, 101–102, 110, 138
Pascual, Carlos 32
PCA *see* Partnership and Cooperation Agreement
Peskov, Dmitry 140
Peter the Great 113, 115
Pifer, Steven 30–31, 132
Pinto Teixeira, José Manuel 50–51
Poland 1, 5–8, 10–13, 20, 22–26, 29, 33–35, 49, 52, 54–56, 63, 66, 68, 72, 74–75, 79, 84, 86, 88, 92–93, 100, 104, 106, 109–111, 114, 116, 122, 124–125, 129–130, 132–133, 138–142
Polish Press Agency 23, 70
Polityka 26
Poroshenko, Petro 101, 111, 141
Poryck 31
Potocki, Michał 76
Powell, Colin 24, 29
Pozharskyi, Vadym 44
Prince Vladimir 118
Prodi, Romano 6, 40
Pshonka, Viktor 46
Putin, Vladimir 26, 28, 33–34, 45, 77, 79–82, 94, 97–99, 113–125, 127–132, 138, 142–143
Pyatt, Geoffrey R. 57

Revolution of Dignity *see* Euromaidan
Rice, Condoleezza 109
Rivne 84
Romania 130
Roosevelt, Franklin D. 130
Roshen 101
Rossiya-1 99
Russia 3, 9–12, 16, 20–23, 26, 28, 33–36, 39, 44–45, 69, 71, 74, 77–83, 85, 90, 96, 99–104, 108, 113–137, 140–143; attitude toward Ukraine 113–116, 118, 128, 130, 134–135, 140, 142; embargo against Ukraine 9, 71, 74, 77–78, 80–83, 101–103, 135; language 6, 46, 79, 122; media 90, 122, 131; trade relations with Ukraine 69, 78, 82–83, 104, 127
Russia Today 122
Rybak, Volodymyr 64–65

Saudi Arabia 52
Scandinavia 18
Scherbak, Yuriy 126
Schröder, Gerhard 26
Schulz, Martin 8–9, 38–*42*, *47*–48, *53*–54, 58–59, *67*, 102, 111–112
Schüssel, Wolfgang 26
Scotland 18
selective justice 8, 55, 57, 60–61, 67, 99, 104, 106
Sevastopol 115–116, 118, 125
Shcherban, Ruslan 110
Shcherban, Yevhen 110
Shell 133
Sikorski, Radek 10, 62–63, 69, 88, 92–94, 97
Simferopol 116–117
Sinatra, Frank 125
Sloviansk 123
Sochi 80, 138
Socialists and Democrats Group 39–40
Solana, Javier 2, 26–28, 30, 34
Solidarity 12–13, 93, 100
South Korea 52
South Ossetia 117
Soviet Union 3, 9, 12, 14, 57, 77, 115–116, 118, 124, 128, 137
Spain 13, 35
Spetsnaz 99, 121
Der Spiegel 105, 132
Stalin, Joseph 113, 115, 128, 130
Stavitsky, Eduard 44
Steinmeier, Frank-Walter 93–94, 97
Strasbourg 2, *6*, *7*, 49, *53*, 57–58, 141
Sumy 84
Svoboda 50
Sweden 10, 19, 44, 63
Szlajfer, Henryk 25

Tarasyuk, Borys 25, 47
Tarnopol 84
Tbilisi 133
Tefft, John F. 57
Tihipko, Serhiy *17*, 27
Tombiński, Jan 50–52
Transnistria 134
Trilateral Commission 123
Turkey 20
Turkmenistan 114
Tymoshenko, Eugenia 54
Tymoshenko, Yulia 2, 7–9, 36–41, 43–50, 54–65, 67–70, 72–73, 80, 85, 95, 99, 102–112, 126, 138, 142; appearance on Maidan Square 95, 108–111; charges against 7, 36; conditions in prison 37, 46, 58, 107; gas deal with Russia 44, 46, 104; medical treatment 9, 43, 45, 52, 59–61, 105, 111; pardon 60, 104; prison sentence 7, 36; tax case 7, 36, 46

Index

UDAR 50
Ukrainian Insurgent Army (UPA) 31
Ukrayinska Pravda 63–64
United Kingdom 17–19
United States 1, 12, 14–17, 19, 21, 24–25, 29–30, 32, 46, 55–57, 91–92, 100, 109–110, 119–122, 123–124, 126–127, 129, 130, 132, 135–136, 140–141, 143
UPA *see* Ukrainian Insurgent Army
U.S.S.R. *see* Soviet Union

Van Rompuy, Herman 38, 55
Venice Commission 62
Verkhovna Rada 27–28, 30, 48, 63–64, 66, 68, 72–74, 86, 88–89, 95, 112, 127
Vienna 5–6, 70–71, 138
Vilnius 2, 8–9, 53–54, 59, 62–64, 66, 68–69, 71, 74–75, 81–82, 84, 95, 98, 104, 106, 116, 137–138, 142
Vlasenko, Serhiy 46, 59–61
Volhynia massacres 31

Wałęsa, Lech 129
The Wall Street Journal 36
Warsaw 13, 25–26, 52, 98, 128, 130–131
Washington, D.C. 9, 11, 15–16, 25, 32, 55–57, 120, 123, 126
Weimar Triangle 93
Wilson, Andrew 127
Wolfowitz, Paul 128

Wolves Are Above the Law: How Yanukovych Lost Ukraine 76
World Bank 128

Yalta 48, 130
Yalta European Strategy 16–*17*, 74, **76**, 112
Yanukovych, Viktor 2, 6, 8–10, 24–25, 27–30, 33–34, 36–37, 39, 41, 43–45, 48, 51–52, 54–56, 58, 60–68, 70–77, 79–100, 103–111, 122, 126–127, 136, 138–139, 141; attitude toward Tymoshenko 37, 103, 105, 138; decision to suspend AA negotiations 69–75; decision to use force 89–90; early life 76, 96; escape 95, 97, 99; integration with EU 36, 52, 68, 74; negotiations with the opposition 87, 89, 92–93; pressure from Putin 77–80, 98, 103, 138
Yatsenyuk, Arseniy 5, *17*, 72, 87, 90, 97
Yefremov, Oleksandr 64–66
Yeltsin, Boris 124
Yushchenko, Viktor 23–30, 33, 48, 79, 126–127

Zajączkowski, Wojciech 25
Zaporizhia 87
Zhytomyr 84
Zlochevsky, Mykola 44–45, 140–141

www.ingramcontent.com/pod-product-compliance
Ingram Content Group UK Ltd.
Pitfield, Milton Keynes, MK11 3LW, UK
UKHW042016140426
5217IPUK00015B/1196